Works 4.5

fast & easy™

Diane Koers

PRIMA TECH

A Division of Prima Publishing

For Timothy, my firstborn and my friend.

God bless you.

 A Division of Prima Publishing

Prima Publishing and colophon are registered trademarks of Prima Communications, Inc. Fast & Easy is a trademark of Prima Communications, Inc. Prima Publishing, Rocklin, California 95765.

Publisher: Matthew H. Carleson

Managing Editor: Dan J. Foster

Acquisitions Editor: Jenny L. Watson

Project Editor: Kevin W. Ferns

Technical Reviewer: Bo Williams

Copy Editor: Judy Ohm

Interior Layout: Shawn Morningstar and Marian Hartsough

Cover Design: Prima Design Team

Indexer: Katherine Stimson

Microsoft and Windows are registered trademarks of Microsoft Corporation.

Important: If you have problems installing or running Microsoft Works 4.5, go to Microsoft's Web site at **www.microsoft.com**. Prima Publishing cannot provide software support.

Prima Publishing and the author have attempted throughout this book to distinguish proprietary trademarks from descriptive terms by following the capitalization style used by the manufacturer.

Information contained in this book has been obtained by Prima Publishing from sources believed to be reliable. However, because of the possibility of human or mechanical error by our sources, Prima Publishing, or others, the Publisher does not guarantee the accuracy, adequacy, or completeness of any information and is not responsible for any errors or omissions or the results obtained from the use of such information. Readers should be particularly aware of the fact that the Internet is an ever-changing entity. Some facts may have changed since this book went to press.

ISBN: 0-7615-1802-9

Library of Congress Catalog Card Number: 98-67615

Printed in the United States of America

98 99 00 01 02 HH 10 9 8 7 6 5 4 3 2 1

Acknowledgments

I am deeply thankful to the many people at Prima Publishing who worked on this book. Thank you for all the time you gave and for your assistance.

To Jenny Watson for the opportunity to write this book and her confidence in me. To Judy Ohm and Bo Williams for their help in making this book technically and grammatically correct, and to Kevin Ferns for all his patience and guidance.

Lastly, a big thank you to my husband, Vern. Your spirit is infectious and I love you for that.

About the Author

Diane Koers owns and operates All Business Service, a software training and consulting business formed in 1988. She specializes in word processing, spreadsheets, and graphics, and she provides training and support for Peachtree Accounting software. Diane's authoring experience includes Prima Tech's *Lotus 1-2-3 97 Fast & Easy, WordPerfect 8 Fast & Easy, Windows 98 Fast and Easy,* and *SmartSuite Millennium Fast & Easy,* and she co-authored Prima Tech's *The Essential Windows 98 Book.* She has also developed and written software training manuals for her clients' use.

Active in her church and civic activities, Diane enjoys spending her free time traveling and playing with her grandson and her three Yorkshire Terriers.

Contents

PART II
USING THE WORD PROCESSOR. 25

Introduction

This *Fast & Easy* book from Prima Publishing will help you use the many and varied features of Microsoft's popular Works 4.5. Works is designed to answer most personal and professional computing needs with a program that has a user-friendly integrated design and a feature-rich environment. *Works 4.5 Fast & Easy* provides the tools to successfully learn Microsoft Works—a word processor, spreadsheet, database manager, and a personal calendar system. This *Fast & Easy* book instructs you with a step-by-step approach, clear language, and detailed illustrations of exactly what you will see on your screen.

WHO SHOULD READ THIS BOOK?

The easy-to-follow, highly visual nature of this book makes it the perfect learning tool for a beginning computer user. It is also ideal for those who are new to this version of Microsoft Works, or those who feel comfortable with computers and software but have never used these types of programs before.

By using *Works 4.5 Fast & Easy*, any level of user can look up steps for a task quickly without having to plow through pages of descriptions.

ADDED ADVICE TO MAKE YOU A PRO

You'll notice that this book uses steps and keeps theory to a minimum to help you learn faster. Included in the book are a few elements that provide some additional comments to help you master the program, without encumbering your progress through the steps:

✦ **Tips** often offer shortcuts when performing an action, or hints about a feature that might make your work in Microsoft Works quicker and easier.

✦ **Notes** give you a bit of background or additional information about a feature, or advice about how to use the feature in your day-to-day activities.

In addition, two helpful appendixes will show you how to install Microsoft Works and how to use the Microsoft TaskWizards, which are included in Works to save you lots of time.

Read and enjoy this *Fast & Easy* book. It certainly is the fastest and easiest way to learn Microsoft Works 4.5.

PART I

Discovering Microsoft Works

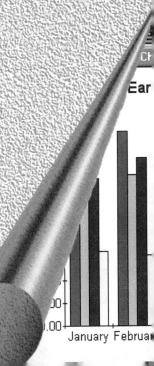

1 Getting Started

Congratulations! You are ready to begin working with Microsoft Works, an excellent integrated software application designed for homes, home offices, or other small businesses. In this chapter, you'll learn how to:

✦ Start the Works program

✦ Discover the Task Launcher

✦ Preview the various Works components

✦ Exit Microsoft Works

STARTING WORKS

When Microsoft Works installs, the setup program creates several startup wizards for you to enter information. If you have not yet installed Microsoft Works, please see Appendix A, "Installing Works."

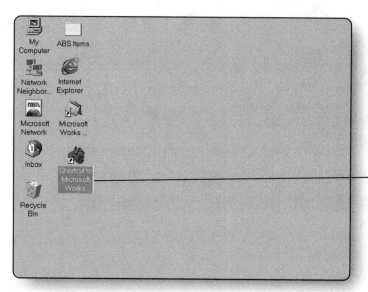

Using the Shortcut Icon

The fastest method to launch the Works program is to use the shortcut placed on your Windows desktop.

1. Double-click on the **Shortcut to Microsoft Works icon**. The Works program will launch.

Using the Start Menu

If your desktop does not have a shortcut, you can access the Works program by using the Start button.

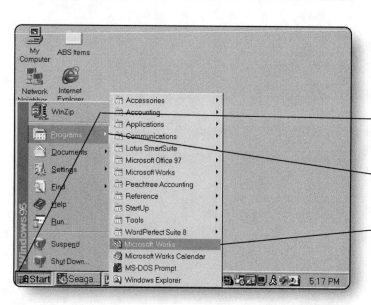

1. Click on **Start**. The Start menu will appear.

2. Click on **Programs**. The Programs menu will appear.

3. Click on **Microsoft Works**. The Works program will launch.

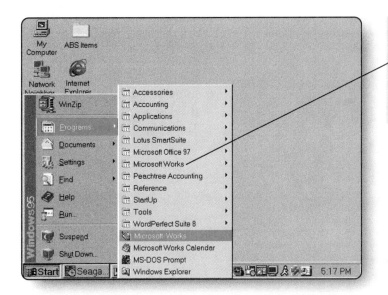

NOTE

You can also click on the Microsoft Works folder and choose Microsoft Works.

Viewing the Demonstration Program

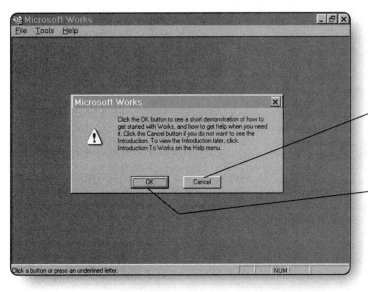

The first time you launch the Works program, you have the option to view a ten-minute demonstration program.

1a. Click on **Cancel**. The Works Task Launcher will display.

OR

1b. Click on **OK**. The demonstration will begin.

DISCOVERING THE TASK LAUNCHER

From the Task Launcher, you can access various components, create new documents, open existing documents, or use one of the Task Wizards.

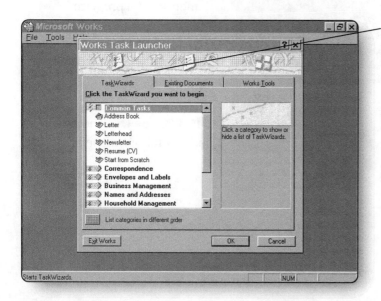

1. Click on the **TaskWizards tab**. A list of available Task Wizards will display. Task Wizards are discussed in Appendix B, "Using Task Wizards."

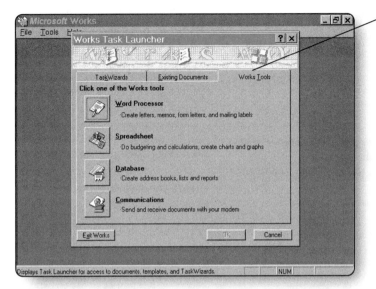

2. **Click** on the **Works Tools tab**. Four of the Works components will display.

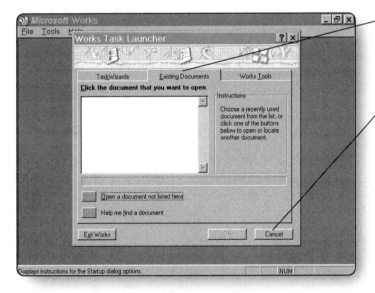

3. **Click** on the **Existing Documents tab**. After you create Works documents, a listing will appear here.

4. **Click** on **Cancel**. The Task Launcher dialog box will close but the Works program remains active.

UNDERSTANDING THE COMPONENTS OF WORKS

Microsoft Works is considered an *integrated* application. This means that all the components work as one single program.

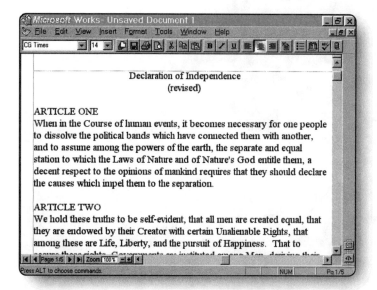

Word Processing

Create memos, letters, proposals, and other text-based documents using the Works word processing module.

NOTE

You'll learn how to format text in Chapter 4, "Formatting a Word Processing Document."

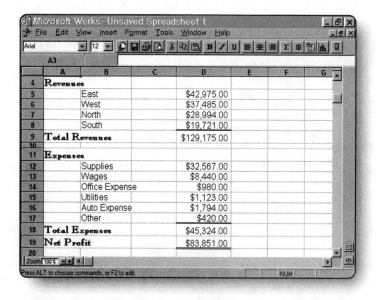

Spreadsheets

Spreadsheets are used to crunch numbers. Save time by letting the spreadsheet do the calculating for you.

NOTE

You'll learn how to create formulas in Chapter 13, "Formatting Worksheets."

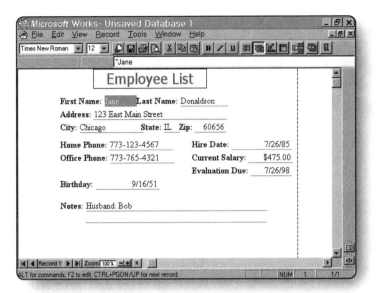

Discovering Databases

Track names, addresses, and other data by designing a Works database.

> **NOTE**
>
> You'll learn how to add records to a database in Chapter 18, "Formatting a Database."

Viewing the Calendar

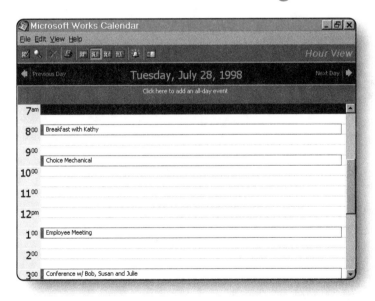

Schedule events and meetings with the newest feature to Microsoft Works—the Calendar.

> **NOTE**
>
> Chapter 24, "Using the Works Calendar," will show you how to keep your calendar up to date.

EXITING WORKS

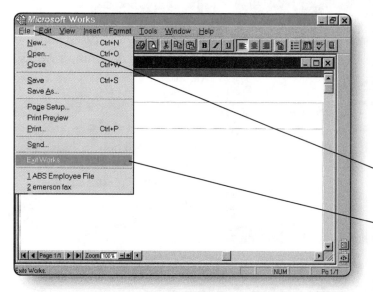

When you are finished with Works, exit the program. This procedure protects your data and avoids possible program damage. It also frees up valuable computer memory that can be used for other programs.

1a. Click on **File**. The File menu will appear.

2a. Click on **Exit Works**. The Works program will be closed.

OR

1b. Click on the **Close box**. The Works program will close.

NOTE

If any documents are open that haven't been saved, Works will ask you whether you want to save changes to those files.

2 Seeking Help

Although you'll find many answers to your questions in this book, sometimes you need additional information. Microsoft supplies you with several types of assistance. In this chapter, you'll learn how to:

✦ **Access the Help window**

✦ **Use the Help Contents and Index**

✦ **Shrink and redisplay the Help window**

✦ **Get help on the Web**

ACCESSING HELP

Help with Microsoft Works is available in several ways. One method, using the Help window, shows you that help is only a mouse-click away. When you begin any type of Works document, the Help window will display a menu of choices applicable to that type of document.

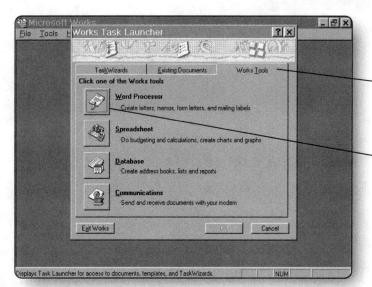

1. **Start Works**. The Works Task Launcher will appear.

2. **Click** on the **Works Tools** tab. The Works Tools tab will come to the front.

3. **Click** on an **application**. A blank document will appear.

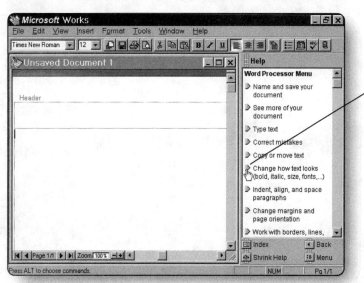

The help topics are displayed to the right of the document window.

4. **Click** on a **task**. A second-level Help window will appear with specific topics for the selected task.

NOTE

Some features may have multiple help topic levels.

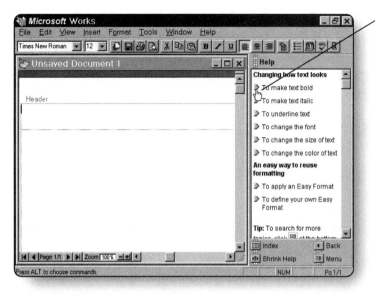

5. **Click** on a **task**. A Step-by-Step help tab will appear.

Step-by-Step help tabs list numbered steps to accomplish a task.

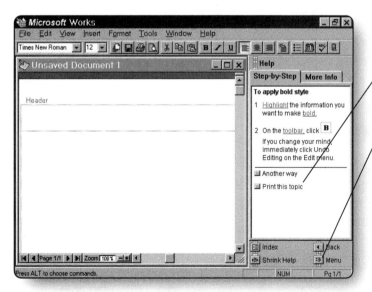

TIP

Click on Print this topic to print a copy of the help information.

6. **Click** on **Menu**. The Help window will return to the document help selections.

USING HELP CONTENTS

The Help Contents feature presents help information in a folder-like format, making it easy for you to browse available topics.

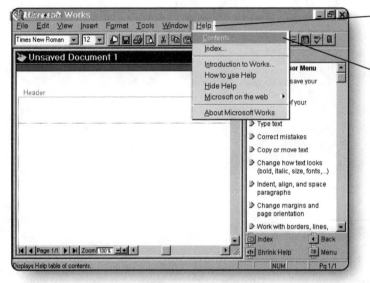

1. **Click** on **Help**. The Help menu will open.

2. **Click** on **Contents.** The Help Topics dialog box will appear with the Contents tab displayed.

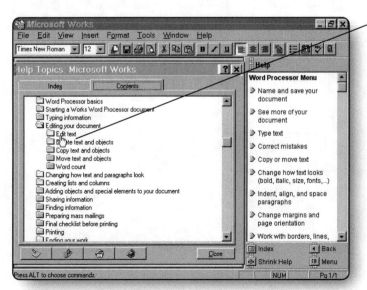

3. **Click** on a **general topic**. The topic folder will open.

NOTE

A *general topic* has specific topics and is signified by a yellow folder, whereas a *specific topic* is indicated by a paper with blue lines on it. Some general topics may have other general topics listed under them.

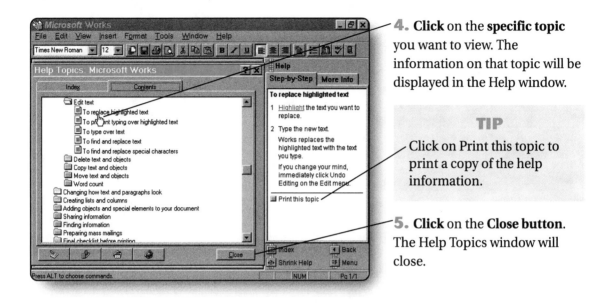

4. Click on the **specific topic** you want to view. The information on that topic will be displayed in the Help window.

TIP

Click on Print this topic to print a copy of the help information.

5. Click on the **Close button**. The Help Topics window will close.

USING THE HELP INDEX

Works' help features also include an extensive index of topics.

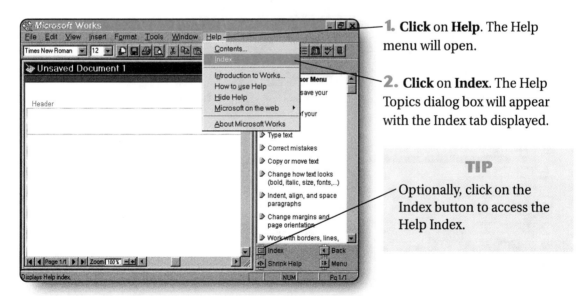

1. Click on **Help**. The Help menu will open.

2. Click on **Index**. The Help Topics dialog box will appear with the Index tab displayed.

TIP

Optionally, click on the Index button to access the Help Index.

The topics are listed alphabetically with some topics displaying a list of subtopics.

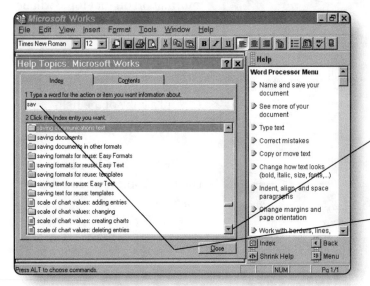

NOTE

The first time the Index is accessed, it may take a moment to display.

3a. **Scroll** through the **list of topics** until you find your topic.

OR

3b. **Type** the **first characters** or **word** of your topic. The topics will jump alphabetically to the word that you typed.

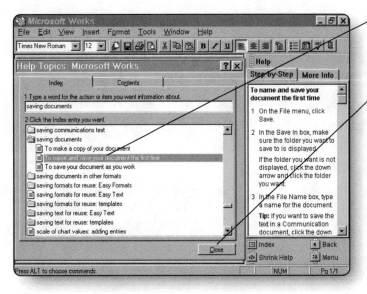

4. **Click** on the desired **topic**. The information will be displayed in the Help window.

5. **Click** on the **Close button.** The Help Topics dialog box will close.

SHRINKING AND REDISPLAYING THE HELP WINDOW

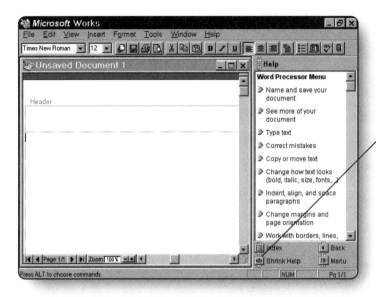

If the Help window is in your way and you don't need it right at the moment, put it away. You can then recall it whenever you need it.

1. **Click** on the **Shrink Help button**. The Help window will close and a small Help icon will appear on the far right side of the Microsoft Works window.

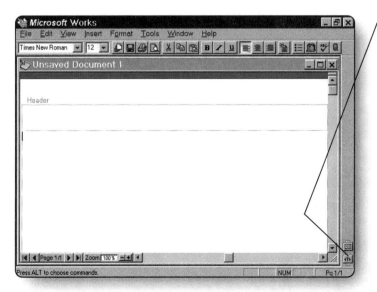

2. **Click** on the **Help icon**. The Help window will reappear.

NOTE

For the remainder of this book, the Help window will not be displayed. Click on the Shrink Help button.

RUNNING THE WORKS TUTORIAL

Works includes a brief introduction of the features available in Microsoft Works. Even though it doesn't show you how to do a specific task, it does give you an overview of the types of projects you can accomplish.

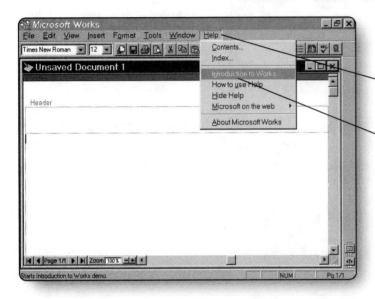

1. **Click** on **Help**. The Help menu will appear.

2. **Click** on **Introduction to Works**. The initial tutorial screen will display.

3. **Click** on the **right arrow button**. The demonstration will begin.

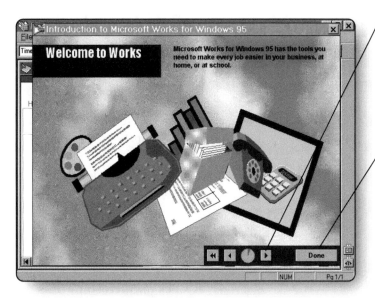

4. **Click** on the **right arrow button**. The next page of the introduction will display.

5. **Repeat step 4** until the tutorial is complete.

6. **Click** on **Done**. The Introduction to Works demonstration will close.

FIRST TIME HELP

Works will automatically display a First Time Help option the first time you select a feature. You can see a demonstration of the feature or get step-by-step instructions.

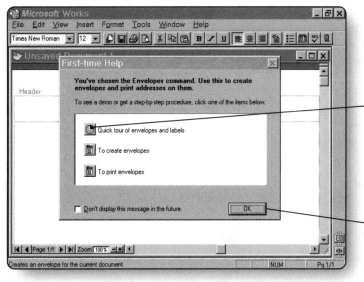

1. **Click** on a **feature** that you have never used before. The First Time Help dialog box will display.

2a. **Click** on the **option** you want to see. The demo or instructions will appear. Follow any instructions on the screen.

OR

2b. **Click** on **OK**. The First Time Help dialog box will close and you can use the feature.

FINDING HELP ON THE WEB

There are many sources of assistance supplied with Microsoft Works. You've already seen several good resources. Another one is the World Wide Web. Microsoft includes technical support at its Web site.

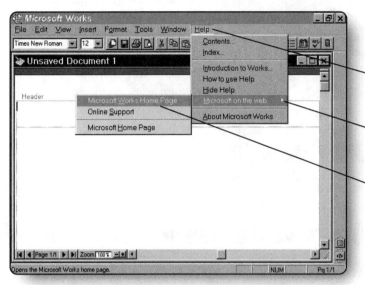

1. Click on **Help**. The Help menu will appear.

2. Click on **Microsoft on the web**. A menu will appear.

3. Click on **Microsoft Works Home Page**. If you are not connected to the Internet, you will be prompted to do so.

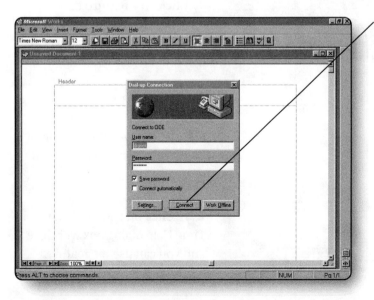

4. Click on **Connect**. Your Internet connection will be established.

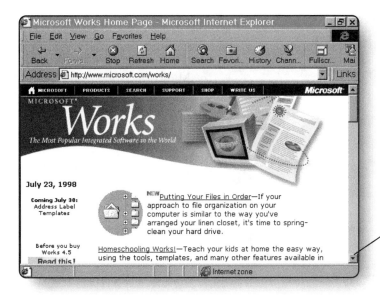

Your Web browser will launch and the Microsoft Works Home Page will be displayed.

NOTE

Because Web pages change frequently, your screen may appear slightly different from the figure.

5. **Scroll down** the Web page. More options will be displayed.

From the Microsoft Works Home page you can obtain technical support, view Frequently Asked Questions, download free templates and task wizards, or even communicate with other Microsoft Works users.

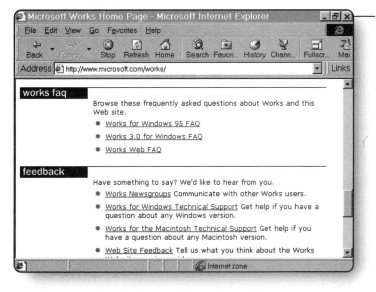

6. **Click** on the **Close button**. The Web browser will close.

You may be prompted to close your Internet connection.

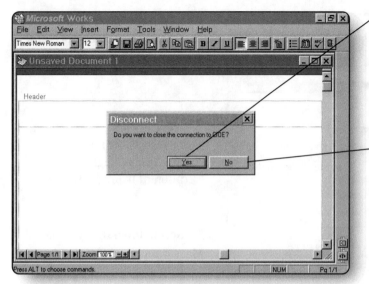

7a. **Click** on **Yes** if you want to disconnect. Your connection will terminate and you will return to the Microsoft Works window.

OR

7b. **Click** on **No**. Your connection will remain open and you will return to the Microsoft Works window.

PART I REVIEW QUESTIONS

1. What is the Task Launcher? *See "Discovering the Task Launcher" in Chapter 1*

2. What are the three types of tasks that you can do with the Task Launcher? *See "Discovering the Task Launcher" in Chapter 1*

3. What are the five major components included with Works? *See "Understanding the Components of Works" in Chapter 1*

4. What is the newest feature added to Works? *See "Viewing the Calendar" in Chapter 1*

5. Where are the help topics displayed when first opening Works? *See "Accessing Help" in Chapter 2*

6. What do Step-by-Step windows do? *See "Accessing Help" in Chapter 2*

7. In the Help Contents window, how are specific help topics indicated? *See "Using Help Contents" in Chapter 2*

8. What can you do to the Help window if it's in your way? *See "Shrinking and Redisplaying the Help Window" in Chapter 2*

9. What is sometimes displayed the first time you access a feature? *See "First Time Help" in Chapter 2*

10. What are some of the ways Microsoft can assist you when you access the Microsoft Works Home Page? *See "Finding Help on the Web" in Chapter 2*

PART II
Using the Word Processor

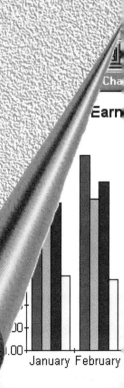

3 Creating a Simple Document

When you need to create a letter, memo, or proposal, use the Word Processing application of Works. Word processing is great for everything text-based—from the simplest letter to a professional-looking newsletter. In this chapter, you'll learn how to:

✦ Create a document

✦ Insert the current date

✦ Move around in a document

✦ Select and delete text

✦ Undo your mistakes

✦ Create and use an Easy Text entry

OPENING A BLANK WORD PROCESSING DOCUMENT

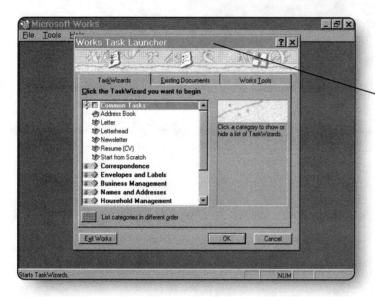

Use the Works Task Launcher to create a new word processing document.

1a. **Start** the Microsoft **Works program**. The Task Launcher will appear when you launch the Works Program.

OR

If you are already using Works, you can access the Task Launcher from the toolbar.

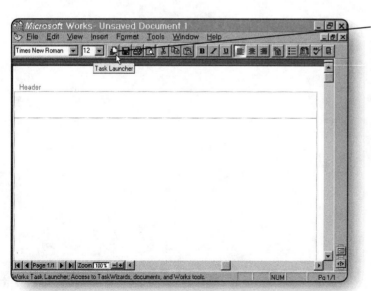

1b. **Click** on the **Task Launcher button**. The Task Launcher will appear.

When the Task Launcher appears, you can select a type of project.

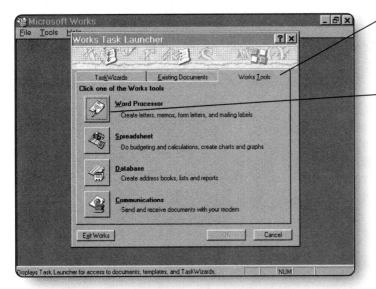

2. **Click** on the **Works Tools tab**. The Works Tools tab will come to the front.

3. **Click** on **Word Processor**. A blank word processing document will appear.

TYPING TEXT IN A DOCUMENT

When typing in a word processing document, press the Enter key only when you get to the end of a paragraph or when you want an extra blank line between paragraphs. Works takes care of the rest. If the word you are typing does not fit entirely at the end of the current line, Works will put it on the next line automatically. This is called *word wrap*.

You will find it to your benefit to follow the "Type First, Edit Later" concept. Type the text into your document and then go back and make any changes.

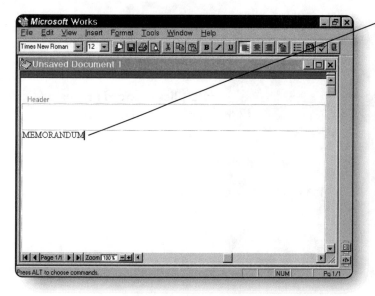

1. **Type** some **text**. The text you type will appear at the location of the insertion point.

If you make any mistakes while typing, you can press the Backspace key to erase any letter to the left of the blinking insertion point. You'll learn how to make other corrections later.

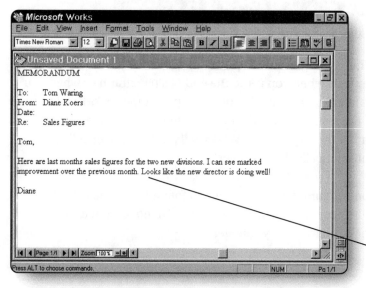

2. **Press** the **Enter key twice** when you have completed a paragraph. The insertion point will move down two lines.

NOTE

A paragraph consists of a single line of text, such as "Dear Sir," or multiple lines of text.

3. **Continue typing** until your document is complete.

INSERTING THE DATE AND TIME

Instead of fishing around your desk looking for your calendar, let
Works put today's date in your document.

1. **Click** the **mouse pointer** where you want to insert the date. The
insertion point will blink.

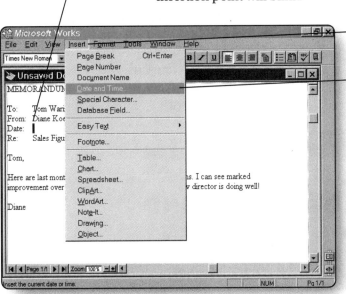

2. **Click** on **Insert**. The Insert
menu will appear.

3. **Click** on **Date and Time**. The
Insert Date and Time dialog box
will open.

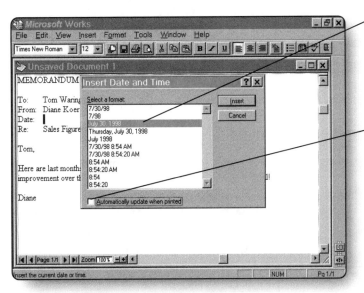

4. **Click** on a **date format**. The
selected date format will be
highlighted.

NOTE

If "Automatically update
when printed" is checked,
the date will change in the
document, every time it is
opened, to reflect the
current date. This is called
a *dynamic* date. If you do
not want the date to
change (a *static* date), do
not check this option.

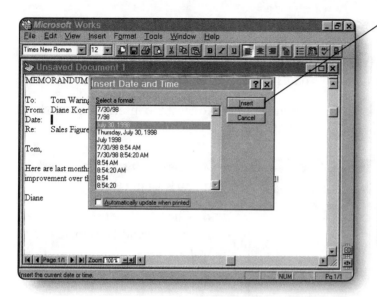

5. **Click** on **Insert**. The date will be inserted into your document at the location of the insertion point.

> **TIP**
>
> A shortcut to insert a dynamic date or time is Ctrl+D for the current date and Ctrl+T for the current time.

MOVING AROUND IN A DOCUMENT

Works provides several quick ways to move around a word processing document.

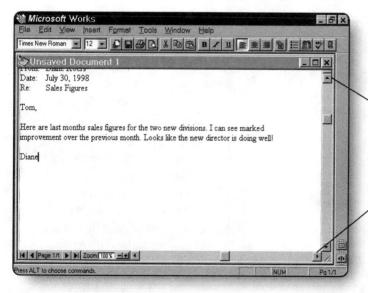

Moving around Using the Scroll Bar

1. **Click** on the **arrows** at either end of the vertical scroll bar. The document onscreen will be moved up or down in the window.

2. **Click** on the **arrows** at either end of the horizontal scroll bar. The document onscreen will be moved left or right in the window.

NOTE

When moving through a document using the scroll bar, the insertion point does not move—only the screen display moves. You must click in the document to move the insertion point to a new location when using the scroll bar.

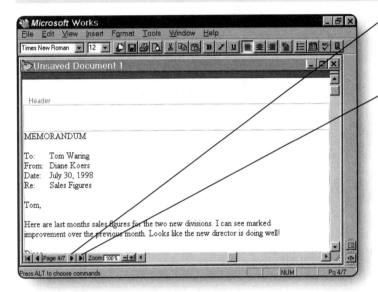

3. **Click** on the **Next page button**. The next page will display.

4. **Click** on the **Last page button**. The last page of the document will display.

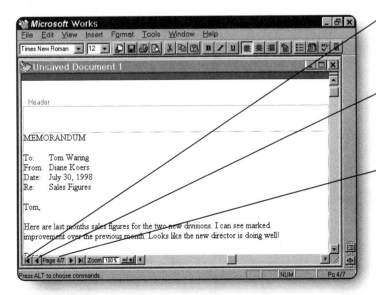

5. **Click** on the **First page button**. The first page of the document will display.

6. **Click** on the **Previous page button**. The previous page will display.

7. **Double-click** on the **Current page indicator**. The Go To dialog box will display.

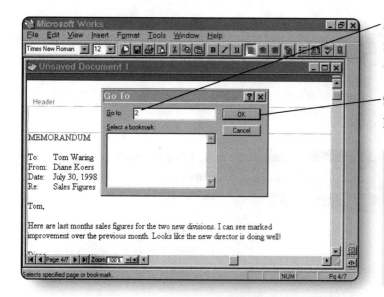

8. Type the desired **page number**. The page number will appear in the Go to: text box.

9. Click on **OK**. The specified page will be displayed.

Moving around Using the Keyboard

You may prefer to use your keyboard to move around in your document. This table illustrates these shortcut keys.

To Move	Do This
Right one word	Press Ctrl+Right Arrow
Left one word	Press Ctrl+Left Arrow
To the beginning of a line	Press Home
To the end of a line	Press End
To the beginning of the paragraph	Press Ctrl+Up Arrow
To the next paragraph	Press Ctrl+Down Arrow
Down one screen	Press Page Down
Up one screen	Press Page Up
To the beginning of the document	Press Ctrl+Home
To the end of the document	Press Ctrl+End
To a specified page number	Press Ctrl+G

INSERTING TEXT

When Works is first installed, word processing initially defaults to *insert* mode. This means that when you want to add new text to a document, any existing text will move to the right to make room for the new text.

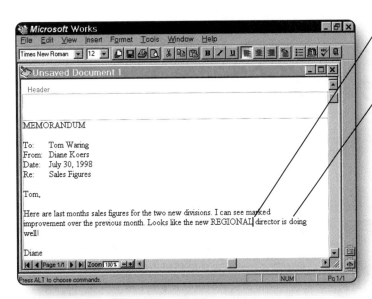

1. **Click** to place an **insertion point** where you want to add additional text.

2. **Type** the **new text**. The new text is inserted into the document.

NOTE

In this figure, the added word is in uppercase letters so you can easily see the effect of inserting text.

SELECTING TEXT

In order to move, copy, delete, or change the formatting of text, you first need to select it. When text is selected, it will appear on your screen as light type on a dark background—just the reverse of unselected text. You can only select a sequential block of text at a time; not bits of text in different places.

1. To select a word, **double-click** on a **word**. The word will be highlighted.

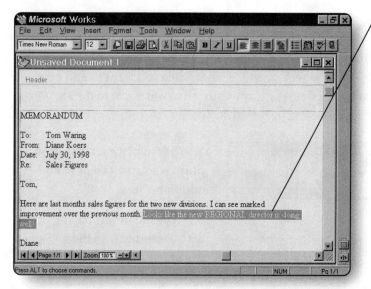

2. To select a sentence, **hold down** the **Ctrl** key and **click** on a **word**. The entire sentence will be highlighted.

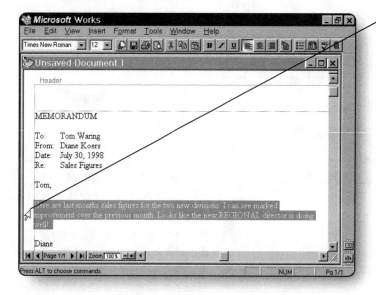

3. To select a paragraph, **position** the **mouse pointer** to the left side of a paragraph. The mouse pointer will point to the right.

4. **Double-click** the **mouse**. The entire paragraph will be highlighted.

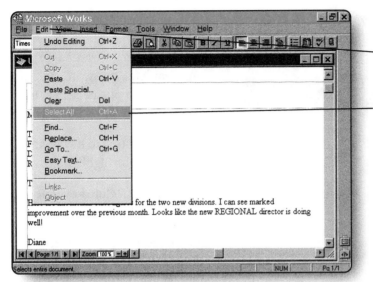

Select the entire document.

5. Click on **Edit**. The Edit menu will appear.

6. Click on **Select All**. The entire document will be highlighted.

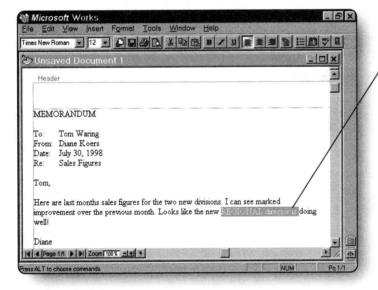

Alternatively, you can select a block of text by clicking at the beginning of the text and pressing and holding the mouse button and dragging across the text. Release the mouse button. The text will be highlighted.

Text can be deselected by clicking anywhere else in the document.

DELETING TEXT

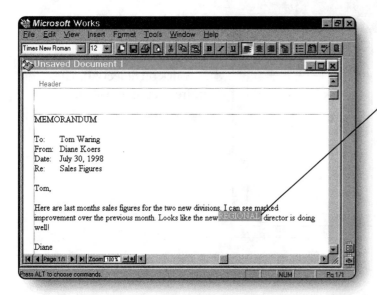

You can delete unwanted text one character, one word, one paragraph, or one page at a time, or any combination thereof.

1. **Select** the **text** to be deleted. The text will be highlighted.

2. **Press** the **Delete key**. The text will be deleted.

As soon as the deleted text disappears, any text below or to the right of the deleted words will move up to remove blank spaces.

UNDOING MISTAKES

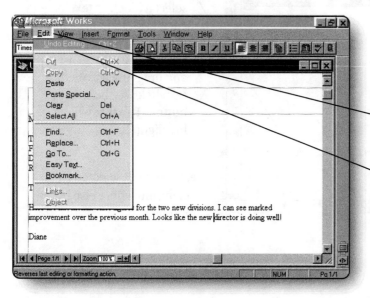

Microsoft Works has a wonderful feature called *Undo*. This feature will reverse the last step you performed.

1. **Click** on **Edit**. The Edit menu will appear.

2. **Click** on **Undo Editing**. The last action you took will be reversed.

USING EASY TEXT

If you use certain phrases or paragraphs of text frequently, you can type the text once and save it as Easy Text. You won't have to type the text in its entirety the next time, only a one word name for it.

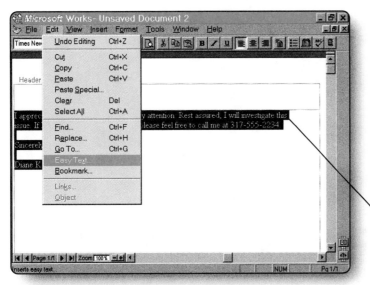

Creating an Easy Text Entry

Save typing time by storing frequently used text as Easy Text.

1. **Type** the **text** to be stored. The text will display in the document.

2. **Highlight** the **text**. The text will be highlighted.

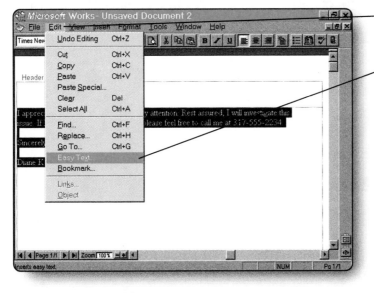

3. **Click** on **Edit**. The Edit menu will appear.

4. **Click** on **Easy Text**. The Easy Text dialog box will open.

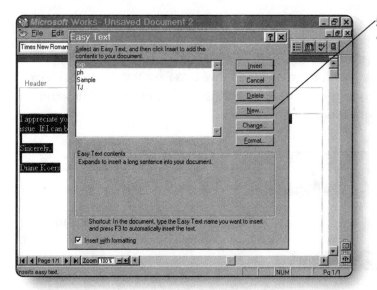

5. **Click** on **New**. The New Easy Text dialog box will open.

The highlighted text will display in the Easy Text contents box.

6. **Type** a **one-word name** for the Easy Text item. The text will appear in the text box.

7. **Click** on **Done**. The New Easy Text dialog box will close.

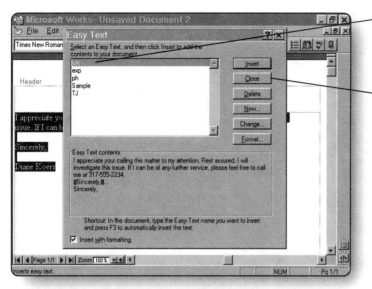

The new Easy Text abbreviation appears in the list of available Easy Text entries.

8. **Click** on the **Close button**. The Easy Text dialog box will close.

> **NOTE**
>
> You can create as many Easy Text entries as you like.

Using an Easy Text Entry

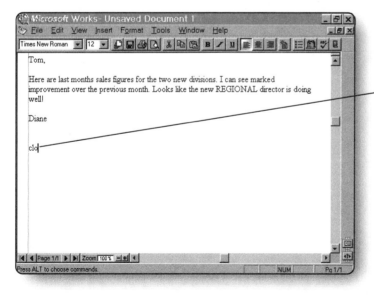

Now that you've saved an Easy Text entry, using it is only a keystroke away!

1. **Click** to **place an insertion point** for the Easy Text. The blinking insertion point will appear.

2. **Type** the **name** for the Easy Text you want to use. The name will appear in the document.

> **TIP**
>
> Make sure the insertion point remains directly on or next to the one-word name.

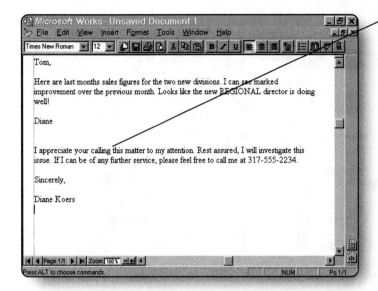

3. **Press** the **F3 key**. The word you typed will be replaced with the Easy Text entry.

4 Formatting a Document

Appearance is everything, so Works offers several ways to improve the appearance of your document through formatting. Formatting allows you to change the look of your document by changing the look of the text. In this chapter, you'll learn how to:

✦ Work with text properties

✦ Set paragraph alignment and indentation

✦ Set and delete tabs

✦ Work with bullets

WORKING WITH TEXT ATTRIBUTES

You can change the appearance of text in a variety of ways. For example, you can make the text boldfaced, underlined, or italicized, as well as change the font typeface and size.

Making Text Bold

Applying the bold attribute to text makes the text characters thicker and darker.

1. Create a new **document** as you learned in Chapter 3. The document will be displayed on the Works screen

2. Select the **text** to be bolded. It will be highlighted.

3. Click on the **Bold button**. The selected text will be boldfaced.

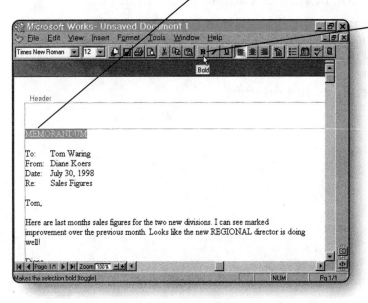

TIP

Repeat steps 1 and 2 to deselect the bold option.

Underlining Text

Using the underline attribute can call special attention to parts of your document.

1. **Select** the **text** you want to underline. The text will be highlighted.

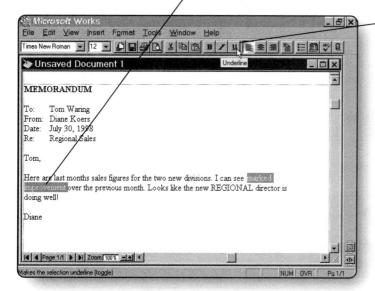

2. **Click** on the **Underline button**. The selected text will be underlined.

TIP

Click on the Italic button to italicize text.

WORKING WITH FONTS

Changing the font typeface is another way to make it stand out from the rest of your document.

Changing the Font Typeface

The font selections you have will vary, depending on which fonts are installed on your computer.

1. **Select** the **text** you want to change. The text will be highlighted.

2. **Click** on the **Font Name drop-down arrow**. A list of available fonts will display.

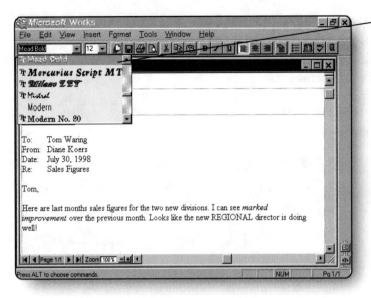

3. **Click** on a **font name** from the list. The font typeface change will be immediately applied to the selected text.

Selecting a Font Size

You may want to make portions of your text larger or smaller than the rest of the text in your document.

1. **Select** the **text** whose font size you want to change. The text will be highlighted.

2. **Click** on the **Font Size drop-down arrow.** A list of font sizes will appear.

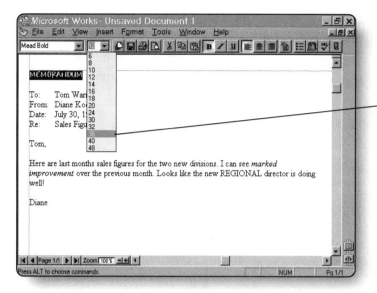

The larger the number, the larger the font size. For example, a 72 point font is approximately 1" tall on the printed page.

3. **Click** on a **new size**. The font size change will be applied to the selected text.

> **NOTE**
>
> Optionally, to select text attributes in a single step, click on Format and choose Font and Style to select font name, size, style (including Strikethrough style), position, and color.

SETTING PARAGRAPH OPTIONS

You may want to align certain paragraphs in your documents so that they are, for example, centered on a page. Headings and titles are examples of text that is usually centered. You also may need to indent paragraphs so that they stand out from other text.

Setting Paragraph Alignment

Four types of alignment are available: left, center, right, and full justified.

✦ **Left Align**. Text is even with the left margin, but jagged on the right margin.

✦ **Center Align**. Text is centered between the left and right margins.

✦ **Right Align**. Text is even with the right margin, but jagged on the left margin.

✦ **Justified**. Text is spaced evenly between the left and right margins.

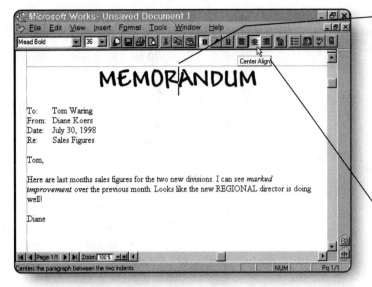

1. Click the **mouse pointer** within the paragraph to align. The insertion point will blink at the selected location.

Three of the four alignment choices are available as selections on the toolbar: Left, Center, or Right.

2a. Click on an **alignment button** to align the selected paragraph.

OR

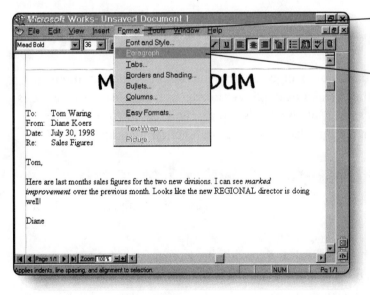

2b. Click on **Format**. The Format menu will appear.

3. Click on **Paragraph**. The Format Paragraph dialog box will open.

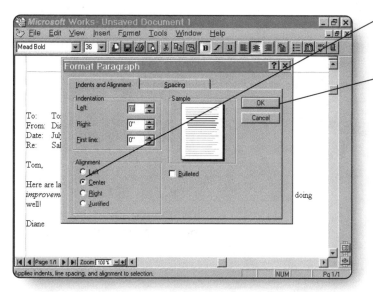

4. **Click** on an **alignment**. The option will be selected.

5. **Click** on **OK**. The Format Paragraph dialog box will close.

Creating Paragraph Borders

Add emphasis to a paragraph by placing a line under it or a border around it. You can have thin lines, thick lines, double lines, or even dashed or dotted lines.

1. **Click** the **mouse** in the paragraph to be modified. The blinking insertion point will appear in the paragraph.

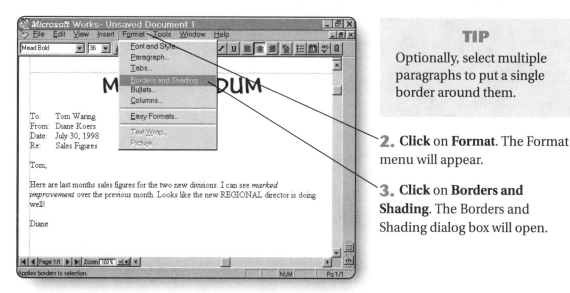

2. **Click** on **Format**. The Format menu will appear.

3. **Click** on **Borders and Shading**. The Borders and Shading dialog box will open.

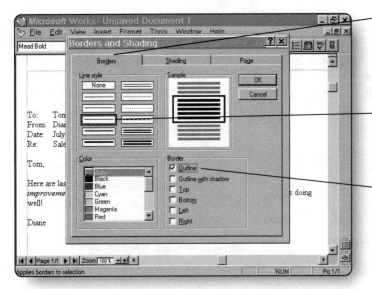

4. **Click** on the **Borders tab**, if necessary, to bring it to the front. The Borders tab will be placed in front.

5. **Click** on a **line style**. The style will have a black border appear around it.

6. **Click** on the **border placement options**. Selected options appear with a check mark.

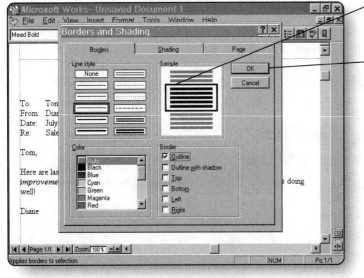

A sample will be displayed in the Sample box.

7. **Click** on **OK**. The Borders and Shading dialog box will close.

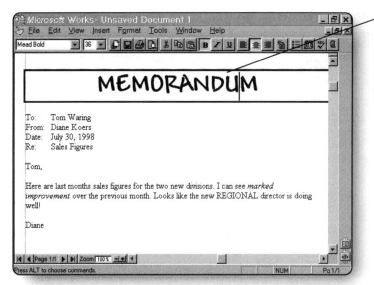

The selected options will be applied to the current paragraph.

Indenting Paragraphs

Sometimes you want to inset an entire paragraph from the left or right margins to emphasize its information. This is known as *indenting*. Different than a tab, all lines of the paragraph are inset when a paragraph is indented.

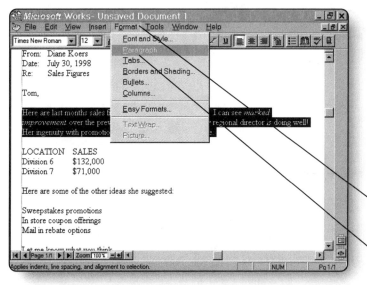

1. **Select** the **paragraphs** to be indented. The paragraphs will be highlighted.

TIP

Optionally, click the mouse in a single paragraph to be modified.

2. **Click** on **Format**. The Format menu will appear.

3. **Click** on **Paragraph**. The Format Paragraph dialog box will open.

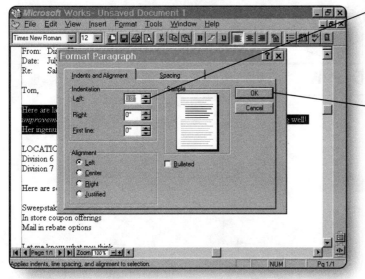

4. **Click** the **up/down arrows** for the Left Indentation. The indentation will increase .10 inch for each click.

5. **Click** on **OK**. The Format Paragraph dialog box will close.

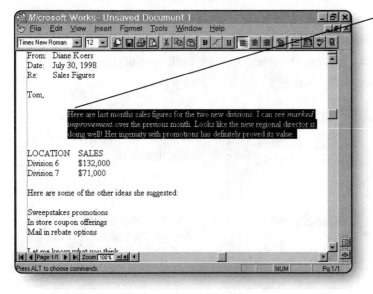

The selected paragraphs will be indented.

WORKING WITH TABS

Often you need to create columns of text in your document. Don't use your space bar to line up these columns because it is better accomplished by using tabs.

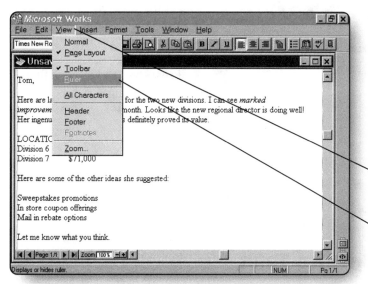

Displaying the Ruler

Setting and deleting custom tabs is easiest by using the ruler. The display of the ruler can be turned on or off as needed.

1. **Click** on **View**. The View menu will appear.

2. **Click** on **Ruler**. The Ruler Bar will be displayed.

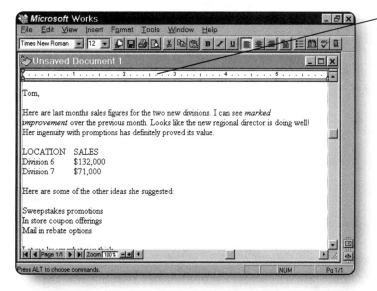

The Ruler Bar is displayed in inches.

TIP

To turn off the display of the ruler, repeat steps 1 and 2.

Using the Default Tabs

By default, tabs are set at every ½ inch.

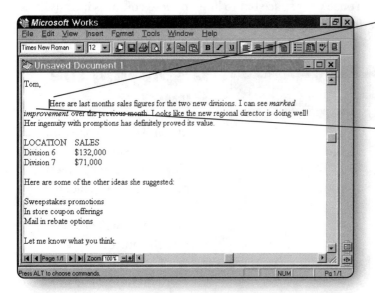

1. **Click** the **mouse pointer** at the beginning of a paragraph. The blinking insertion point will appear at the beginning of the paragraph.

2. **Press** the **Tab key**. The first line of the paragraph moves to the right ½ inch.

TIP

Press the Tab key again to indent the first line an additional ½ inch.

Setting Tabs

Use the ruler to create your own tab settings using a left aligned tab.

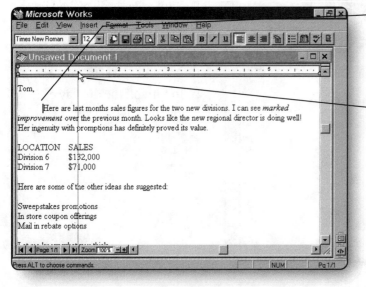

1. **Click** the **mouse pointer** in the paragraph to be modified. The blinking insertion point will appear in the paragraph.

2. **Position** the **mouse pointer** on the ruler. The mouse pointer will become a white arrow.

3. **Click** the **point of the arrow** on the ruler where you want to create a new tab. The tab will be set at that point.

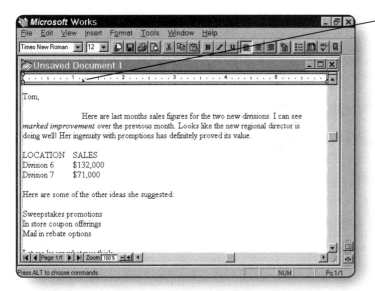

Custom tabs are indicated by a small L-shaped character on the ruler.

Modifying Tab Styles

When you set a custom tab by clicking on the ruler, Works inserts a left-aligned tab. You can modify any tab to be a right, centered, or decimal tab.

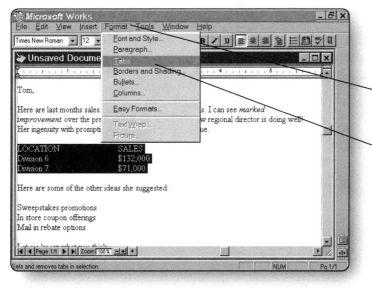

1. **Select** the **paragraphs** to be modified. The paragraphs will be highlighted.

2. **Click** on **Format**. The Format menu will appear.

3. **Click** on **Tabs**. The Format Tabs dialog box will open.

A list of custom tabs for the selected paragraphs is displayed.

4. Click on the **tab stop** you want to modify. The tab stop position will be highlighted.

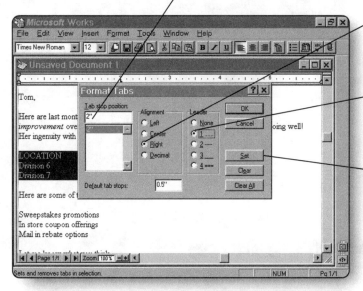

5. Click on an **alignment**. The alignment option will be selected.

6. Click on a **leader** for the tab. The leader option will be selected.

7. Click on **Set**. The changes will be recorded to the tab.

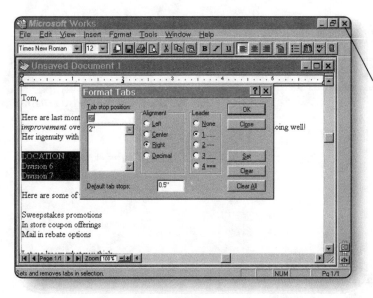

8. Repeat steps 4–7 for each tab that you want to modify.

9. Click on **Close**. The Format Tabs dialog box will close.

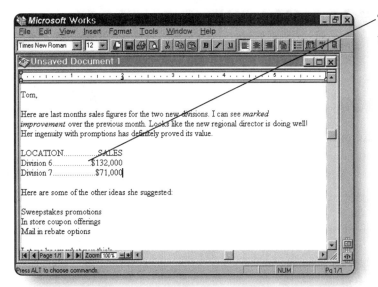

The tab changes will be applied to the selected paragraphs.

Deleting Tabs

Delete any tabs placed in error or no longer wanted in the paragraph. Make sure your insertion point is in the paragraph that contains the tab that you want to delete.

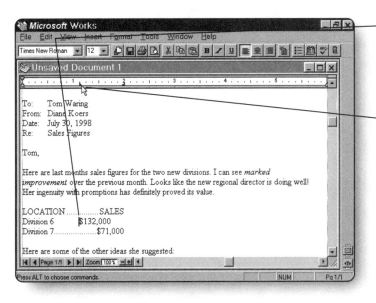

1. **Click** the **mouse** in the paragraph to be modified. The blinking insertion point will appear in the paragraph.

2. **Drag** the **unwanted tab** anywhere off the ruler. The tab will be removed.

WORKING WITH BULLETS

Works makes it easy to create a bulleted paragraph.

Adding a Bullet

Often indenting a paragraph or group of paragraphs is not enough to draw attention to it, so you might want to add a symbol in front of it. This is known as a *bullet*.

1. **Select** the **paragraphs** to bullet. The paragraphs will be highlighted.

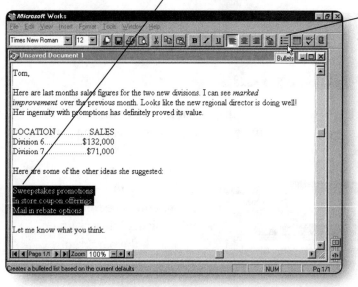

2. **Click** on the **Bullets button**. The paragraph will be immediately bulleted and indented.

TIP

Repeat steps 1 and 2 to remove the bullet from a paragraph.

Changing a Bullet Style

Choose from a collection of bullet styles ranging from small, black, filled circles to check marks to funny little icons.

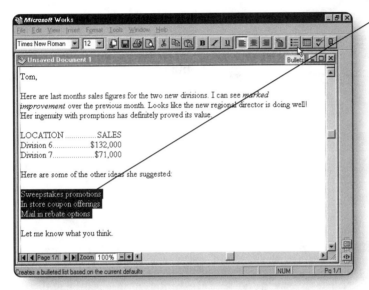

1. **Select** the **paragraphs** to modify the bullet. The paragraphs will be highlighted.

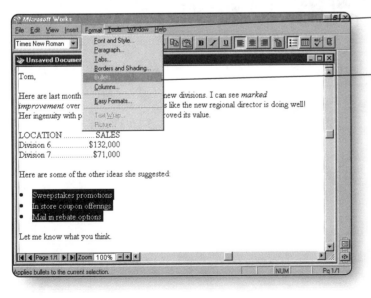

2. **Click** on **Format**. The Format menu will appear.

3. **Click** on **Bullets**. The Format Bullets dialog box will open.

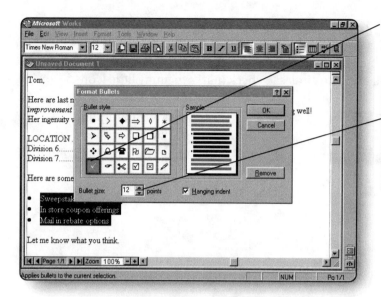

4. **Click** on a **bullet style**. The bullet style will be highlighted.

TIP

Optionally, click on the up/down arrows to increase the size of the bullet.

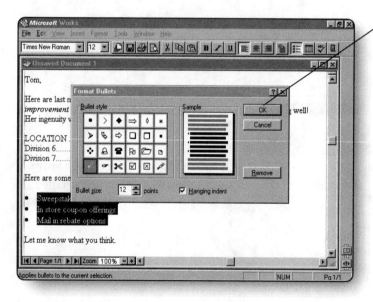

5. **Click** on **OK**. The Format Bullets dialog box will close and the bulleted paragraphs will reflect the newly selected bullet style.

5 Working with Tables

Prior to tables, a typist had to spend a lot of time pressing the Tab key or spacebar to line up text in columns. Tables have greatly simplified this process. Tables have columns and rows, making it easy to enter columnar text. In this chapter, you'll learn how to:

✦ Create a table

✦ Modify a table size

✦ Format a table

CREATING A TABLE

Tables created in Works can be up to 99 columns wide and 99 rows in length. Creating a table is done through the Insert menu.

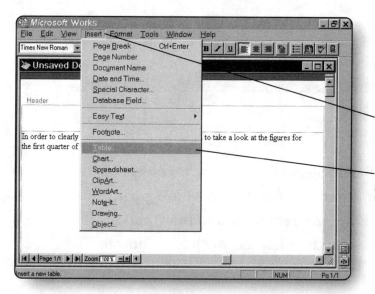

1. **Click** the **mouse** where you want the table to appear. The blinking insertion point will be displayed.

2. **Click** on **Insert**. The Insert menu will appear.

3. **Click** on **Table**. The Insert Table dialog box will open.

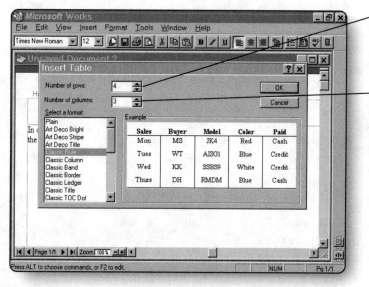

4. **Click** on the **up/down arrows** to indicate the Number of rows for the table.

5. **Click** on the **up/down arrows** to indicate the Number of columns for the table. The number of rows and columns can be modified later.

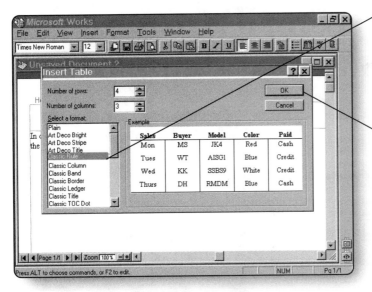

6. **Click** on a predefined **format** for the table. A sample will display in the Example box. You'll learn how to modify the format later in this chapter.

7. **Click** on **OK**. The table will be inserted into your document.

ENTERING TEXT INTO A TABLE

Text that is typed into a table cell is restricted by the boundaries of each table cell. The Tab key is used to move from one cell to the next, whereas the combination Shift+Tab keys moves the insertion point backwards to the previous cell. You can also use your arrow keys to move from cell to cell.

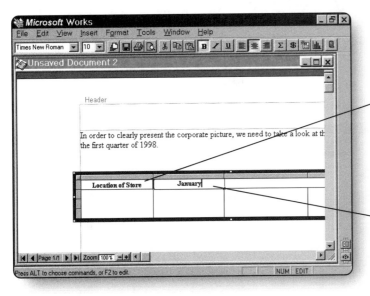

1. **Click** on the **cell** where you want to enter data. The border around the cell will be highlighted.

2. **Type** some **text**. The text will appear in the cell.

3. **Press** the **Tab** key. The insertion point will move to the next cell.

4. **Type** some **text**. The text will appear in the next cell.

5. **Repeat steps** 1–4 to enter your data.

SELECTING TABLE CELLS

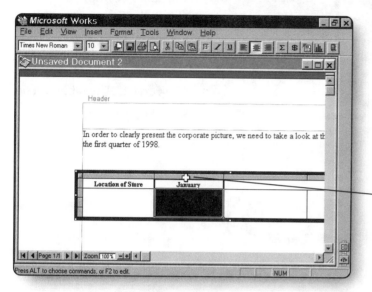

To modify a table, you'll need to select the cells you want to change. When selecting cells, the first cell selected does not appear highlighted, but will be included in the selection.

✦ To select a single cell, click on a cell.

✦ To select an entire column, position the mouse at the top of a column where the mouse turns into a white plus. Click on the small gray box (column selection markers).

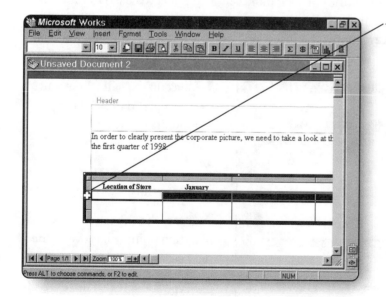

✦ To select an entire row, position the mouse at the left of a row where the mouse turns into a white plus. Click on the small gray box (row selection markers).

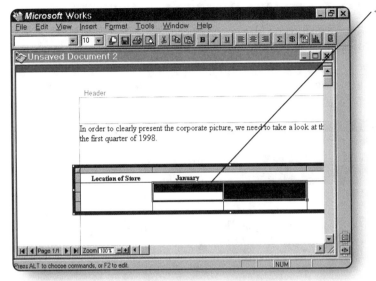

◆ To select a block of cells, click on the beginning cell, hold down the mouse button and drag across the additional cells. Then release the mouse button. (The first cell does not appear selected, but is included.)

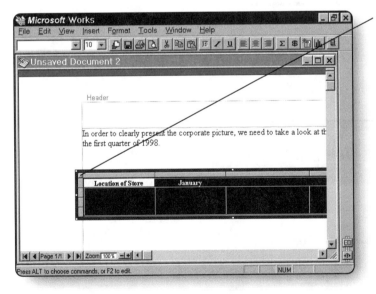

◆ To select the entire table, click in the small gray box above the row selection markers and to the left of the column selection markers.

MODIFYING TABLE SIZE

After you start working with a table, you may find that you need to add rows and columns or you may want to make a column narrower or wider based on the text in that column.

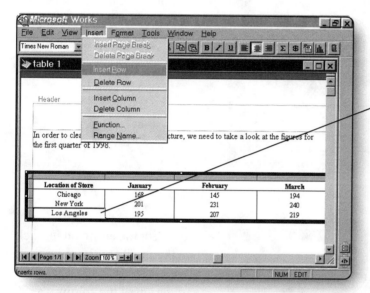

Adding Rows

All existing rows below the new row will be moved down.

1. **Click** on the **row** below where you want the new row to appear. A cell in that row will be selected.

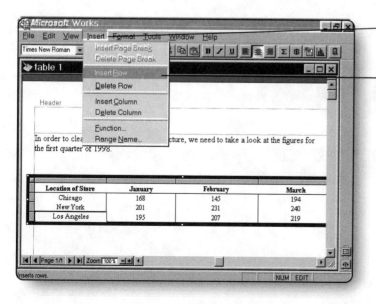

2. **Click** on **Insert**. The Insert menu will appear.

3. **Click** on **Insert Row**. The new row will be inserted after the selected row.

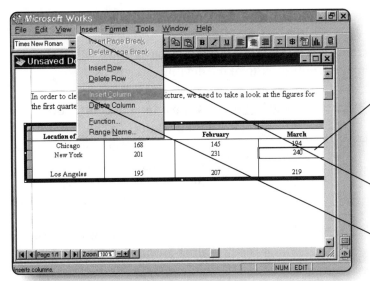

Adding Columns

Existing columns will be moved to the right of a new column.

1. **Click** on the **column** to the right of where you want the new column to appear. A cell in that column will be selected.

2. **Click** on **Insert**. The Insert menu will appear.

3. **Click** on **Insert Column**. The new column will be inserted to the left of the selected column.

Deleting Rows or Columns

If a row or column is no longer necessary, you can delete it.

1. **Click** on the **column** or **row** you want to delete. A cell in that column or row will be selected.

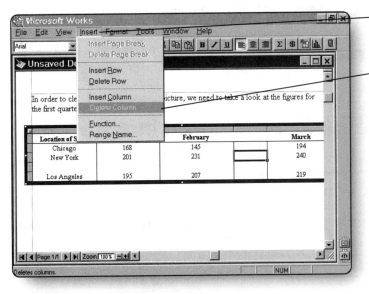

2. **Click** on **Insert**. The Insert menu will appear.

3a. **Click** on **Delete Column**. The selected column will be deleted.

OR

3b. **Click** on **Delete Row**. The selected row will be deleted.

Changing Column Width

By default, all columns are equally spaced and a table expands across the entire width of the document margins.

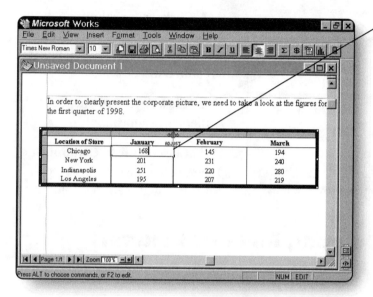

1. Position the **pointer** over the right border of a column selection marker. The pointer will change to a horizontal, double-headed arrow with the word "adjust."

2. Press the mouse button and drag the **border** until the column is the desired size. A dotted line will indicate the new column size.

3. Release the **mouse button**. The column will be resized.

FORMATTING A TABLE

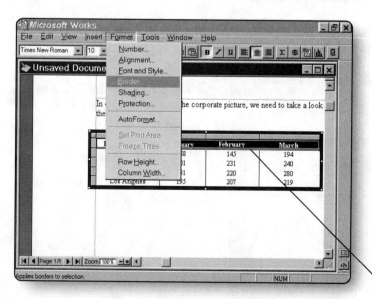

When you first created your table, you were able to select a formatting style. You can change any of the formatting options that you earlier selected.

Placing Borders around Cells

Many varieties of borders are available to appear around individual cells, rows, or columns.

1. Select the **cells** to be modified. The selected cells will be highlighted.

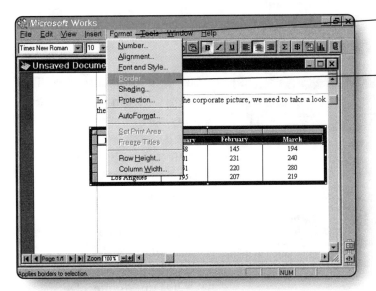

2. Click on **Format**. The Format menu will appear.

3. If necessary, **click** on **Border**. The Format Cells dialog box will open with the Border tab in front.

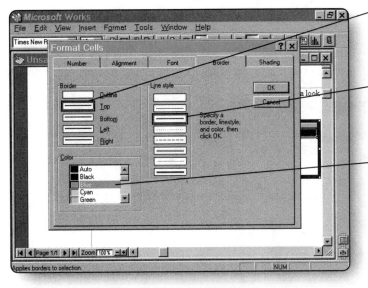

4. Click on a border **location**. The option will appear with a line around it.

5. Click on a border **Line style**. The style will appear in the border location box.

6. Optionally, **click** on a border **color**. The color will appear in the border location box.

7. Click on **OK**. The Format Cells dialog box will close and the border style will be applied to your selection.

Setting Number Formats for Cells

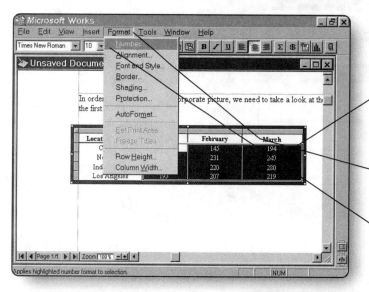

Make your numbers appear like currency, percentages, or other numerical formats.

1. **Select** the **cells** to be formatted. The cells will be highlighted.

2. **Click** on **Format**. The Format menu will appear.

3. **Click** on **Number**. The Format Cells dialog box will appear with the Number tab in front.

4. **Click** on a **format**. The option will be selected and a sample will be displayed at the bottom right of the dialog box.

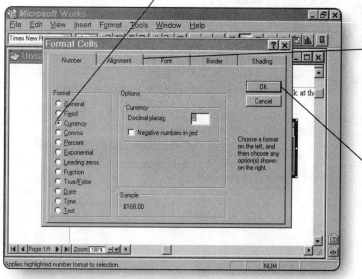

TIP

Optionally, click on the Alignment tab and select any desired alignment options for the selected cells.

5. **Click** on **OK**. The number formatting will be applied to the selection.

Connecting Cells

You may want to connect cells when creating a heading for your table.

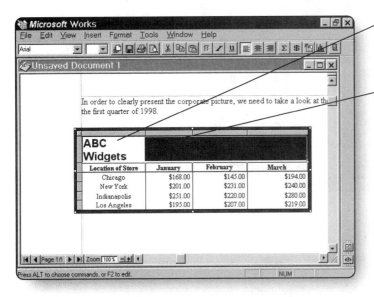

1. **Enter** the **heading text** in the first cell to the left. The text may wrap to the bottom of the cell.

2. **Press** and **hold** the **mouse button** and **drag** across the cells you want to connect. The cells will be selected.

NOTE

Other than the heading text in the first cell, no other text should be in any of the selected cells.

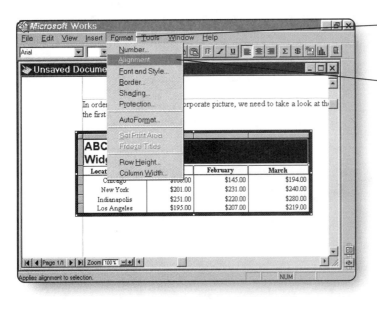

3. **Click** on **Format**. The Format menu will appear.

4. **Click** on **Alignment**. The Format Cells dialog box will open with the Alignment tab in front.

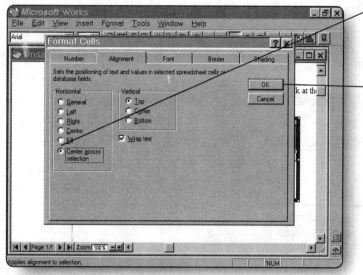

5. **Click** on **Center across selection**. The option will be selected.

6. **Click** on **OK**. The Format Cells dialog box will close.

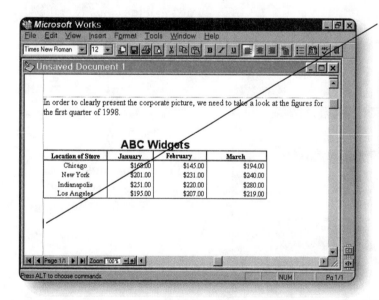

Click anywhere outside of the table to deselect the table.

TIP

Double-click on the table to return to editing it.

6 Working with Page Layout

In the world of word processing documents, one size doesn't always fit all. You may need to adjust the size of the text area of a document. Headers and footers are often used to repeat key information on each page of a document such as a company's name or the page number. These types of page layout features give your document a professional look. In this chapter, you'll learn how to:

✦ Set margins

✦ Change page size

✦ Change page orientation

✦ Add a header or footer

SETTING MARGINS

The size of the text area is determined by the page margins. You can set left, right, top, and bottom margins. By setting the margins, you control the amount of text area available. The default margin setting is 1" for the top and bottom margins and 1.25" for the left and right margins.

1. **Click** on **File**. The File menu will appear.

2. **Click** on **Page Setup**. The Page Setup dialog box will open.

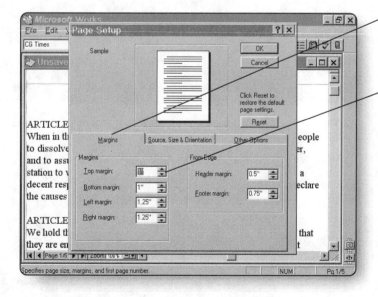

3. **Click** on the **Margins tab,** if necessary**.** The Margins tab will come to the front.

4. **Click** on the **up/down arrows** for each margin in the Top margin, Bottom margin, Left margin, and Right margin list boxes. The values in these boxes are measured in inches.

5. **Click** on **OK**. The Page Setup dialog box will close.

CHANGING PAGE SIZE

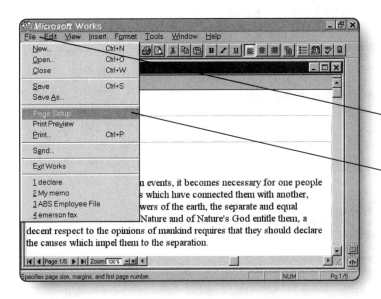

Works lets you select from several page size options, which are based on the page size settings of your printer.

1. **Click** on **File**. The File menu will appear.

2. **Click** on **Page Setup**. The Page Setup dialog box will open.

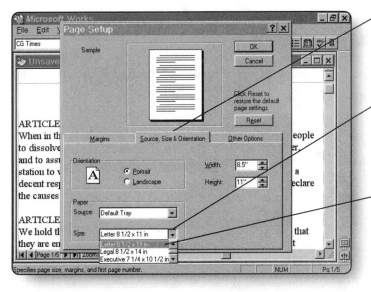

3. **Click** on the **Source, Size & Orientation tab.** The Source, Size & Orientation tab will come to the front.

4. **Click** on the **down arrow** at the right of the Size: list box. The list of available page size options will appear.

5. **Click** on a **page size**. The page size will be selected.

6. **Click** on **OK**. The Page Setup dialog box will close.

CHANGING PAGE ORIENTATION

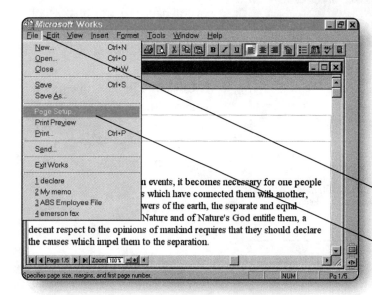

Works lets you print a document using either a portrait or landscape orientation. Portrait orientation will print the document in a vertical layout whereas landscape orientation will print horizontally across the page.

1. **Click** on **File**. The File menu will appear.

2. **Click** on **Page Setup**. The Page Setup dialog box will open.

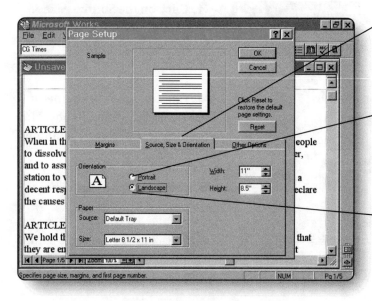

3. **Click** on the **Source, Size & Orientation tab.** The Source, Size & Orientation tab will come to the front.

4a. **Click** on the **Portrait button**. The document's orientation will be portrait.

OR

4b. **Click** on the **Landscape button**. The document's orientation will be landscape.

5. **Click** on **OK**. The Page Setup dialog box will close.

ADDING A HEADER OR FOOTER

Two areas in a document are reserved for repeating text. When this text is at the top of a page, it is called a *header*. When this text is at the bottom of a page, it is called a *footer*. The header or footer area is displayed as a box with a light gray outline at the top or bottom of the document.

Creating a Header or Footer

Examples of text you may want to place in a header or footer are the date the document was created, the document name, your company's name, or the current page number. The header and footer area are automatically created when you create a new document.

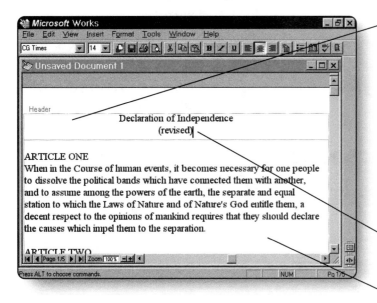

1a. **Click** in the **Header area** of your document. The insertion point will be located in the header area of the document.

OR

1b. **Click** in the **Footer area** of your document. The insertion point will be located in the footer area of the document.

2. **Type text**. The text will be added to the header or footer.

3. **Click** on an area **outside** of the Header or Footer. The blinking insertion point will be located in the body of your document.

TIP

Format header or footer text using the same methods used to format the document body text. Formatting text was discussed in Chapter 4.

Inserting a Page Number in a Header or Footer

When creating a header or footer, do not type a number for the page number because Works requires a special field to increment them.

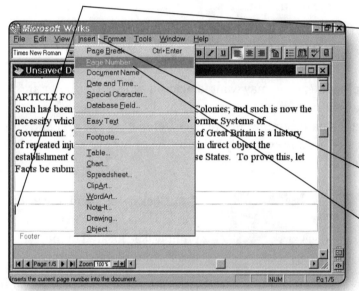

1. **Position** the **insertion point** at the location in the Header or Footer where you want the page number to be printed. The insertion point will be located in the header or footer area of the document.

2. **Click** on **Insert**. The Insert menu will appear.

3. **Click** on **Page Number**. A code for the current page number will be inserted into the header or footer.

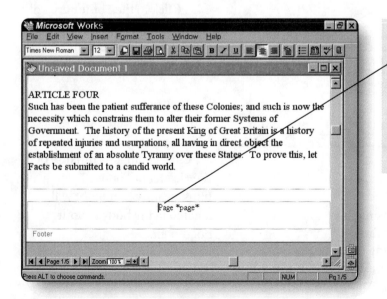

If you want the page number to be preceded by text, such as the word "Page," type the text in front of the page numbering field.

7 Creating Reports

Reports are second only to letters in popularity and use. Whether you are a student, consultant, or other professional, you will have many uses for reports. Students are often called upon to do reports as part of their class work; professionals often need to do reports for a variety of reasons ranging from cost and project justifications to recommendations and strategic directions. In this chapter, you'll learn how to:

✦ Add page breaks

✦ Add page borders

✦ Add footnotes

INSERTING PAGE BREAKS

When a page is full with text, Works automatically begins a new page. Sometimes, however, you want a new page to begin at a specific location. This is called a *page break*.

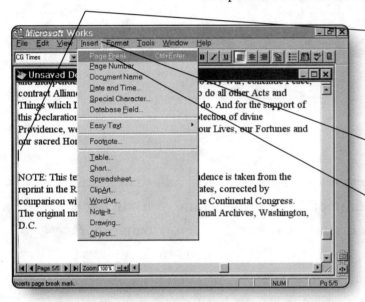

1. **Click** the **mouse** at the position where you want the new page to begin. The blinking insertion point will appear at that position.

2. **Click** on **Insert**. The Insert menu will appear.

3. **Click** on **Page Break**. The insertion point will appear at the beginning of a new page.

ADDING PAGE BORDERS

Decorate your page with a border. Works offers a variety of borders that you can use. You can opt for a border around all pages of your document or only the first page.

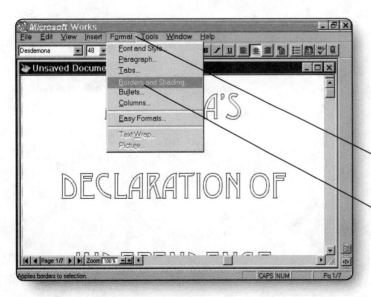

1. **Click** on **Format**. The Format menu will appear.

2. **Click** on **Borders and Shading**. The Borders and Shading dialog box will open.

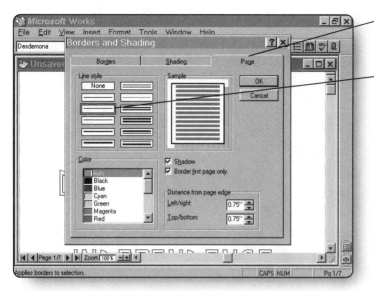

3. Click on the **Page tab**. The Page tab will come to the front.

4. Click on a **Line style**. A black box will surround the selected style and a sample will appear in the Sample box.

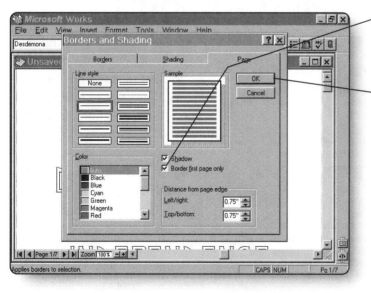

5. Optionally, **click** on **Border first page only**. A check mark will appear in the selection.

6. Click on **OK**. The Borders and Shading dialog box will close.

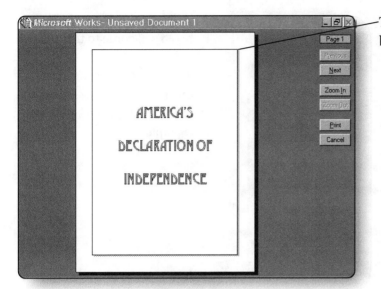

The page border selections will be applied to the document.

ADDING FOOTNOTES

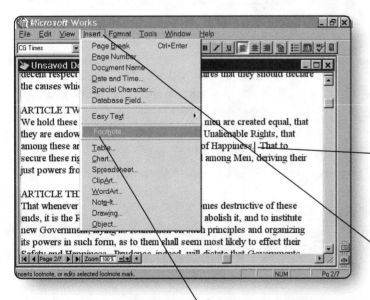

Footnotes comment on and provide reference information for the text in your document. Works allows you to insert footnotes or endnotes, but not both.

1. Click on the **location** for the footnote. The blinking insertion point will be moved to that location.

2. Click on **Insert**. The Insert menu will appear.

3. Click on **Footnote**. The Insert Footnote dialog box will open.

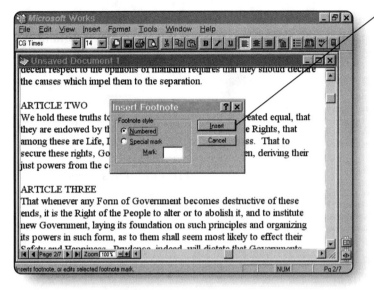

4. **Click** on **Insert**. The footnote reference number will be added to the document and the Insert Footnote dialog box will close. The insertion point will be placed in the footnote area of the document.

Works automatically includes a separator line for your footnotes.

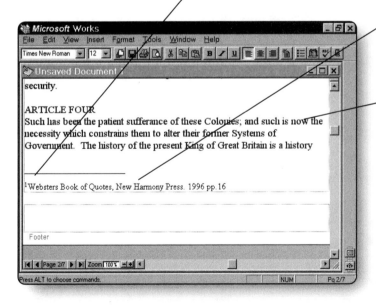

5. **Type** the **text** of the footnote. The text will be entered for this footnote.

6. **Click** in the **document body**. You will return to the main text of the document.

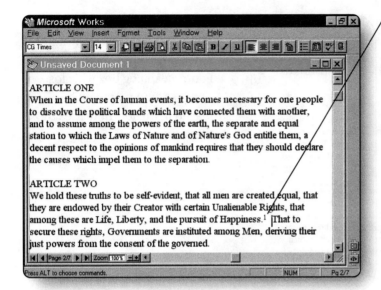

The footnote reference number is displayed in the document body.

TIP

For endnotes instead of footnotes, choose File, Page Setup, Other, and click on Print footnotes at end.

8 Improving Your Writing

One of the goals of Microsoft Works is to make document creation as easy as possible. To reach this goal, several features are included to improve your writing. For example, the Spell Correct feature of Works can catch many misspellings for you, and if you can't think of the exact word you want to use, the Thesaurus can help you out. These and other features such as Find and Replace can be used to improve your writing style. In this chapter, you'll learn how to:

✦ Use the Find and Replace features

✦ Check your spelling

✦ Use the Thesaurus feature

USING FIND TO LOCATE TEXT

Do you have a long document that you created, but you can't remember where you used a particular word or phrase? Use the Find feature to search for words or phrases in a document.

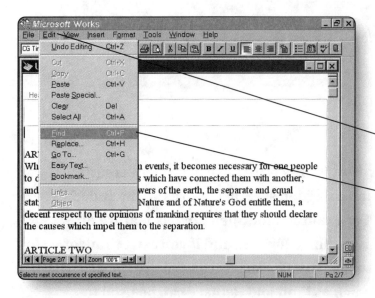

1. **Click** the **mouse** at the location to begin the search—usually the beginning of the document. The insertion point will appear at that location.

2. **Click** on **Edit**. The Edit menu will appear.

3. **Click** on **Find**. The Find dialog box will open.

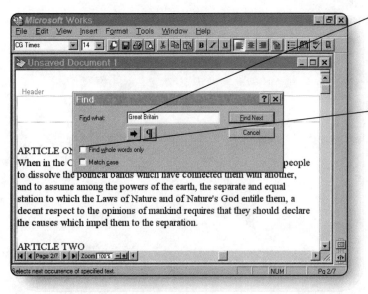

4. **Type** the **word** or **phrase** you want to locate. The text will appear in the Find what: text box.

5. Optionally, **click** on **Find whole words only** or **Match case**. These items will be selected.

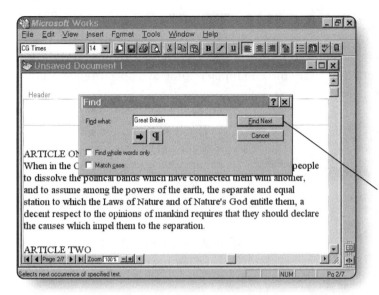

For example, if you type "and" in the Find box and select Find whole words only, Works will not find the words "Anderson," "candy," or "band." If you choose Match case, Works would only find "and." It would not find "AND" or "And."

6. **Click** on **Find Next**. The first occurrence of the found text will be highlighted.

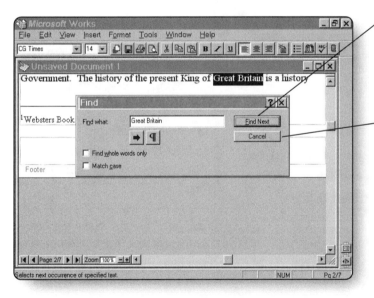

7a. **Click** on **Find Next**. Works will locate the next occurrence of the found text.

OR

7b. **Click** on **Cancel**. The Find dialog box will close and the found text will remain highlighted.

REPLACING TEXT

Use the Replace feature to exchange a word or phrase for something else. You can replace some or all occurrences of the text with other text.

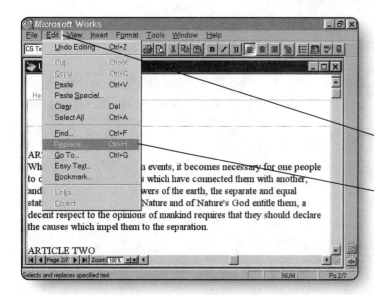

1. **Click** the **mouse** at the beginning of the document or where you wish to begin the search. The insertion point will appear at that location.

2. **Click** on **Edit**. The Edit menu will appear.

3. **Click** on **Replace**. The Replace dialog box will open.

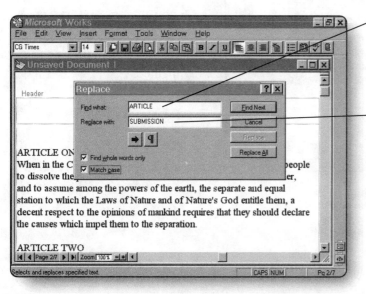

4. **Type** the **text** that you want to find in the Find what: text box. The text will appear in the box.

5. **Type** the **text** in the Replace with: text box that will replace the Find text in step 4. The text will appear in the box.

6. **Click** on **Find Next**. The first location of the Find text will be highlighted.

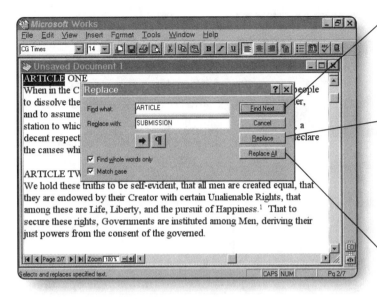

7a. **Click** on **Find Next**. Works will leave the found text alone and go to the next occurrence.

OR

7b. **Click** on **Replace**. The replacement text will be placed in the document and Works will search for the next occurrence of the text.

TIP

Click on Replace All to replace all occurrences of the search text at the same time.

NOTE

If the Replace box is left blank and you click on Replace, Works will delete the word or phrase.

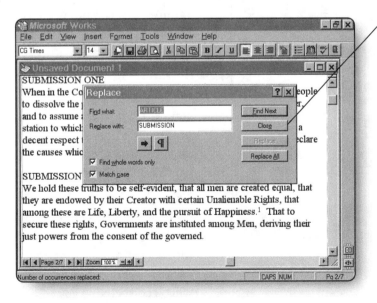

8. **Click** on the **Close button**. The Replace dialog box will close.

CORRECTING YOUR SPELLING

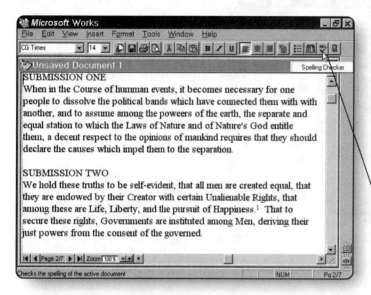

Works has a feature that locates and corrects misspelled words after you are finished typing. Be aware that Works considers any word that it doesn't recognize a misspelled word. This means that proper names, like your last name, will probably be identified as misspelled.

1. Click on the **Spelling Checker button**. The Spelling: American English dialog box will open with the first error highlighted.

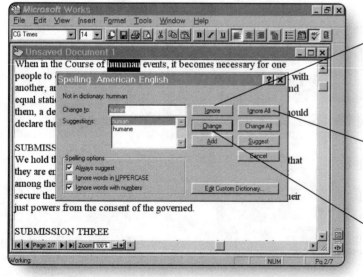

2. Choose from these **options**:

✦ **Ignore**. If you do not want to change the spelling of this word and you want to skip this occurrence, click on Ignore.

✦ **Ignore All**. If you do not want the Spelling Checker to stop on any occurrences of this word, click on Ignore All.

✦ **Change**. To replace this single occurrence of this word, click on the correct spelling from the suggestions: list box and click on Change. The word will be corrected in your document.

TIP

Optionally, click in the Change to Box and type your
own correction of the word prior to choosing Change.

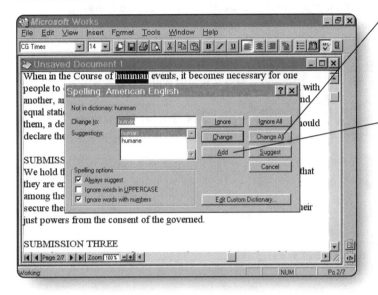

◆ **Change All**. To replace all
occurrences of this word,
click on the correct spelling
from the suggestions: list box
and click on Change All.

◆ **Add**. If the word is correctly
spelled and you want to avoid
having the Spelling Checker
stop on it in the future, click
on Add.

3. Repeat step 2 until all the
highlighted words have been
checked. A message box will
display letting you know that the
spelling check is complete.

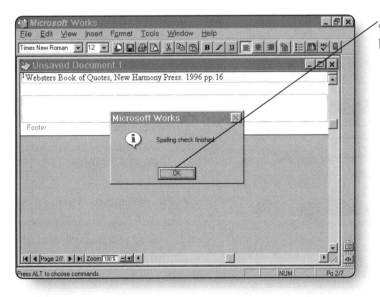

4. Click on **OK**. The message
box will close.

USING THE THESAURUS

The Works Thesaurus gives you an easy way to find just the right words to use in your document.

1. **Click** in the **word** you want to replace. The blinking insertion point will appear in the word.

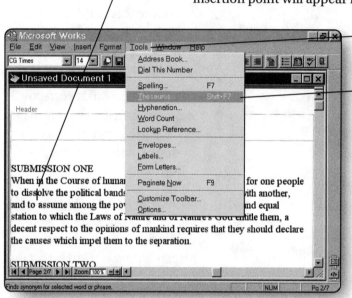

2. **Click** on **Tools**. The Tools menu will appear.

3. **Click** on **Thesaurus**. The Thesaurus dialog box will open.

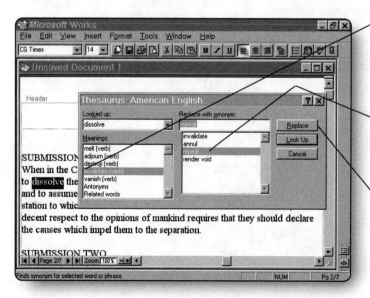

4. **Click** on a **meaning** in the Meanings: list box. A list of synonyms for that meaning will be displayed.

5. **Click** on a **word** from the Replace with synonym: list box. The word will be highlighted.

6. **Click** on **Replace**. The Thesaurus dialog box will close and the word will be replaced in the document.

9 Completing Your Document

One of the most important things that you learn to do with any application is save your work. Who wants to spend hours on a document and then lose it when the power flickers because it wasn't saved? Saving a document also allows you to exit from Works and return to your document later to work on it. You'll also need to know how to print your work. In this chapter, you'll learn how to:

✦ Save a document

✦ Print a document

✦ Close and open a document

SAVING A DOCUMENT

Your computer could fail you at any time due to any number of reasons. Saving your work not only preserves changes you make in the process of creating a document, but also files it electronically so that you can find it and use it again at a later time.

Saving a Document the First Time

When you first create a document, it has no name. If you want to use that document later, you must name it so that Works is able to find it.

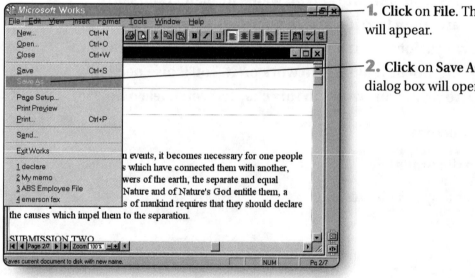

1. **Click** on **File**. The File menu will appear.

2. **Click** on **Save As.** The Save As dialog box will open.

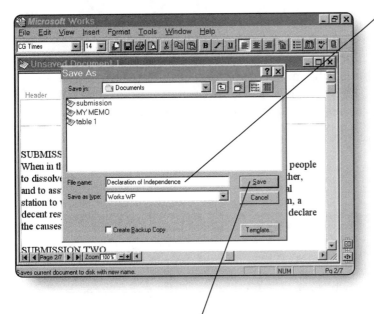

3. **Type** a **name** for your file in the File name: text box. The file name will be displayed.

4. **Click** on **Save**. Your document will be saved and the name you specified will appear in the title bar.

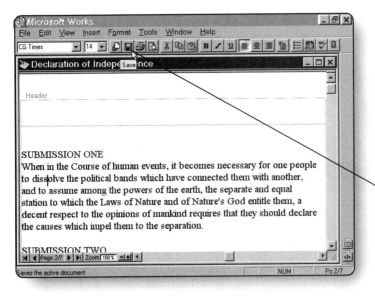

Resaving a Document

As you continue to work on your document, you should resave it every ten minutes or so to help ensure that you do not lose any changes.

1. **Click** on the **Save button**. The document will be resaved with any changes. No dialog box will appear, because the document is resaved with the same name and in the same folder as previously specified.

PRINTING A DOCUMENT

Works is a what-you-see-is-what-you-get (WYSIWYG) word processing program which means that text and other elements, such as graphics, appear on the screen the same way that they will look when they print out.

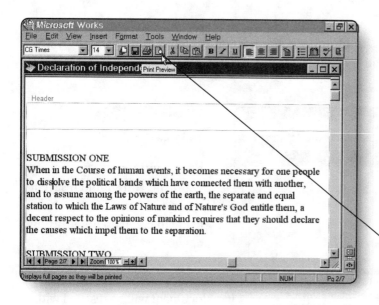

Using Print Preview

Before you print your document, you should preview it full-screen. Previewing a document allows you to get an idea of how document layout settings, such as margins, will look on the printed document.

1. Click on the **Print Preview button**. The document will be sized so that an entire page is visible on the screen. You won't be able to edit the document from this screen.

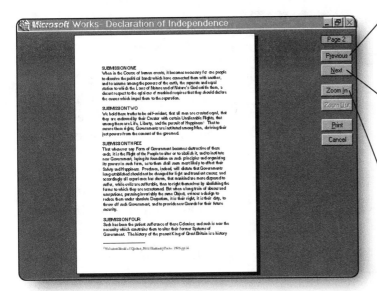

2. **Click** on **Previous**. The previous page of the document will be displayed.

3. **Click** on **Next**. The next page of the document will be displayed.

4. **Click** on **Zoom In**. The text will become larger on the screen.

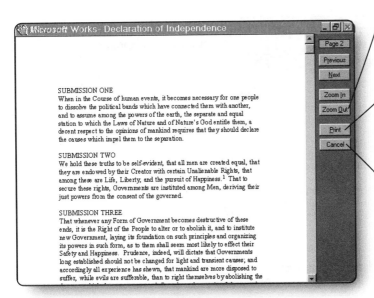

5. **Click** on **Zoom Out**. The text will become smaller on the screen.

6. Optionally, **click** on **Print**. The document will automatically print with standard options.

7. **Click** on **Cancel**. The document will be returned to the normal editing view.

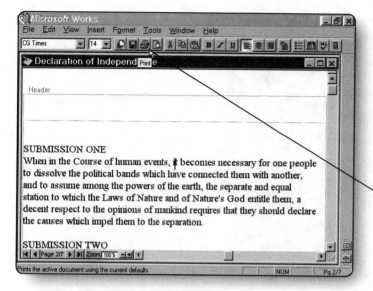

Printing Your Work

Typically, the end result of entering a document into Works is to get text onto paper. Works gives you a quick and easy way to get that result.

1a. Click on the **Print button**. The document will print with standard options.

OR

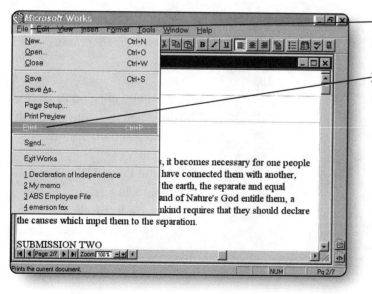

1b. Click on **File**. The File menu will appear.

2. Click on **Print**. The Print dialog box will open.

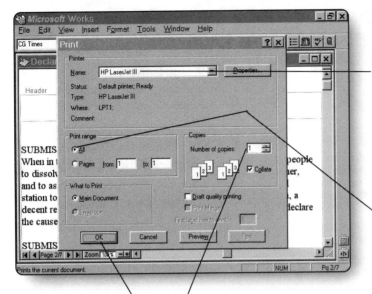

Many options are available from the Print dialog box including:

✦ **Name**. If you are connected to more than one printer, you can choose which one to use for this print job. Click on the down arrow in the Name drop-down list box and make a selection.

✦ **Print range**. You can choose which pages of your document to print with the Print range options.

✦ **Number of copies**. Choose the number of copies to be printed by clicking on the up/down arrows at the right of the Number of copies: list box.

3. **Click** on any desired **option.** The option will be activated.

4. **Click** on **OK** after you have made your selections. The document will be sent to the printer.

CLOSING A DOCUMENT

When you are finished working on a document, you should close it. Closing is the equivalent of putting it away for later use. When you close a document, you are only putting the document away—not the program. Works is still active and ready to work for you.

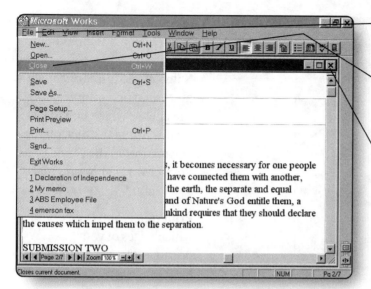

1. **Click** on **File**. The File menu will appear.

2. **Click** on **Close**. The document will be put away.

OR

3. **Click** on the **Close Button**. The document will be closed. By choosing this method, you combine steps 1 and 2.

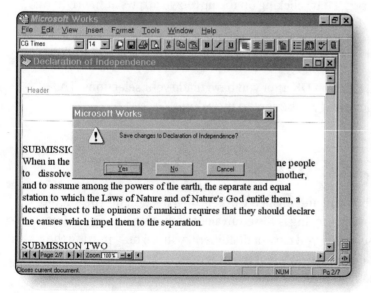

NOTE

If you close a document with changes that have not been saved, Works will prompt you with a dialog box. Choose Yes to save the changes or No to close the file without saving the changes.

If you have no other documents open, the Task Launcher will reappear.

OPENING A DOCUMENT

Opening a document is putting a copy of that file up into the computer's memory and onto your screen so that you can work on it. If you make any changes, be sure to save the file again.

Opening a Document from the Task Launcher

You can open a document from the Works Task Launcher that appears when you first start the Works program.

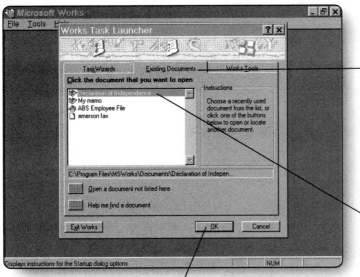

1. **Start Microsoft Works**. The Task Launcher will appear.

2. **Click** on the **Existing Documents tab**. The Existing Documents tab will come to the front.

If the document you want to open is listed:

3a. **Click** on the **file name** that you want to open. The file name will be highlighted.

4a. **Click** on **OK**. The file will be placed on your screen, ready for you to edit.

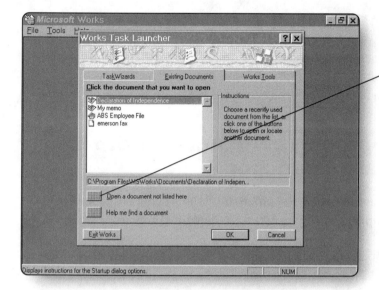

If the document you want to open is not listed:

3b. **Click** on **Open a document not listed here**. The Open dialog box will open.

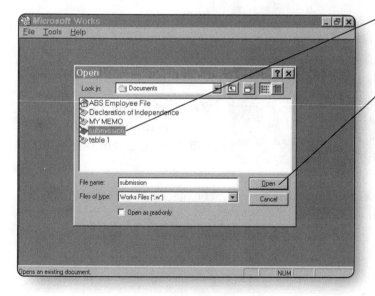

4b. **Click** on the **file name** you wish to open. The file name will be highlighted.

5. **Click** on **Open**. The file will be placed on your screen, ready for you to edit.

Opening Multiple Documents

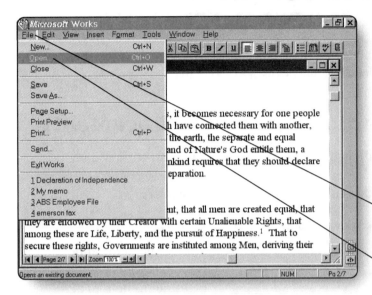

1. **Click** on **File**. The File menu will appear.

2. **Click** on **Open**. The Open dialog box will open.

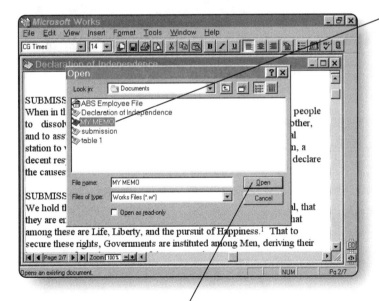

3. **Click** on the **file name** you wish to open. The file name will be highlighted and appear in the File name: text box.

4. **Click** on **Open**. The file will be placed onscreen, ready for you to edit.

WORKING WITH MULTIPLE DOCUMENTS

When more than one document is open at a time, one document will be displayed on top of all the others.

Switching between Documents

Although multiple documents can be open, only one document can be edited at a time. Use the Window menu to locate and switch to a different open document.

1. **Click** on **Window**. The Window menu will appear, and a list of all open documents will appear at the bottom of the window.

2. **Click** the **document name** that you wish to edit. The document appears on top of the stack of open documents.

Viewing Multiple Documents Together

Occasionally you may need to view more than one document at the same time. You can use the Tile feature to accomplish this. Tiling will divide up the screen space among the open documents. It is not recommended for more than three documents at a time.

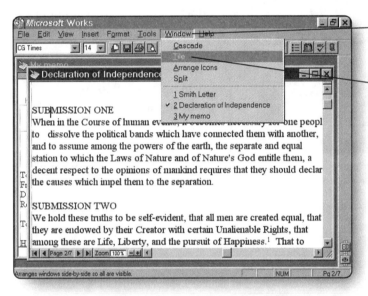

1. Click on **Window**. The Window menu will appear.

2. Click on **Tile**. The entire work area will be divided between the open documents.

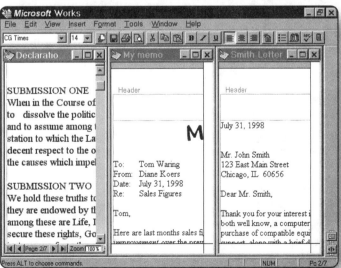

TIP

To edit a document, click anywhere on the window for that document.

Moving Data from One Document to Another

If you have information that needs to be copied from one document to another, use the Tiled windows to drag the information. The feature you'll use is called "Drag and Drop."

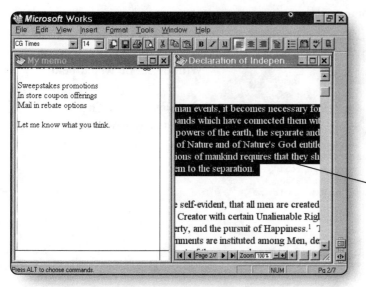

1. Tile the **windows** of two documents. Both documents will be displayed on the screen.

2. Click in the **document** from which you want to copy information. The document will be the active document.

3. Select the **text** to be copied. The text will be highlighted.

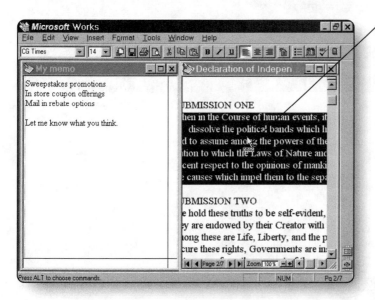

4. Press and hold the **mouse pointer** over the highlighted text. The mouse pointer will display the word "DRAG."

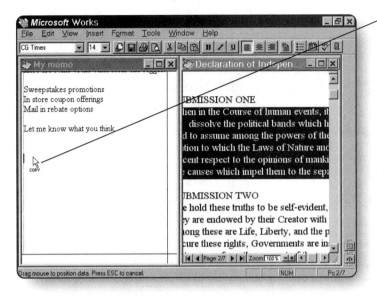

5. Drag the **mouse pointer** across to the second document. The mouse pointer will display the word "COPY" as you reach the second document.

6. Release the **mouse button** when the blinking insertion point is at the position you want the text to be copied. The text will be duplicated.

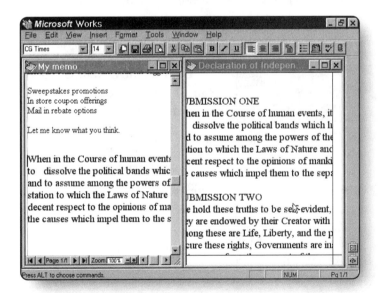

The text remains in the original document.

NOTE

You can also use the Windows Cut, Copy, and Paste commands to copy or move information from one document to another. You'll learn more about those commands in Chapter 11, "Working with Functions and Formulas."

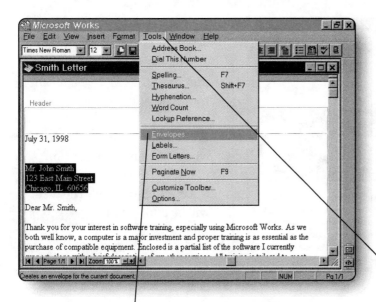

CREATING AN ENVELOPE

With a laser or inkjet printer and Microsoft Works, you can easily print a professional looking envelope.

1. **Select** the **recipient address** in the letter. The address will be highlighted.

2. **Click** on **Tools**. The Tools menu will appear.

3. **Click** on **Envelopes**. The Envelopes dialog box will open.

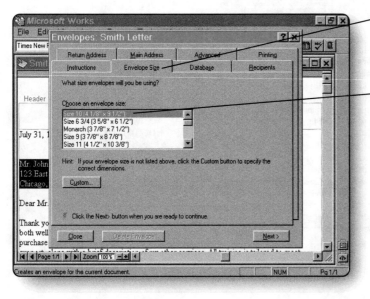

4. **Click** on the **Envelope Size tab**. The Envelope Size tab appears on top.

5. **Click** on an **envelope size**. The selection will be highlighted.

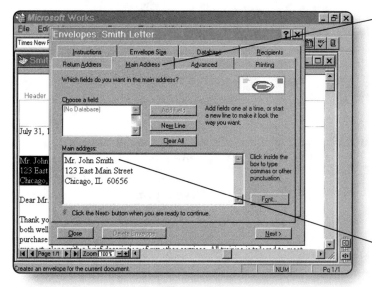

6. **Click** on the **Main Address tab**. The Main Address tab appears on top.

7. Optionally, **type** any necessary **changes** in the Main Address: text box. The changes will affect the envelope only, not the letter.

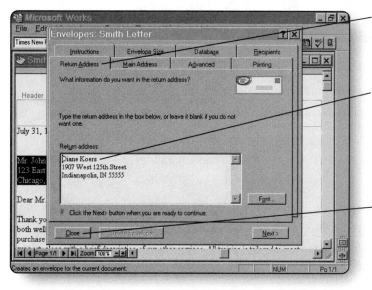

8. **Click** on the **Return Address tab**. The Return Address tab appears on top.

9. **Click** in the **Return Address: text box** and **type** the **return address**. Leave this area blank if you are using preprinted envelopes.

10. **Click** on the **Close button**. A message box will open.

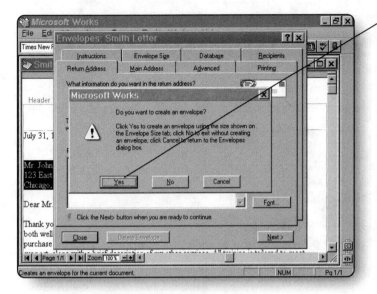

11. **Click** on **Yes** if you want to create the envelope. The message box will close and the envelope will be created.

NOTE

Refer to your printer manual for instructions on placing an envelope into your printer.

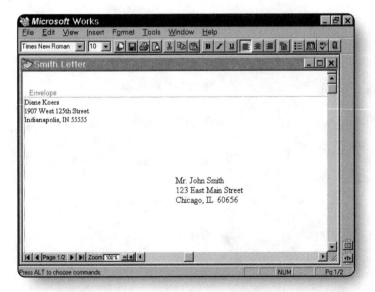

The envelope will appear as page one of the letter.

PART II REVIEW QUESTIONS

1. **What is a dynamic date?** *See "Inserting the Date and Time" in Chapter 3*

2. **What feature can you use to store frequently used text?** *See "Using Easy Text" in Chapter 3*

3. **What are the four types of text alignment?** *See "Setting Paragraph Alignment" in Chapter 4*

4. **What should you display if you are going to be working with tabs?** *See "Displaying the Ruler" in Chapter 4*

5. **What is the maximum number of rows and columns available for a table?** *See "Creating a Table" in Chapter 5*

6. **What two areas of a document are reserved for repeating text?** *See "Adding a Header or Footer" in Chapter 6*

7. **Page borders can be placed around which pages of a document?** *See "Adding Page Borders" in Chapter 7*

8. **When using Spell Correct, what is the difference between the options Ignore and Ignore All?** *See "Correcting Your Spelling" in Chapter 8*

9. **How often should you save a document?** *See "Resaving a Document" in Chapter 9*

10. **How can you view multiple documents at the same time?** *See "Viewing Multiple Documents Together" in Chapter 9*

PART III

Using Spreadsheets

Cha

Earni

January February

New York

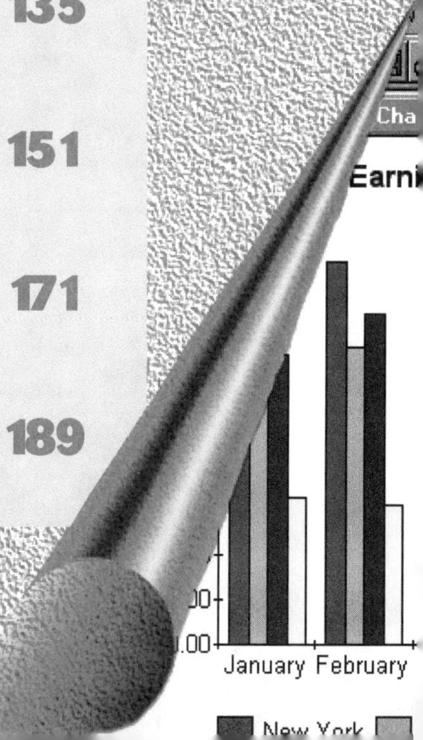

10 Creating a Simple Spreadsheet

Works has a full-featured spreadsheet program that you can use to make calculations, create charts, and even sort data! In this chapter, you'll learn how to:

✦ Create a new spreadsheet

✦ Explore and move around in the spreadsheet screen

✦ Enter and edit labels and values

✦ Undo mistakes

OPENING A NEW SPREADSHEET

Create a new spreadsheet by using the Works Task Launcher.

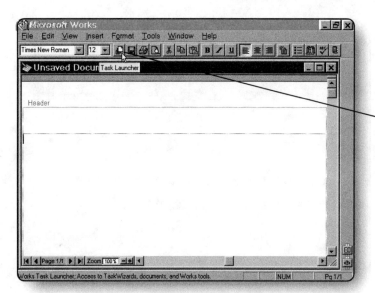

1a. **Start** Microsoft **Works**. The Task Launcher will appear.

OR

1b. **Click** on the **Task Launcher button**. The Task Launcher will appear.

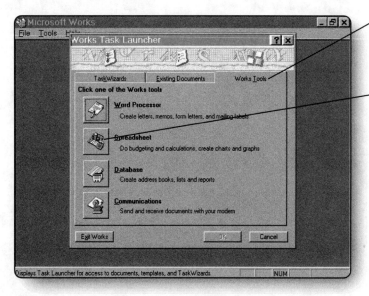

2. **Click** on the **Works Tools tab**. The Works Tools tab will come to the front.

3. **Click** on **Spreadsheet**. A blank spreadsheet will appear on your screen.

EXPLORING THE SPREADSHEET SCREEN

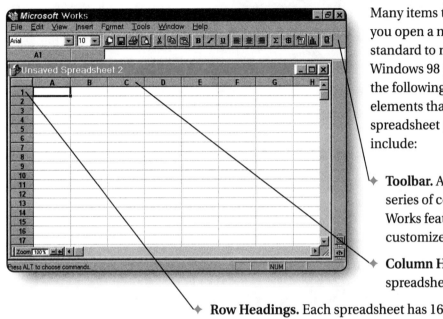

Many items that you see when you open a new spreadsheet are standard to most Windows 95 or Windows 98 programs. However, the following list illustrates a few elements that are specific to a spreadsheet program. These include:

✦ **Toolbar.** A toolbar with a series of commonly used Works features. You can customize the toolbar.

✦ **Column Headings.** Each spreadsheet has 256 columns.

✦ **Row Headings.** Each spreadsheet has 16,384 rows.

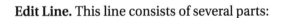

Edit Line. This line consists of several parts:

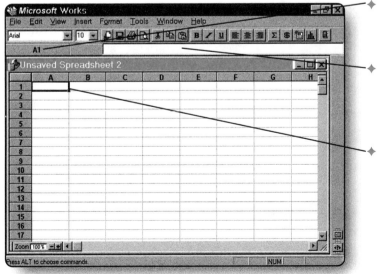

✦ **Selection Indicator.** This shows the address or name of the current selection.

✦ **Contents box.** This area displays the entry you are typing or editing, or the contents of the current cell.

✦ **Cell.** An intersection of a column and row, sometimes called a *cell address*. It is indicated by a heavy border around the selected cell.

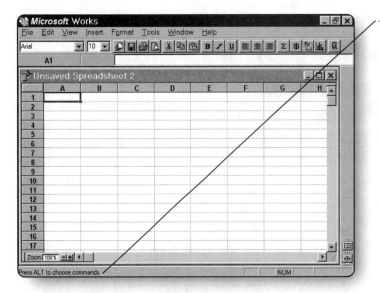

✦ **Status Bar.** Gives you information about the current selection and tells you what Works is doing. You can use the status bar to perform many functions with the mouse.

MOVING AROUND THE SPREADSHEET SCREEN

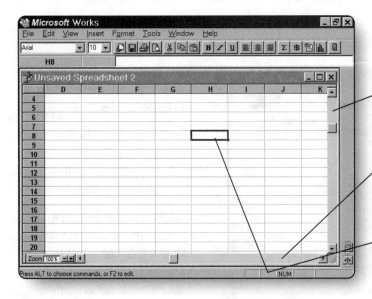

You can use your mouse or keyboard to quickly move around in a spreadsheet.

1. **Click** on the **vertical scroll bar** until the row you are looking for is visible.

2. **Click** on the **horizontal scroll bar** until the column you are looking for is visible.

3. **Click** on the **desired cell**. It will become the current cell.

The following table describes keyboard methods for moving around in your spreadsheet:

KEYSTROKE	RESULT
Arrow keys	Move one cell at a time up, down, left, or right
Page Down	Moves one screen down
Page Up	Moves one screen up
Home	Moves to column A of the current row
Ctrl+Home	Moves to cell A1
F5	Displays the GoTo dialog box, which enables you to specify a cell address

ENTERING DATA

Spreadsheet data is made up of three components: labels, values, and formulas. Labels are traditionally descriptive pieces of information, such as names, months, or types of products. Works identifies a cell as a label if it begins with a letter or a prefix character.

Entering Labels into Cells

1. **Click** on the **cell** where you want to place the label. A border will appear around the selected cell.

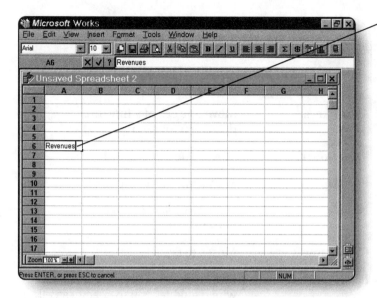

2. Type text. A blinking insertion point will appear.

TIP

If you make a mistake and you have not yet pressed Enter, press the Backspace key to delete characters and type a correction, or press the Escape key to cancel the typing.

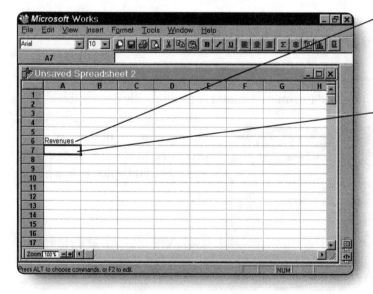

3. Press the **Enter key** to accept the label. The text will be entered and will align along the left edge of the cell.

4. Press an **arrow key**. The next cell is selected.

5. Repeat steps 1 through 4 for each label you want to enter.

NOTE

Optionally, you could press an arrow key instead of the Enter key. This will not only accept the cell you were typing in, but move to the next cell in the direction of the arrow key at the same time.

Entering Values into Cells

Values are the raw numbers that you track in a spreadsheet. There is no need to enter commas or dollar signs. You'll let Works do that for you later.

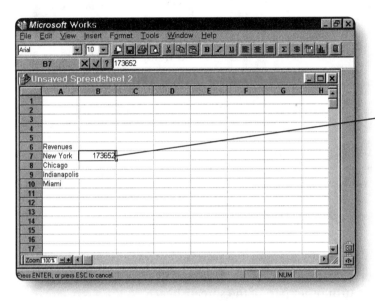

1. **Click** on the **cell** where you want to place the value. A border will appear around the selected cell.

2. **Type** the numerical **value**. A blinking insertion point will appear.

3. **Press Enter** to accept the value. The number will be entered into the cell.

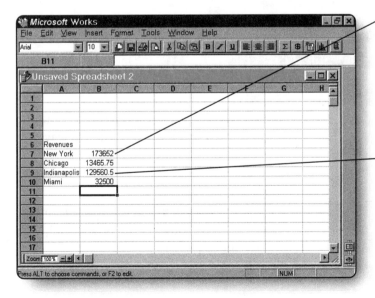

Notice how values are aligned along the right edge of the cell.

4. **Press** an **arrow key**. The next cell will be selected.

NOTE

If you entered a number such as 39.95, that is exactly what will be displayed in the cell; however, if you entered 39.50, the spreadsheet will display 39.5 (without the trailing zero). Don't worry, nothing is lost. You will change the appearance later.

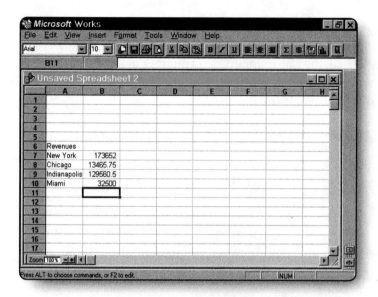

5. Repeat steps 1 through 4 for each value you want to enter.

TIP

To enter a value as a label, type a quotation (") character before the number, such as "1997. The quotation character tells Works that the information is a label.

EDITING DATA

You can edit your data in a variety of ways. You may need to change the contents of a cell, or you may want to move the data to another part of the spreadsheet.

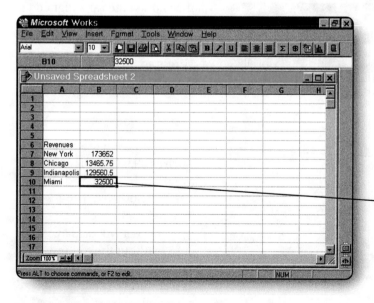

Replacing the Contents of a Cell

You can make changes to the contents of a cell in two ways. One is by typing over the contents of a cell.

1. Click on a cell. The cell and its contents will be selected.

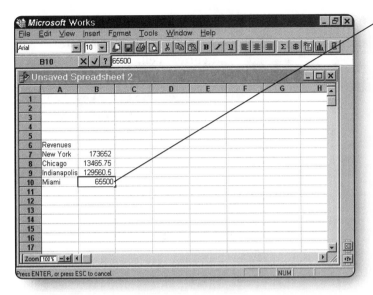

2. **Type** new **text**. The new text will appear in the cell.

3. **Press** the **Enter key**. The text will be entered in the selected cell.

Editing the Contents of a Cell

The other method to make changes to the contents of a cell is by using the Edit feature.

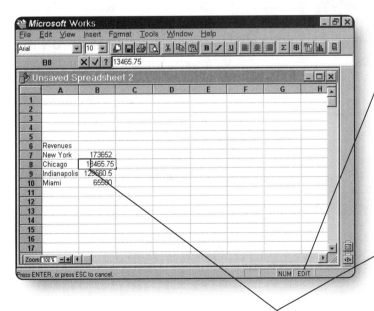

1. **Double-click** on the **cell** to be edited. The insertion point will blink within the cell.

Edit mode is indicated on the status bar.

TIP

You can also press the F2 key to edit the contents of a cell.

2. **Press** the **left arrow key**. The insertion point will be relocated within the current cell.

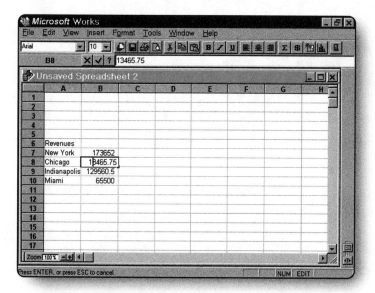

3. **Type** the **changes**. The changes will appear in the current cell.

4. **Press** the **Enter key**. The changes will be entered into the current cell.

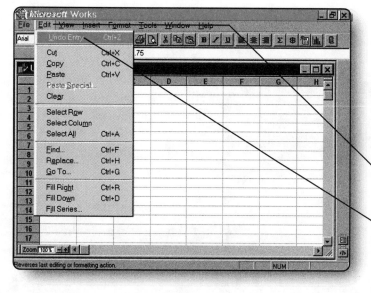

Undoing Mistakes

If you make a mistake while working in a spreadsheet, STOP! Don't go any further. Works will reverse the last step you took.

1. **Click** on **Edit**. The Edit menu will appear.

2. **Click** on **Undo Entry**. The last step you took will be reversed.

11 Editing a Spreadsheet

Frequently after data is entered into a spreadsheet, you'll need to change the location of the data. You can insert or delete rows or columns as needed or just move the data to a new location. In this chapter, you'll learn how to:

◆ Select cells, rows, and columns

◆ Insert and delete rows and columns

◆ Move data

◆ Use the fill feature

LEARNING SELECTION TECHNIQUES

To move, copy, delete, or change the formatting of data in the spreadsheet, the cells to be modified must first be selected. When cells are selected, they appear black onscreen—just the reverse of unselected text. An exception to this is if a block of cells is selected. In this case, the first cell will not be black—it will have a black border around it. The following table describes some of the different selection techniques.

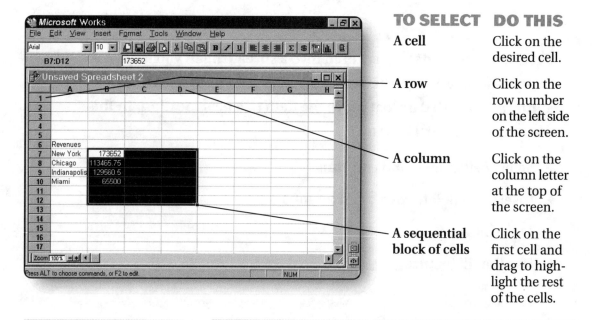

TO SELECT	DO THIS
A cell	Click on the desired cell.
A row	Click on the row number on the left side of the screen.
A column	Click on the column letter at the top of the screen.
A sequential block of cells	Click on the first cell and drag to highlight the rest of the cells.

TIP

To deselect a block of cells, click the mouse in any other cell.

TIP

Make sure the mouse pointer is a white arrow before attempting to select cells.

NOTE

Microsoft Works does not allow for a group of non-sequential cells to be selected.

INSERTING ROWS AND COLUMNS

Occasionally you need a column or a row to be inserted into the middle of information that you have already entered. Inserting a row or column moves existing data to make room for blank rows or columns. Each worksheet always has 256 columns and 16,384 rows.

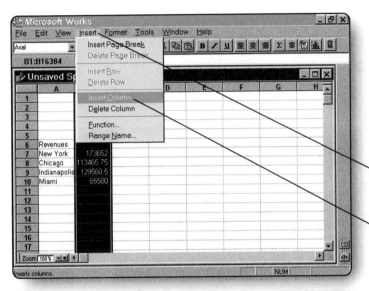

Inserting Columns

1. Click on the **Column Heading letter** where you want to insert the new column. The entire column will be selected.

2. Click on **Insert**. The Insert menu will appear.

3. Click on **Insert Column**. A new column will be inserted.

Existing columns move to the right.

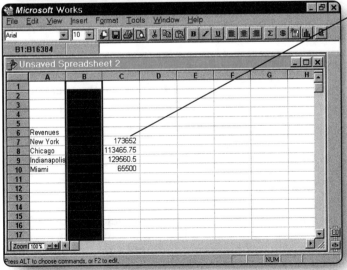

Inserting Rows

1. **Click** on the **Row Heading number** where you want to insert the new row. The entire row will be selected.

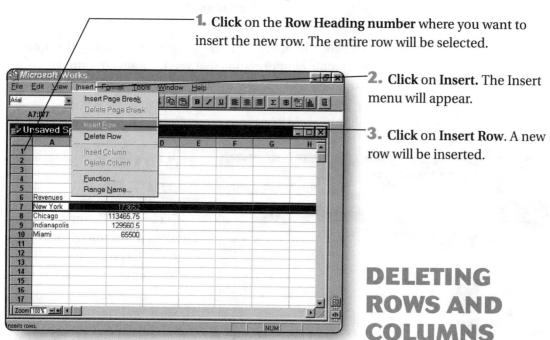

2. **Click** on **Insert**. The Insert menu will appear.

3. **Click** on **Insert Row**. A new row will be inserted.

DELETING ROWS AND COLUMNS

Use caution when deleting a row or column. Deleting a row will delete it across all 256 columns; deleting a column will delete it down all 16,384 rows.

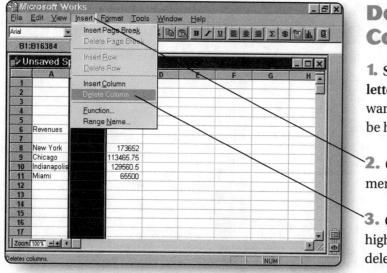

Deleting Columns

1. **Select** the **Column Heading letter** of the column that you want to delete. The column will be highlighted.

2. **Click** on **Insert**. The Insert menu will appear.

3. **Choose Delete Column**. The highlighted column will be deleted.

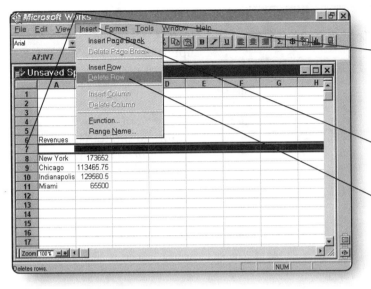

Deleting Rows

1. **Select** the **Row Heading number** of the row that you want to delete. The Row will be highlighted.

2. **Click** on **Insert**. The Insert menu will appear.

3. **Choose Delete Row**. The highlighted row will be deleted.

Remaining columns move to the left; remaining rows move up.

MOVING DATA AROUND

If you're not happy with the placement of data, you don't have to delete it and retype it. Works makes it easy for you to move it around.

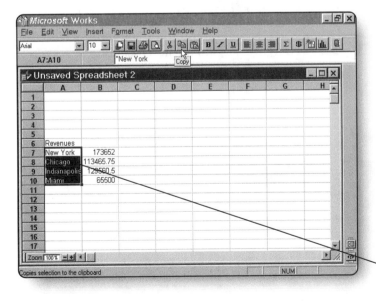

Copying and Pasting Cells

Windows comes with a feature called the Clipboard. The Clipboard temporarily holds information in memory. It is extremely helpful if you want to transfer information from one place to another. To copy information, Works uses the Copy and Paste features.

1. **Select** some **cells** to be duplicated. The cells will be highlighted.

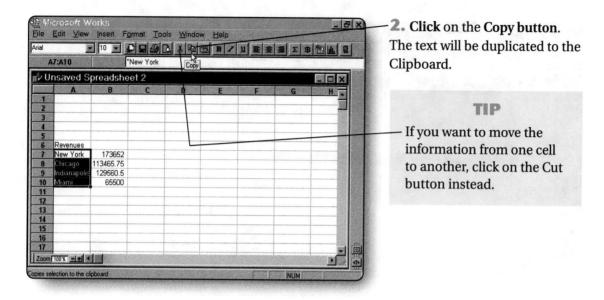

2. Click on the **Copy button.** The text will be duplicated to the Clipboard.

TIP

If you want to move the information from one cell to another, click on the Cut button instead.

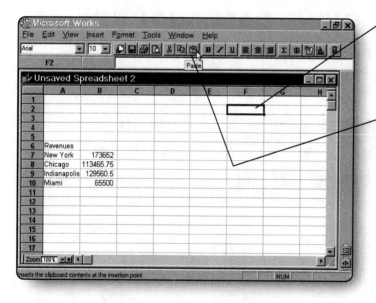

3. Click on the beginning **cell** where you want to place the duplicated information. The cell will be highlighted.

4. Click on the **Paste button.** The information will be copied to the new location.

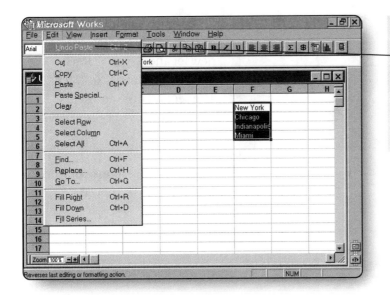

TIP

If you pasted the cells to the wrong area, click on the Edit menu and choose Undo Paste to reverse the step.

Using Drag-and-Drop to Move Cells

Another method that you can use to move information from one location to another is the drag-and-drop method.

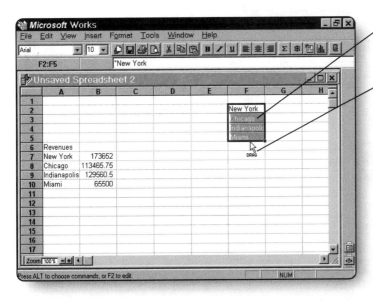

1. **Select** some **cells** to move. The cells will be highlighted.

2. **Position** the **mouse pointer** around one of the outside edges of the selection. The mouse pointer will become a small white arrow with the word "DRAG" displayed.

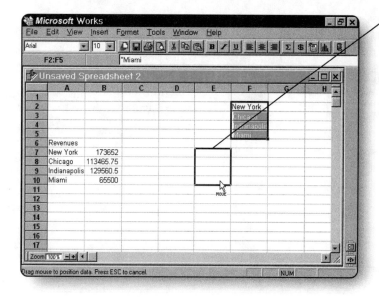

3. **Press** and **hold** the **mouse button** and **drag** the **cell** to a new location. The "DRAG" command changes to "MOVE." The second box represents where the moved cells will be located.

4. **Release** the **mouse button**. The cells will be moved.

CLEARING CELL CONTENTS

If you have data in cells that you no longer want, you can easily delete the data.

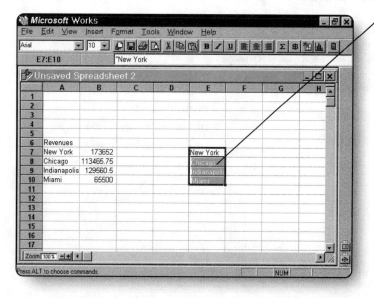

1. **Select** some **cells** to be cleared. The cells will be highlighted.

2. **Press** the **Delete key**. The contents of the cells will be removed.

USING THE FILL FEATURE

Works has a great built-in time saving feature called Fill. If you give Works the beginning Month, Day, Season, or numbers, it can fill in the rest of the pattern for you. For example, if you type January, Works fills in February, March, April, and so on.

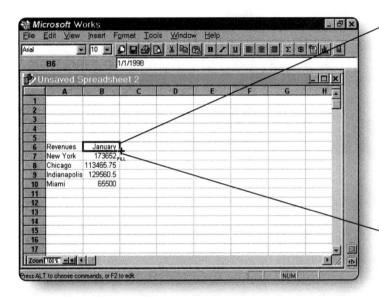

1. Type the **beginning Month, Day, or Season** in the beginning cell. The text will be displayed in the cell.

If you want Works to fill in numbers, you must first give it a pattern. For example, enter the value of "1" in the first cell, then enter "2" in the second cell.

2. **Position** the **mouse pointer** on the lower-right corner of the beginning cell. The mouse pointer will change to become a small black cross with the word "FILL" displayed.

TIP

For numbers, select both the first and second cells before proceeding to step 3.

3. **Press** and **hold** the **mouse button** and **drag** to select the next cells to be filled in. The cells will have a gray border surrounding them.

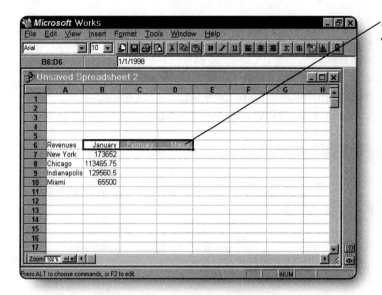

4. **Release** the **mouse button.**
The pattern will be repeated.

12 Working with Functions and Formulas

Formulas in a Works spreadsheet will do the calculations for you. For example, by referencing cell addresses in a formula, if the data changes, so will the formula answer. In this chapter, you'll learn how to:

✦ Create simple and compound formulas

✦ Copy formulas

✦ Create an absolute reference

✦ Use functions

CREATING FORMULAS

All formulas must begin with the equal (=) sign, regardless of whether the formula consists of adding, subtracting, multiplying, or dividing.

Creating a Simple Formula

An example of a simple formula might be =B5–B6.

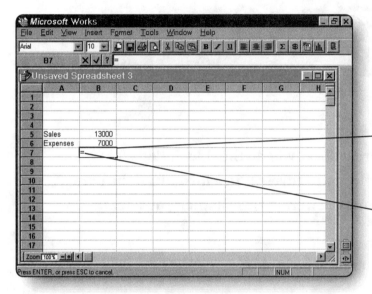

1. **Click** on the **cell** in which you want to place the formula answer. The cell will be selected.

2. **Type** an **equal sign** (=) to begin the formula. The symbol will display in the cell.

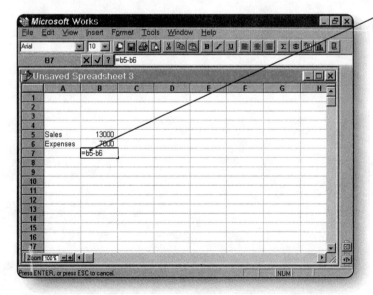

3. **Type** the **cell address** of the first cell to be included in the formula. This is called the cell *reference.*

NOTE

Spreadsheet formulas are not case sensitive. For example, B5 is the same as b5.

A formula needs an *operator* to suggest the next action to be performed.

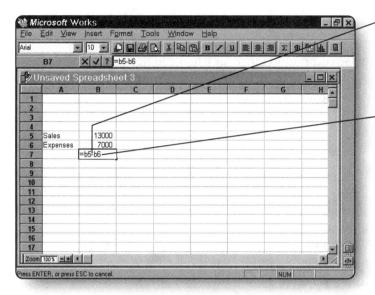

4. Type the **operator**: plus (+), minus (–), multiply (*), or divide (/). The operator will display in the formula.

5. Type the **reference** to the second cell of the formula. The reference will display in the cell.

6. Press the **Enter key**. The result of the calculation will appear in the cell.

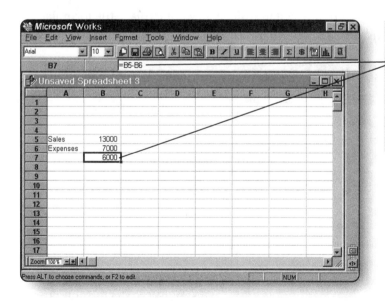

NOTE

Notice how the result appears in the cell, but the actual formula, =B5–B6, appears in the Contents box of the Edit line.

Creating a Compound Formula

You use compound formulas when you need more than one operator. Examples of a compound formula might be =B7+B8+B9+B10 or =B11–B19*A23.

> **NOTE**
>
> When you have a compound formula, Works will do the multiplication and division first, then the addition and subtraction. If you want a certain portion of the formula to be calculated first, put it in parentheses. Works will do whatever is in the parentheses before the rest of the formula. Such a formula as =B11–B19*A23 will give a totally different answer than =(B11–B19)*A23.

1. **Click** on the **cell** in which you want to place the formula answer. The cell will be selected.

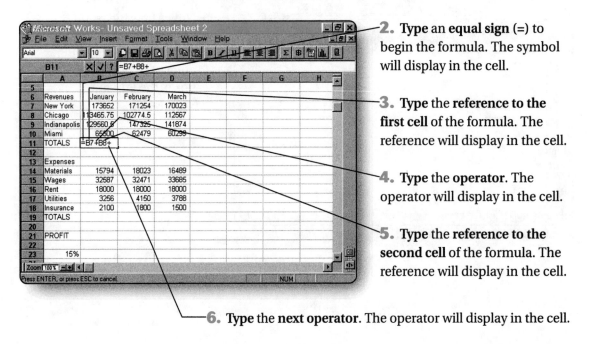

2. **Type** an **equal sign** (=) to begin the formula. The symbol will display in the cell.

3. **Type** the **reference to the first cell** of the formula. The reference will display in the cell.

4. **Type** the **operator**. The operator will display in the cell.

5. **Type** the **reference to the second cell** of the formula. The reference will display in the cell.

6. **Type** the **next operator**. The operator will display in the cell.

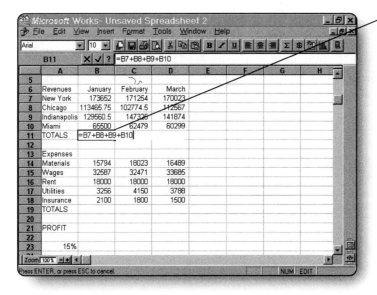

7. Type the **reference to the third cell** of the formula. The reference will display in the cell.

8. Repeat steps 6 and **7** until the formula is complete, adding the parentheses wherever necessary.

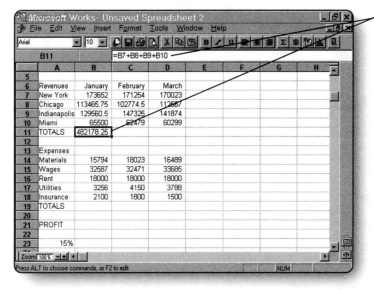

9. Press the **Enter key** to accept the formula. The calculation answer will be displayed in the cell and the formula will be displayed in the content bar.

Try changing one of the values you originally typed in the spreadsheet and watch the answer to the formula change.

COPYING FORMULAS

If you're going to copy a formula to a surrounding cell, you can use the Fill method. If the cells are not sequential, you can use Copy and Paste. Fill and Copy and Paste were discussed in Chapter 11, "Editing a Spreadsheet."

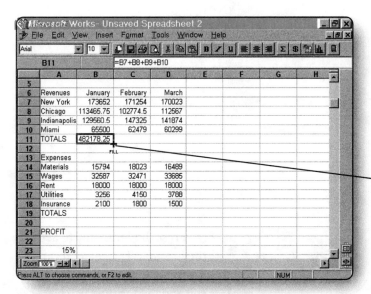

Copying Formulas Using Fill

1. Click on the **cell** that has the formula. The cell will be selected.

2. Position the **mouse pointer** on the lower-right corner of the beginning cell. The mouse pointer will become a black cross with the word "FILL" below it.

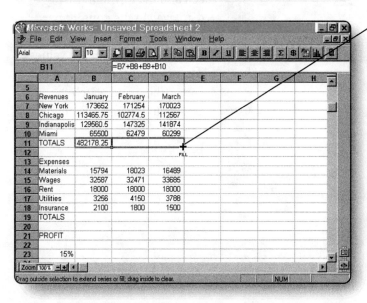

3. Press and **hold** the **mouse button** and **drag** to select the next cells to be filled in. The cells will be selected.

4. Release the **mouse button**. The formula will be copied.

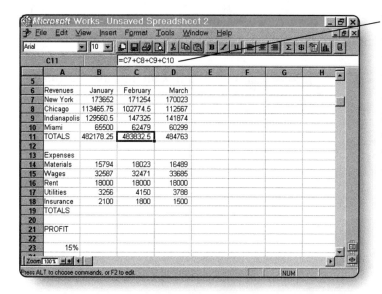

When Works copies a formula, the references change as the formula is copied. If the original formula was =B11–B19 and you copied it to the next cell to the right, the formula would read =C11–C19. Then, if you copied it to the next cell to the right, it would be =D11–D19, and so on.

Copying Formulas with Copy and Paste

1. **Select** the **cells** with the formula that you want to duplicate. The cell will be selected.

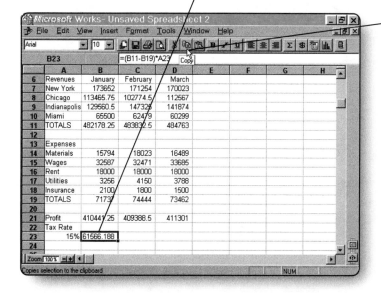

2. **Click** on the **Copy button**. The formulas will be copied to the Clipboard.

3. **Highlight** the **cells** in which you want to place the duplicated formula. The cells will be selected.

4. **Click** on the **Paste button**. The information will be copied to the new location.

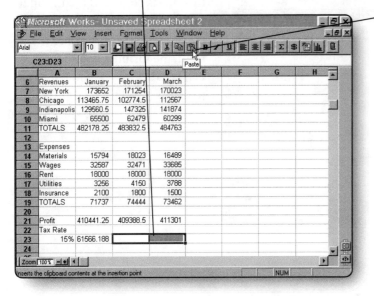

If you are following the examples in the book, don't be alarmed by the answers you see in the exercise. You'll discover why the answers are incorrect in the next section.

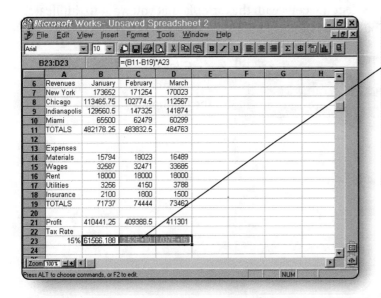

CREATING AN ABSOLUTE REFERENCE IN A FORMULA

Occasionally when you copy a formula, you do not want one of the cell references to change. That's when you need to create an absolute reference. You use the dollar sign ($) to indicate an absolute reference.

It's called an *absolute reference* because when you copy it, it absolutely and positively stays that cell reference and never changes. An example of a formula with an absolute reference might be =B21*B23. The reference to cell B23 will not change when copied.

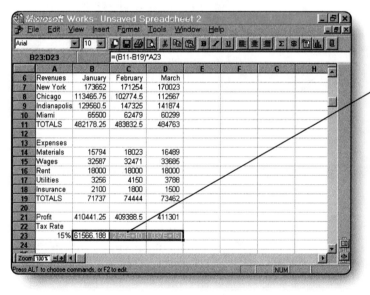

For this exercise, you'll need to delete the original formulas and start again.

1. **Highlight** the **cells** in which the original formulas exist. The cells will be selected.

2. **Press** the **Delete key**. The information in these cells will be deleted.

3. **Click** on the **cell** in which you want to place the formula answer. The cell will be selected.

4. **Type** an **equal sign** (=) to begin the formula.

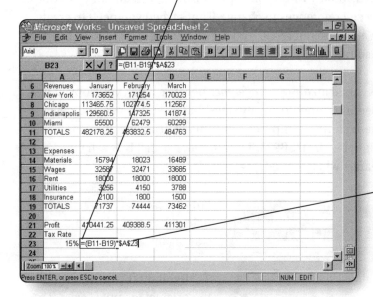

5. **Type** the **reference to the first cell** of the formula. If this reference is to be an absolute reference, add dollar signs ($) in front of both the column reference and the row reference.

6. **Type** the **operator**.

7. **Type** the **reference to the second cell** of the formula. If this reference is to be an absolute reference, add dollar signs ($) in front of both the column reference and the row reference.

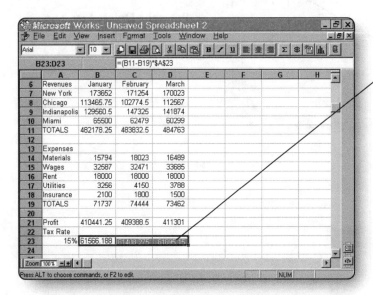

8. **Press** the **Enter key** to complete the formula.

9. **Copy** the **formula** to the adjacent cells using one of the methods in steps 1 through 4 of the preceding section.

NOTE

Compound formulas can also have absolute references.

USING FUNCTIONS

Sometimes, formulas can be quite complex and time consuming to build. Works has more than 70 different functions to assist you with your calculations. All Works functions begin with the equal (=) sign and have the basis (arguments) for the formula in parentheses.

Using the SUM Function

The SUM function totals a range of values. The syntax for this function is =SUM(*range of values to total*). An example might be =SUM(B7:D7).

NOTE

There are two ways to reference a range of values. If the cells to be included are sequential, they are separated by a colon (:). If the range is nonsequential, the cells are separated by a comma (,). For example, the range (B7:D7) would include cells B7, C7, and D7; the range (B7:D7,F4) would include cells B7, C7, D7, and F4.

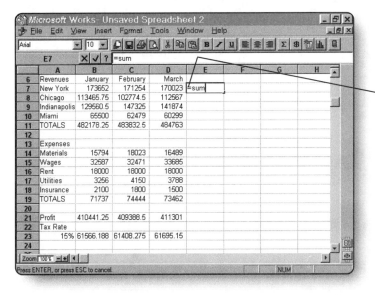

1. **Click** on the **cell** in which you want to place the sum of values. The cell will be selected.

2. **Type** the **equal (=) sign**. The symbol will display in the cell.

NOTE

Remember that functions are complex formulas and all formulas must begin with the equal (=) sign.

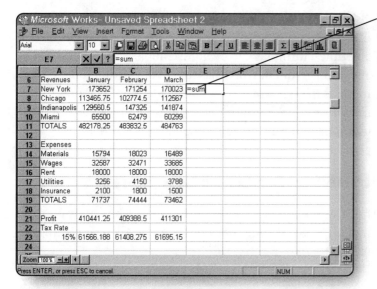

3. **Type** the function name **sum.** The characters will display in the cell.

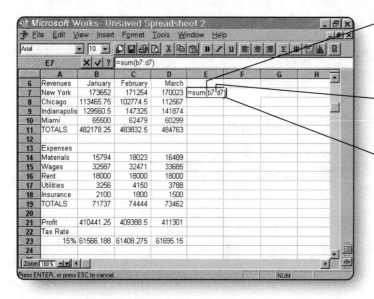

4. **Type** the **open parentheses** symbol. The symbol will display in the cell.

5. **Type** the **range** to be totaled. The range will display in the cell.

6. **Type** the **close parentheses** symbol. The symbol will display in the cell.

7. **Press** the **Enter key**. The total of the range will be displayed in the selected cell.

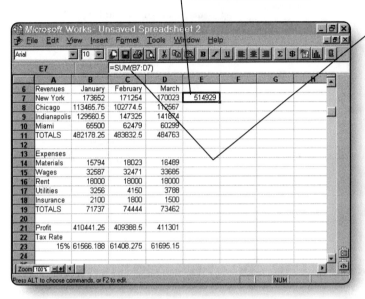

Again, while the result displays in the selected cell, the formula is displayed in the contents box.

Using the AutoSum Button

Works includes the SUM function as a button on the toolbar. This makes creating a simple addition formula a mouse click away.

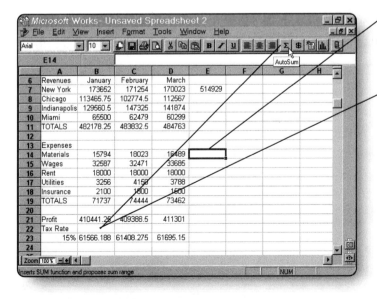

1. **Click** on the **cell** below or to the right of the values to be totaled. The cell will be selected.

2. **Click** on the **AutoSum button**. The cells to be totaled are highlighted.

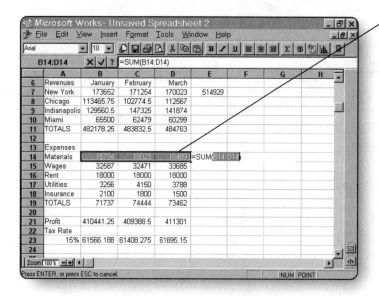

3. Press the **Enter key**. Works enters the sum of the values above it or to the left of it.

Using the AVG Function

The AVG function finds an average of a range of values. The syntax for this function is =AVG(*range of values to average*). An example might be =AVG(B7:D7).

1. Click on the **cell** in which you want to place the average. The cell will be selected.

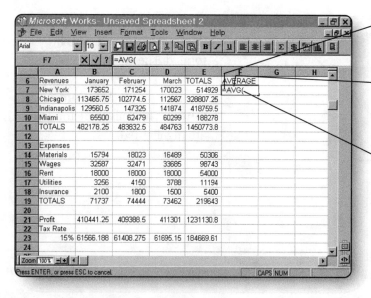

2. Type the **equal** (=) sign. The symbol will display in the cell.

3. Type the function name **AVG**. The characters will display in the cell.

4. Type the **open parentheses** symbol. The symbol will display in the cell.

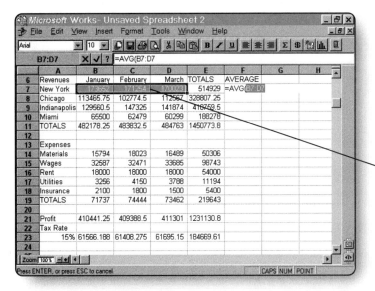

5. **Type** or **highlight** the **range** to be averaged. The range will display in the cell.

6. **Type** the **close parentheses** symbol. The symbol will display in the cell.

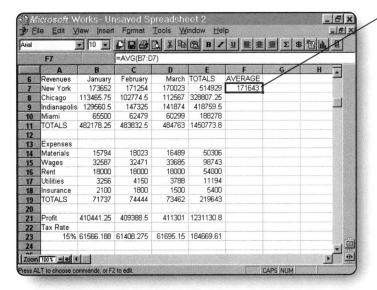

7. **Press** the **Enter key**. Works will average the values in the selected range.

13 Formatting Worksheets

The days of the dull spreadsheet are gone. Liven up your spreadsheet by changing its appearance. In this chapter, you'll learn how to:

+ Set number formatting

+ Change alignment

+ Select fonts

+ Adjust column width

+ Add borders to cells

+ Use AutoFormat

+ Adjust the view of the spreadsheet

FORMATTING NUMBERS

By default, values are displayed as general numbers. Values can be displayed as currency, percentages, fractions, dates, and many other formats.

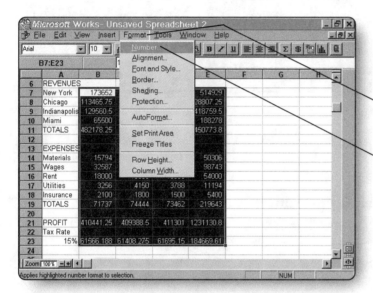

1. **Select** some **cells** to be formatted. The cells will be highlighted.

2. **Click** on **Format**. The Format menu will appear.

3. **Click** on **Number**. The Format Cells dialog box will open with the Number tab in front.

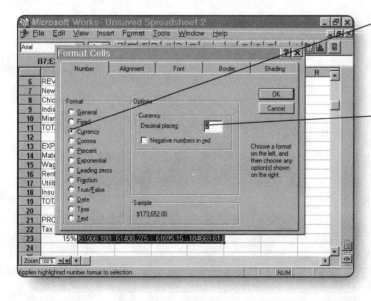

4. **Click** on the **format** of your choice. The format will be selected and any available options will appear.

5. **Change** any desired **option**. The option will be selected.

6. **Click** on **OK**. The Format Cells dialog box will close.

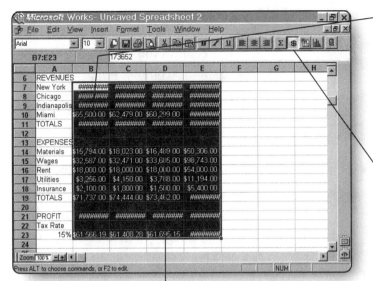

The new number format will be applied to the selected cells. Notice the dollar signs and two decimal points. These cells had the currency style applied to them.

TIP

A quick way to apply currency style is to select the cells and click on the currency button.

NOTE

Don't be alarmed if some of the cells display a series of number signs (######) or in scientific format (1E+08) instead of your values. This is due to the column width being too small. You will learn to change this in the next section.

ADJUSTING COLUMN WIDTH

The default width of a column is ten characters, but each individual column can be from one to 240 characters wide.

A line located at the right edge of each column heading divides the columns. You will use this line to change the column width.

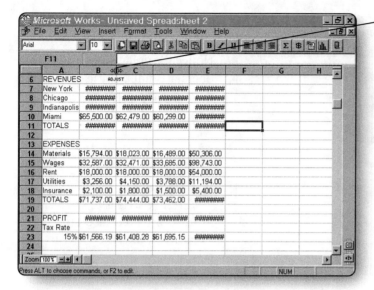

1. Position the **mouse pointer** on the right column line for the column you want to change. The mouse pointer will become a double-headed white arrow with the word "ADJUST" displayed under it.

2. Press and **hold** the **mouse button** and **drag** the column line. If you drag it to the right, the column width will increase; if you drag it to the left, the column width will decrease.

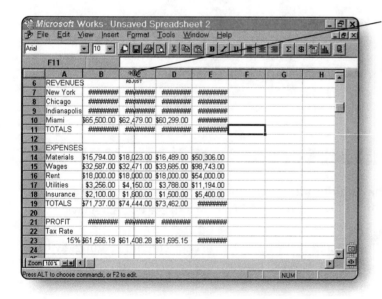

3. Release the **mouse button**. The column width will be changed.

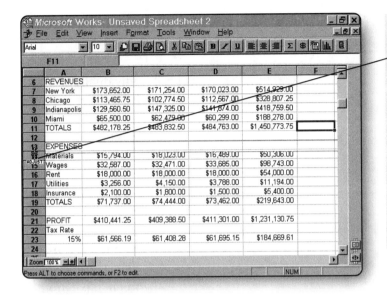

TIP

Row Height can be adjusted in a similar manner. Position the mouse pointer on the bottom edge of the row heading. Again, the mouse will change to a double-headed white arrow. Drag the line down to increase row height or up to decrease row height.

SETTING WORKSHEET ALIGNMENT

Labels are left-aligned and values are right-aligned by default; however, you can change the alignment of either one to be left, right, centered, or full justified. Also by default, both are vertically aligned to the bottom of the cell.

Wrapping text in cells is useful when text is too long to fit in one cell and you don't want it to overlap to the next cell.

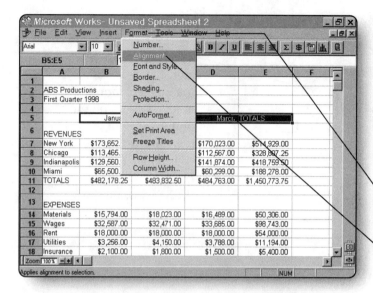

Adjusting Cell Alignment

Adjust cells individually or adjust a block of cells at once.

1. **Select** the **cells** to be formatted. The cells will be highlighted.

2. **Click** on **Format**. The Format menu will appear.

3. **Click** on **Alignment**. The Format Cells dialog box will open with the Alignment tab in front.

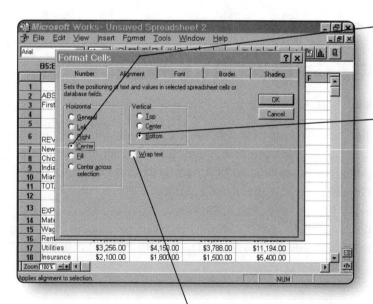

4. **Click** on an **option** under Horizontal alignment. The horizontal alignment of the text in the cell will change.

5. **Click** on an **option** under Vertical alignment. The vertical alignment of the text in the cell will change.

TIP

The Wrap text feature treats each cell like a miniature word processor, with text wrapping around in the cell.

6. **Click** on the **Wrap text check box** if desired. A check will appear in the selection box.

7. **Click** on **OK**. The selections will be applied to the highlighted cells.

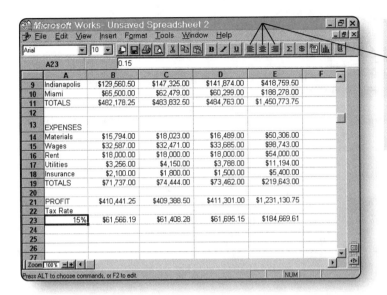

TIP

Optionally, select cells to be aligned and click on one of the three alignment buttons on the toolbar: Left, Center, or Right.

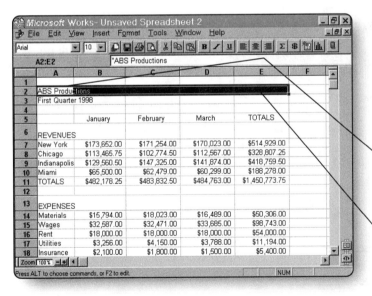

Centering Headings

Text also can be centered across a group of columns to create attractive headings.

1. **Type** the **heading text** in the first column of the worksheet body. This is usually column A.

2. **Select** the **heading cell** and **the cells to be included** in the heading. The cells will be highlighted.

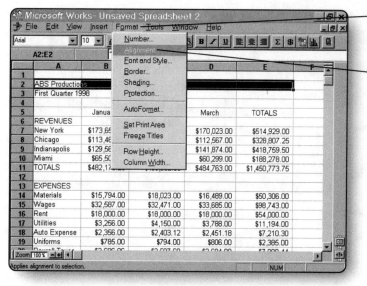

3. **Click** on **Format**. The Format menu will appear.

4. **Click** on **Alignment**. The Format Cells dialog box will open with the Alignment tab in front.

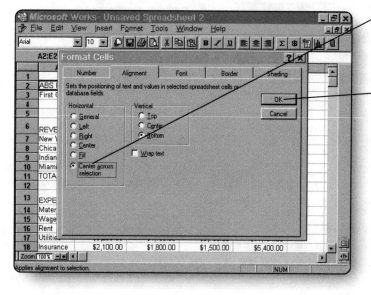

5. **Click** on **Center across selection**. The option will be selected.

6. **Click** on **OK**. The Format Cells dialog box will close and the title will be centered.

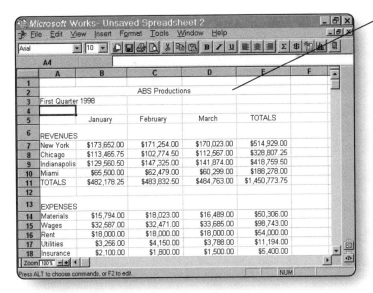

Notice the gridlines have disappeared and the cells appear to be joined together.

TIP

In this example, it appears the headings are located in Column C; however, the text is still in Column A. If you are going to make other changes, be sure to select Column A, not Column C.

FORMATTING WITH FONTS

The default font in a spreadsheet is Arial 10 points, but both the typeface or size can be easily changed.

Selecting a Font Typeface

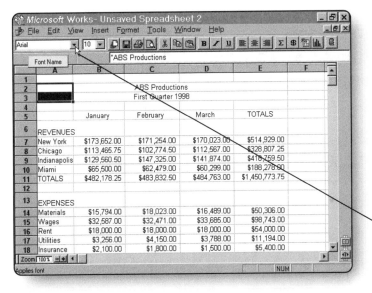

Your font choices will vary depending on the software installed on your computer.

1. **Select** some **cells** to change the typeface. The cells will be highlighted.

2. **Click** on the **Font Name drop-down arrow.** A list of available fonts will appear.

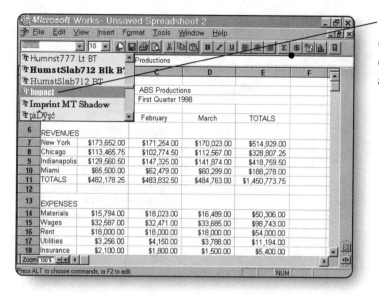

3. **Click** on the **font** of your choice. The selection list will close and the new font will be applied to the selected cells.

Selecting a Font Size

The default font size in a Works spreadsheet is 10 points. There are approximately 72 points in an inch, so a 10-point font is slightly less than one-seventh of an inch tall.

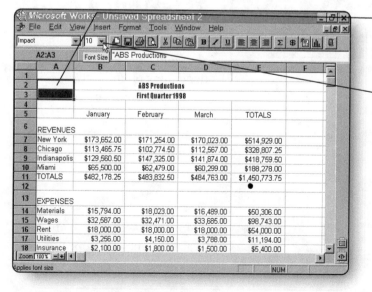

1. **Select** some **cells** to change the font size. The cells will be highlighted.

2. **Click** on the **Font Size drop-down arrow**. A list of available font sizes will appear.

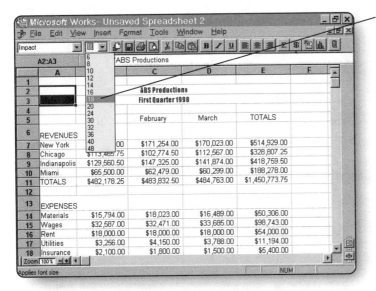

3. **Click** on the **size** of your choice. The selection list will close and the new font size will be applied to the selected cells.

Selecting a Font Style

Font styles include attributes like **boldface**, *italics,* and underlining.

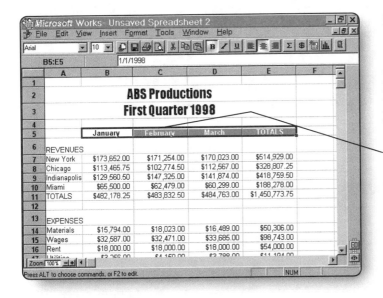

1. **Select** some **cells** to change the style. The cells will be highlighted.

2. Click on any of the following **options:** The attributes will be applied to the text in the cell.

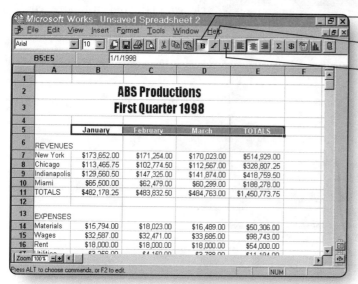

◆ Bold button

◆ Italics button

◆ Underline button.

The Bold, Italics, and Underline buttons are toggle switches. Click on them a second time to turn off the attribute.

TIP

Shortcut keys include Ctrl+B for Bold, Ctrl+I for Italics, and Ctrl+U for Underline.

NOTE

Underlining is not the same as a cell border. Cell borders are discussed in the next section.

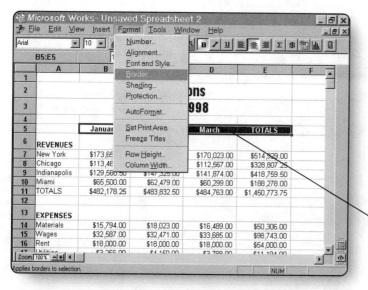

ADDING BORDERS

You can add borders or lines to cells to emphasize important data. Borders are different from the gridlines that separate cells in the sheet. You can change the style and color of borders.

1. Select the **cells** you want to have borders or lines. The cells will be highlighted.

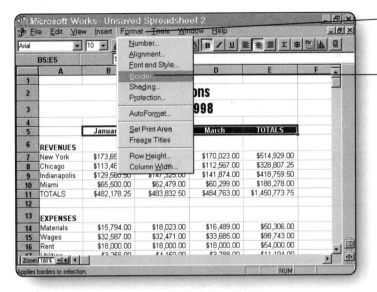

2. **Click** on **Format**. The Format menu will appear.

3. **Click** on **Border**. The Format Cells dialog box will open with the Border tab in front.

4. **Choose** a border **Line style**. The selected style will have a black box around it.

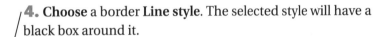

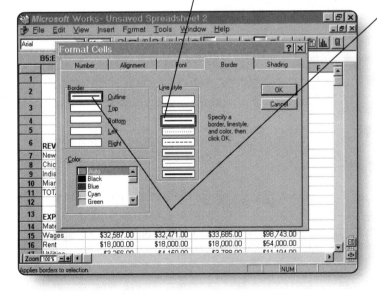

5. **Choose** from the **Border placement options**. A sample of the chosen line style from step 4 will appear in the selected placement options.

TIP

Click on the Shading tab and select shading options for the selected cells.

6. **Click** on **OK**. The Format Cells dialog box will close and the border choices will be applied to the highlighted cells.

SAVING TIME WITH AUTOFORMAT

Save time by letting Works format your spreadsheet using the AutoFormat feature. You can choose from sixteen different styles.

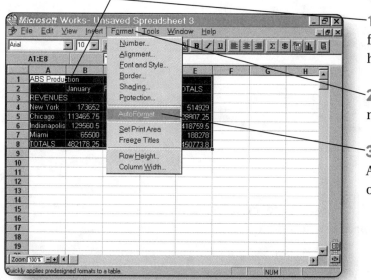

1. **Select** the **cells** to be formatted. The cells will be highlighted.

2. **Click** on **Format**. The Format menu will appear.

3. **Click** on **AutoFormat**. The AutoFormat dialog box will open.

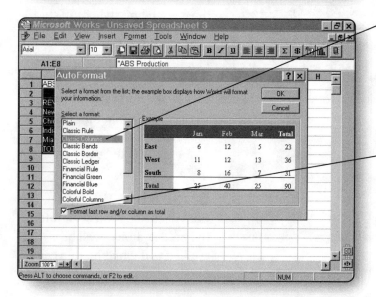

4. **Click** on a **format** from the Select a format list. A sample will display in the Example box.

Works assumes the last row of your selection is a Total row.

5. Optionally, **click** on the **Format last row and/or column as total** check box. The option will be deselected.

6. **Click** on **OK**. The Autoformat dialog box will close and the selected cells will be formatted.

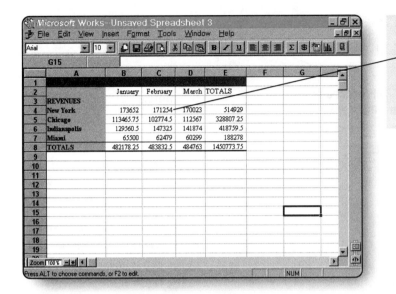

You can still change any format option (such as number format) manually as necessary.

CHANGING THE SPREADSHEET DISPLAY

Works includes several options to modify the display of your spreadsheet. Most display options do not affect how the spreadsheet prints, only the way you see it on the monitor.

Freezing Spreadsheet Titles

You can freeze columns, rows, or both so that column and row titles remain in view as you scroll through the sheet instead of scrolling off the screen with the rest of the spreadsheet. This is particularly helpful with larger spreadsheets.

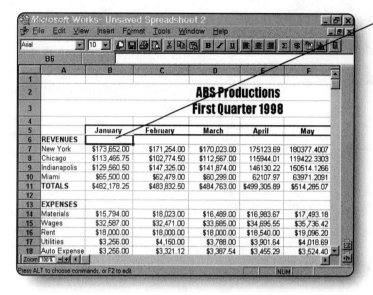

1. **Click** the **mouse** on the desired cell:

✦ To freeze columns, position the mouse pointer one cell to the right of the columns you want to freeze.

✦ To freeze rows, position the cell pointer one cell below the rows you want to freeze.

✦ To freeze both columns and rows, position the cell pointer in the cell below the rows and to the right of the columns you want to freeze.

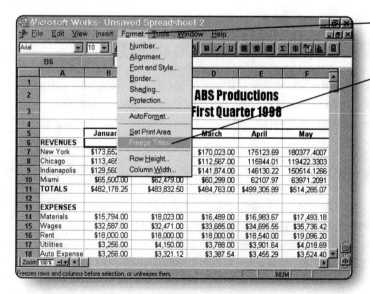

2. **Click** on **Format**. The Format menu will appear.

3. **Click** on **Freeze Titles**. Lines will appear on the document indicating the frozen areas.

As you scroll downward or across in your document, the frozen part stays stationary on the screen while the rest of the text moves.

TIP

Repeat steps 2 and 3 to unfreeze the windows.

Using Zoom

Zoom enlarges or shrinks the display of your spreadsheet to allow you to see more or less of it. Zooming in or out does not affect printing. The normal display of your spreadsheet is 100%.

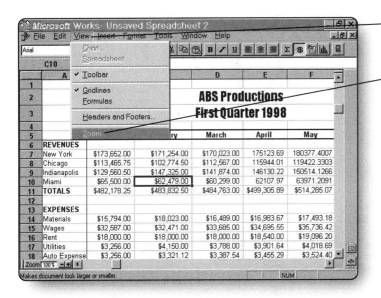

1. **Click** on **View**. The View menu will appear.

2. **Click** on **Zoom**. The Zoom dialog box will open.

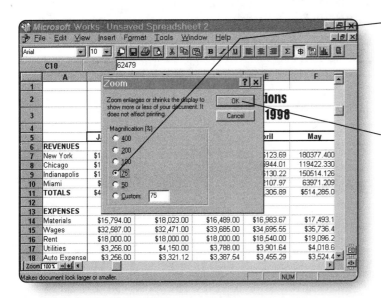

3. **Click** on a **magnification** (%) **choice**. The higher the number, the larger the cells will appear onscreen. The option will be selected.

4. **Click** on **OK**. The Zoom dialog box will close and the display of your screen will adjust according to your selection.

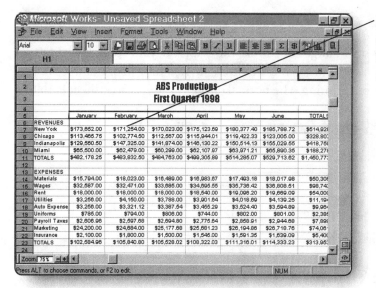

In this example, the zoom was set to 75%, which allowed more of the worksheet to display onscreen.

Hiding Gridlines

Gridlines are the light gray lines displayed on the screen that separate one cell from another. If you do not want the gridlines to display on the screen, you can quickly turn them off.

1. Click on **View**. The View menu will appear.

2. Click on **Gridlines**. The option will be deselected.

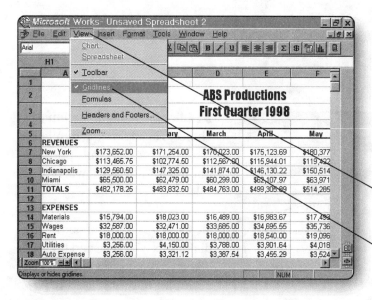

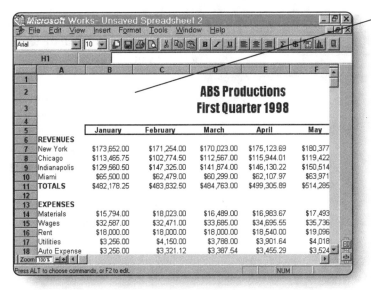

The display of gridlines will be turned off.

3. **Repeat steps** 1 and 2. The gridlines will redisplay.

By default, gridlines do not print whether you have them displayed on the spreadsheet or not. The option to print them must be selected separately. See Chapter 14, "Completing Your Spreadsheet," for instructions on printing gridlines.

Viewing Formulas

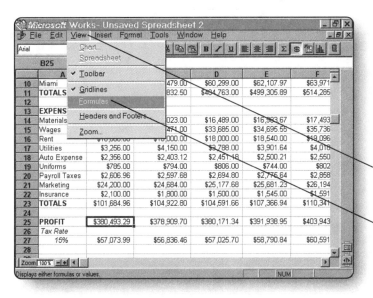

When you create formulas, the result of the formula is displayed in the spreadsheet, not the formula itself. Having the formula displayed is a wonderful tool for troubleshooting formula errors in your spreadsheet.

1. **Click** on **View**. The View menu will appear.

2. **Click** on **Formulas**. The option will be selected.

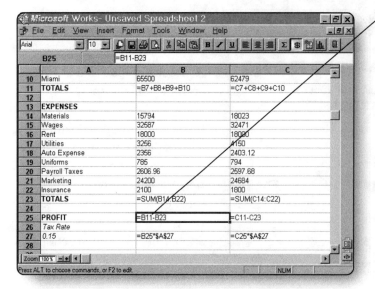

The spreadsheet formulas will be displayed in each cell instead of the result of the formula.

3. **Repeat steps 1** and **2.** The formula results will redisplay.

NOTE

If you print the spreadsheet while the formulas are displayed, the formulas will print, but not the formula results.

14 Completing Your Spreadsheet

Now that you have created your spreadsheet with all its text, values, and formulas, you'll want to prepare it for final output. You should proof it for errors as well as specify what area you want to print. In this chapter, you'll learn how to:

✦ Check your spelling

✦ Save, close, and open a spreadsheet

✦ Use Print Preview

✦ Print a spreadsheet

CHECKING YOUR SPELLING

The spell-check feature of Works checks for common misspellings.

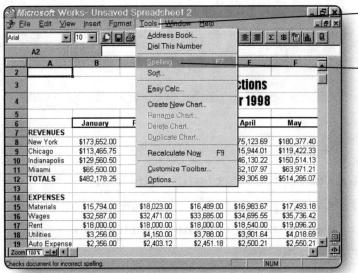

1. **Click** on **Tools**. The Tools menu will appear.

2. **Click** on **Spelling**. The Spelling: American English dialog box will open and highlight the first found error.

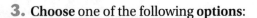

3. **Choose** one of the following **options**:

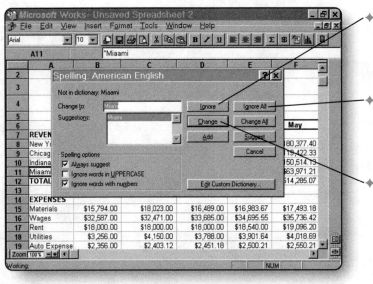

♦ **Ignore**. If you do not want to change the spelling of this word and you want to skip this occurrence, click on Ignore.

♦ **Ignore All**. If you do not want the Spelling Checker to stop on any occurrences of this word, click on Ignore All.

♦ **Change**. To replace this single occurrence of this word, click on the correct spelling from the Suggestions list and click on Change. The word will be corrected in your spreadsheet.

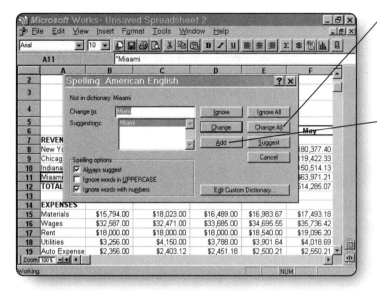

✦ **Change All**. To replace all occurrences of this word, click on the correct spelling from the Suggestions list and click on Change All.

✦ **Add**. If the word is correctly spelled and you want to avoid having the Spelling Checker stop on it in the future, click on Add.

4. **Repeat step 3** until all the highlighted words have been checked. A message box will display and let you know that the spell-check is complete.

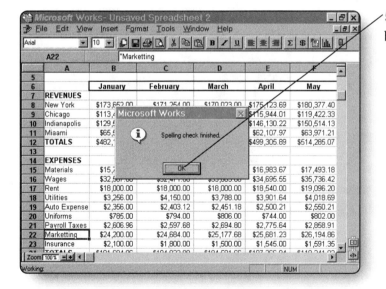

5. **Click** on **OK**. The message box will close.

SAVING A SPREADSHEET

As you create a spreadsheet in Works, it is stored temporarily in the computer's memory. That memory is erased when you exit Works or when you turn the computer off. To prevent losing your work, you need to save it.

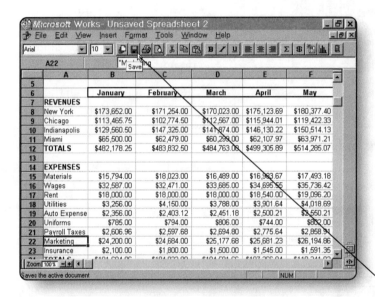

Saving a Spreadsheet the First Time

When you first create a spreadsheet, it is untitled. To save the spreadsheet for use again at a later date, you must give it a name. When you have saved a spreadsheet, the name will appear at the top of the screen in the title bar.

1. **Click** on the **Save button**. The Save As dialog box will open.

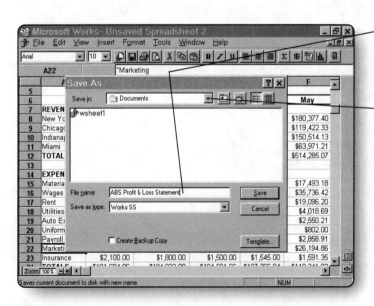

2. **Type** a **name** for your file in the File name: text box. The file name will be displayed.

The Save in: drop-down box lists the folder where the file will be saved. The default folder that appears is "documents". If you want to save to a different folder or disk, you can select another one. Click on the down arrow to browse.

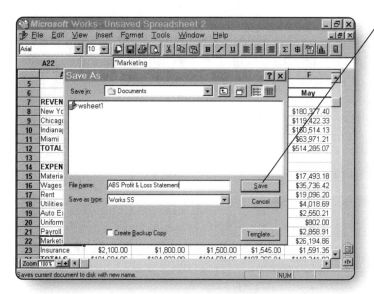

3. **Click** on **Save**. Your spreadsheet will be saved and the name you specified will appear in the title bar.

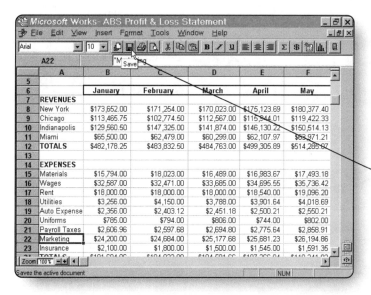

Resaving a Spreadsheet

You should resave your spreadsheet every ten minutes or so to ensure that you do not lose any changes.

1. **Click** on the **Save button**. The spreadsheet will be resaved with any changes. No dialog box will appear because the spreadsheet is being resaved with the same name and in the same folder as previously specified.

TIP

If you want to save the spreadsheet with a different name or in a different folder, click on File, then choose Save As. The Save As dialog box will prompt you for the new name or folder. The original document will remain as well as the new one.

CLOSING A SPREADSHEET

When you finish working on a spreadsheet, you should close it. As you learned in Chapter 9, "Completing Your Document," closing is the equivalent of putting it away for later use. When you close a spreadsheet, you put the spreadsheet away—not the program. Works is still active and ready to work for you.

1. Click on **File**. The File menu will open.

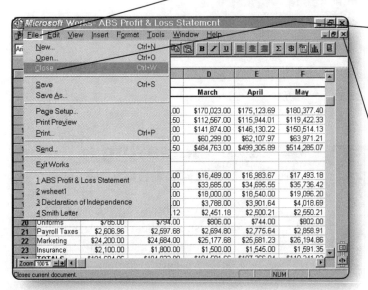

2. Click on **Close**. The spreadsheet will close; however, the Works program will remain active.

TIP

Optionally, you can click on the Close Document button. The file will close in a single step.

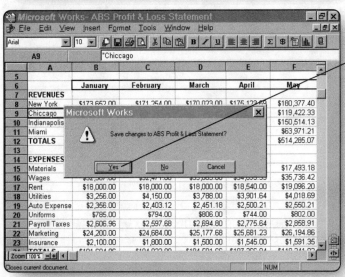

NOTE

If you have not saved any changes to your file, you will be prompted to do so. If you want to save the changes, click on Yes; if you do not want to save the changes, click on No.

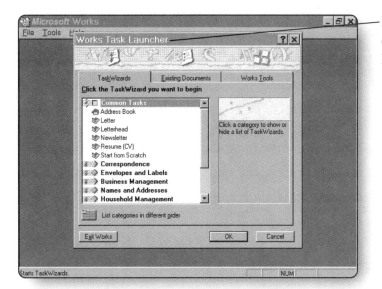

If no other documents are currently open, the Works Task Launcher will appear.

OPENING A SAVED SPREADSHEET

To edit a spreadsheet you have already closed, you must open that spreadsheet again. If you want to open a spreadsheet when you begin the Works program, the screen will look different from the screen that appears if you are already in a spreadsheet and want to open another one.

Opening a Spreadsheet from Another Document

Even if you already have a Works document open on your screen, you can open another. In fact, you can have up to eight documents open at a time. These documents can be any combination of spreadsheets, word processing documents, or database files.

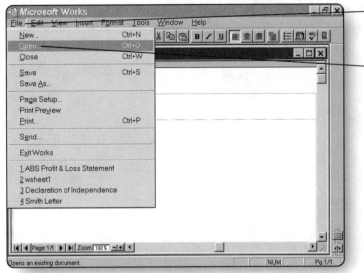

1. Click on **File**. The File menu will appear.

2. Click on **Open**. The Open dialog box will open.

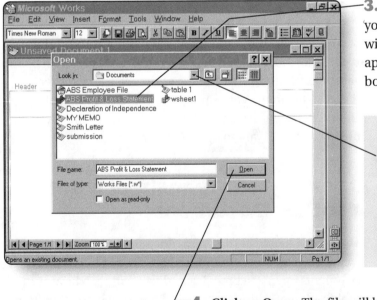

3. Click on the **file name** that you wish to open. The file name will be highlighted and will appear in the File name: text box.

NOTE

If your file is located in a different folder than the one displayed in the Look in: list box, click on the down arrow to navigate to the proper folder.

4. Click on **Open**. The file will be placed on your screen, ready for you to edit.

Opening a Document from the Task Launcher

You can open a document from the Works Task Launcher, which appears when you first start the Works program.

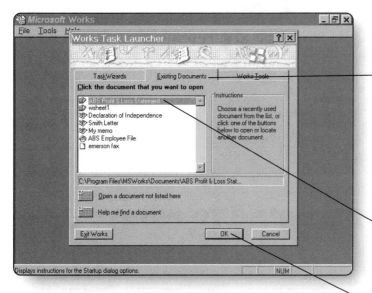

1. **Start Microsoft Works**. The Task Launcher will appear.

2. **Click** on the **Existing Documents tab**. The Existing Documents tab will come to the front.

If the spreadsheet you want to open is listed:

3a. **Click** on the **file name** you want to open. The file name will be highlighted.

4a. **Click** on **OK**. The file will be placed on your screen, ready for you to edit.

OR

If the spreadsheet you want to open is not listed:

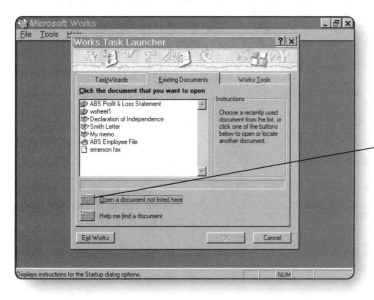

3b. **Click** on **Open a document not listed here**. The Open dialog box will open.

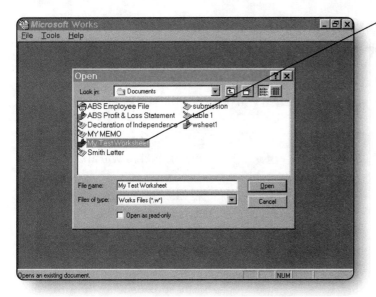

4b. **Double-click** on the **file name** you wish to open. The spreadsheet will be placed on your screen, ready for you to edit.

PREPARING TO PRINT

Before you print your spreadsheet, you may want to tell Works what size paper you'd like to use, how large the margins should be, and whether to print the gridlines or not. These options and others are selected from the Page Setup feature of Works.

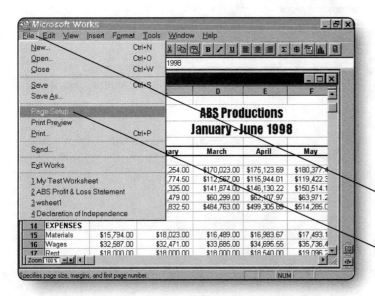

Setting Up Margins

By default, the top and bottom margins are set at 1" and the left and right margins are set at 1.25". You can change these margins.

1. **Click** on **File**. The File menu will appear.

2. **Click** on **Page Setup**. The Page Setup dialog box will open.

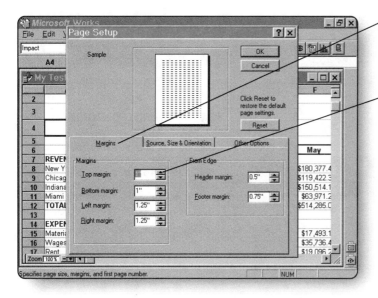

3. If necessary, **click** on the **Margins tab**. The Margins tab will come to the front.

4. **Click** on the **up/down arrows** on each margin you want to change. A sample is displayed in the sample box.

5. **Click** on **OK**. The Page Setup dialog box will close.

Setting Up Page Orientation and Size

If your spreadsheet uses quite a few columns, you may want to change the orientation or paper size. The default size is 8½" by 11" paper in portrait orientation—the short side at the top. Changing to landscape orientation will print with the long edge of the paper at the top.

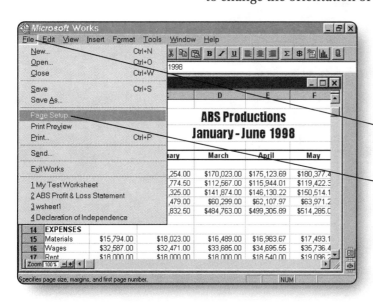

1. **Click** on **File**. The File menu will appear.

2. **Click** on **Page Setup**. The Page Setup dialog box will open.

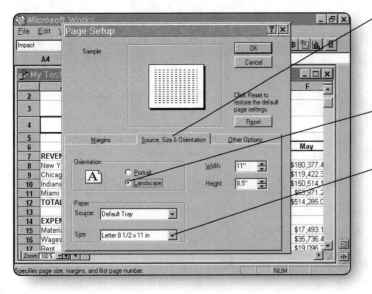

3. If necessary, **click** on the **Source, Size & Orientation tab**. The Source, Size & Orientation tab will come to the front.

4. Click on an **Orientation**. The option will be selected.

5. Click on the **down arrow** at the right of the Size: list box. The list of available page size options will appear.

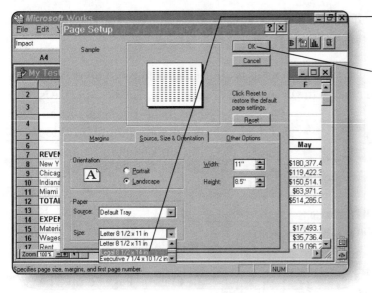

6. Click on a **page size**. The page size will be selected.

7. Click on **OK**. The Page Setup dialog box will close.

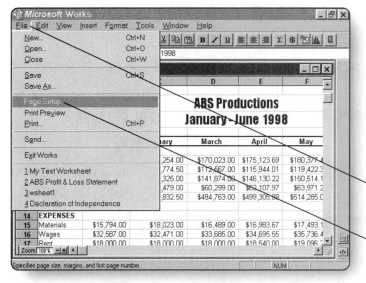

Setting Other Printing Options

You may want to consider other options for your worksheet, such as whether to print the gridlines or the row and column headings.

1. **Click** on **File**. The File menu will appear.

2. **Click** on **Page Setup**. The Page Setup dialog box will open.

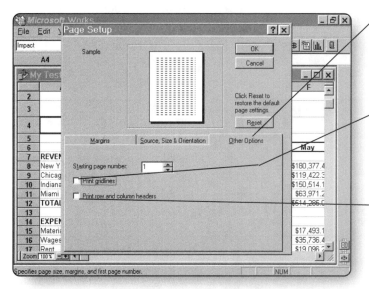

3. If necessary, **click** on the **Other Options tab**. The Other Options tab will come to the front.

4. **Click** on **Print Gridlines** if you want to print the gridlines. A check mark will appear in the selection box.

5. **Click** on **Print row and column headers** if you want the column headings or row headings to print on the spreadsheet. A check mark will appear in the selection box.

6. **Click** on **OK**. The Page Setup dialog box will close.

PRINTING A SPREADSHEET

After you have created your spreadsheet, you can print a hard copy for your records or to send to someone else.

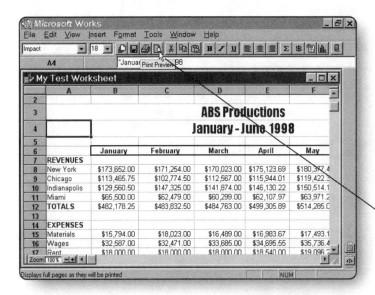

Using Print Preview

Printing can be a slow, expensive process that uses valuable resources. Print Preview allows you to check the overall spreadsheet onscreen prior to printing.

1. **Click** on the **Print Preview button**. The document will be sized so that an entire page is visible on the screen.

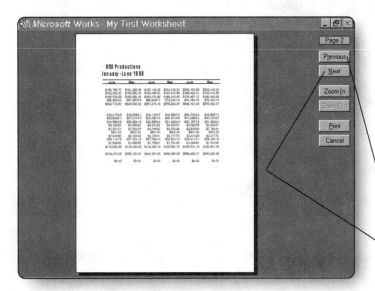

Don't strain your eyes trying to read the text in the Preview windows. You are looking at the overall perspective here, not necessarily the individual cells. The document is not editable on this screen.

2. **Click** on **Previous**. The previous page of the spreadsheet will be displayed.

3. **Click** on **Next**. The next page of the spreadsheet will be displayed.

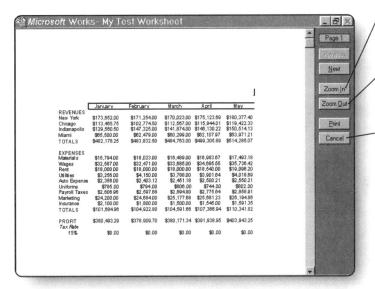

4. Click on **Zoom In**. The text will become larger onscreen.

5. Click on **Zoom Out**. The text will become smaller onscreen.

6. Click on **Cancel**. The spreadsheet will be returned to the normal view.

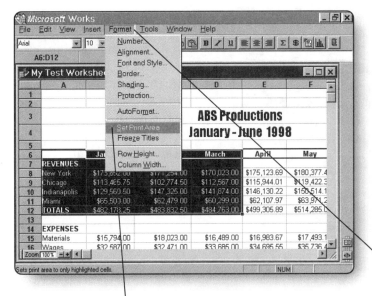

Printing a Range

By default, Works assumes you want to print the entire spreadsheet. If this is not the case, you need to specify the area you want to print.

1. Select the **cells** you want to print if you do not intend to print the entire spreadsheet. The cells will become highlighted.

2. Click on **Format**. The Format menu will open.

3. Click on **Set Print Area**. A confirmation dialog box will open.

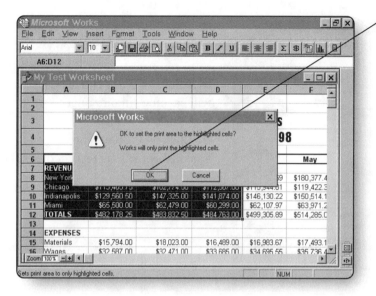

4. **Click** on **OK**. The dialog box will close.

Now when you print your spreadsheet, only the cells you selected in step 1 will print.

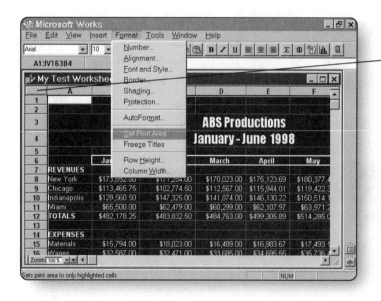

If you later want to print the entire spreadsheet, select the entire spreadsheet by clicking in the small gray box above the row headings and to the left of the column headings, then choose Format, Set Print Area, then click on OK.

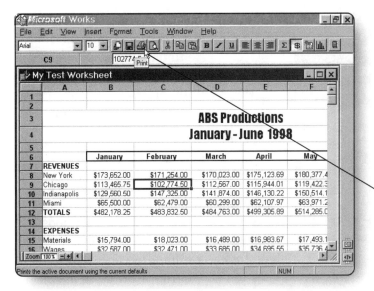

Printing Your Work

Typically, the end result of entering a document into Works is to get text onto paper. Works gives you a quick and easy way to get that result.

1a. **Click** on the **Print button**. The spreadsheet will print with standard options.

OR

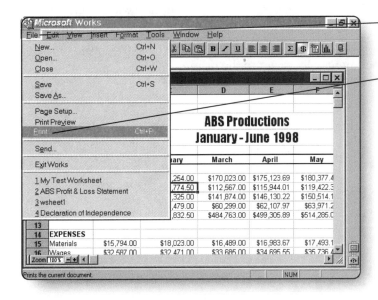

1b. **Click** on **File**. The File menu will appear.

2. **Click** on **Print**. The Print dialog box will open.

Many options are available from the Print dialog box including:

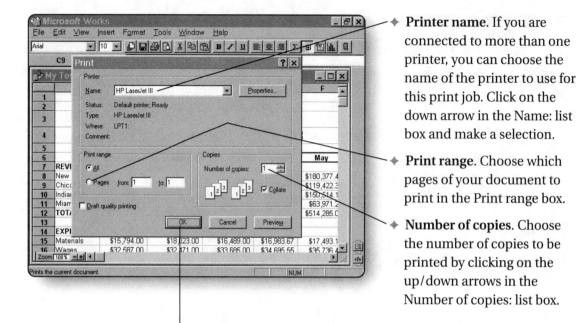

◆ **Printer name.** If you are connected to more than one printer, you can choose the name of the printer to use for this print job. Click on the down arrow in the Name: list box and make a selection.

◆ **Print range.** Choose which pages of your document to print in the Print range box.

◆ **Number of copies.** Choose the number of copies to be printed by clicking on the up/down arrows in the Number of copies: list box.

3. Click on any desired **option.** The option will be activated.

4. Click on **OK** after you have made your selections. The document will be sent to the printer.

15 Creating Charts

A chart is an effective way to illustrate the data in your spreadsheet. It can make relationships between numbers easier to see because it turns numbers into shapes, and the shapes can then be compared to one another. In this chapter, you'll learn how to:

✦ Create a chart

✦ Modify a chart

✦ Delete a chart

CREATING A CHART

Creating a chart is a simple process using the Works Chart Wizard. You first decide what you want to chart and how you want it to look.

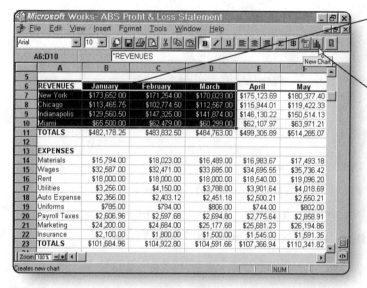

1. **Select** the **range** that you want to chart. The range will be highlighted.

2. **Click** on the **New Chart button**. The New Chart wizard will display onscreen.

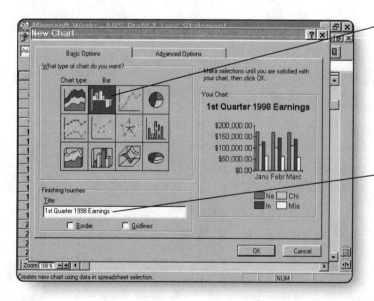

3. **Click** on a **Chart type**. A sample will be displayed in the Your Chart area.

4. **Click** in the **Title: text box**. A blinking insertion point will appear.

5. **Type** a **Title** for your chart. The title will appear in the Title: text box.

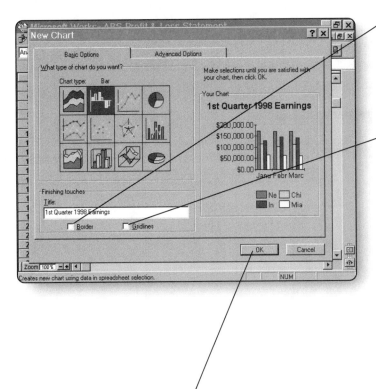

6. **Click** on the **check box** for Border if you want a border around the entire chart. A check mark will display in the check box.

7. **Click** on the **check box** for Gridlines if you want gridlines displayed in your chart. A check mark will display in the check box.

NOTE

If Works does not read the data in the order you expected it, click on the Advanced Options tab and experiment with the options listed.

8. **Click** on **OK**. The chart will be displayed as a new window.

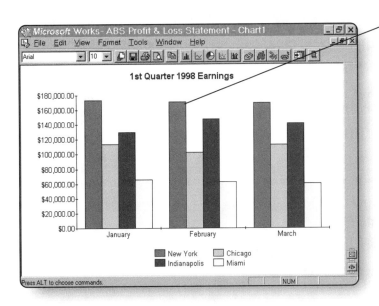

The data from the selected cells of the spreadsheet is plotted out in a chart. If the data in the spreadsheet changes, the chart will also change.

SWITCHING VIEWS

After creating the chart, you may need to return to the spreadsheet window to edit the data.

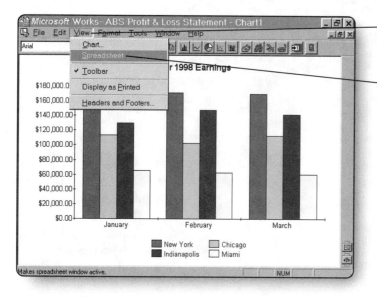

1. **Click** on **View**. The View menu will appear.

2. **Click** on **Spreadsheet**. The Spreadsheet will be displayed.

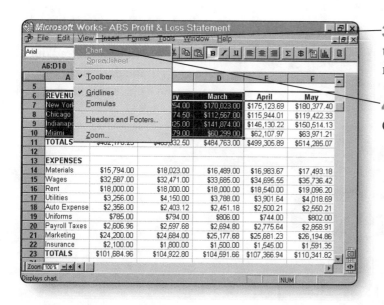

3. **Click** on **View** to return to the Chart window. The View menu will appear.

4. **Click** on **Chart**. The View Chart dialog box will open.

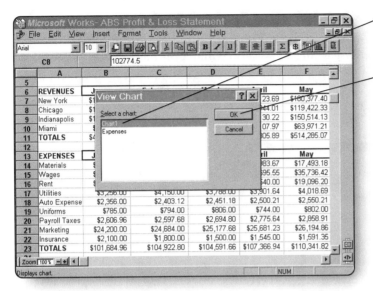

5. **Click** on the **chart** to display. The option will be highlighted.

6. **Click** on **OK**. The Chart window will be displayed.

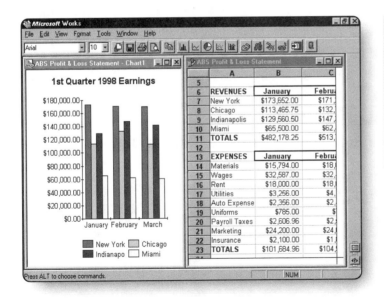

MODIFYING A CHART

Creating a chart is so simple that it probably made you want to enhance the chart to improve its appearance. You can change the style, make it 3-D, or add titles to the chart to further explain its use.

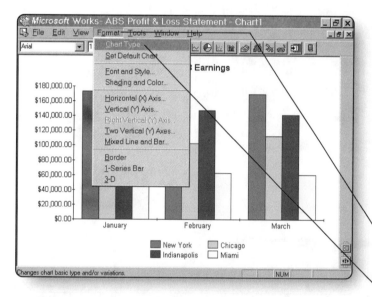

Changing a Chart Style

If you want to change the style of the chart, you can select a bar, area, pie, or line chart, and make it 3-D.

1. **Display** the **chart**. The chart window will be active.

2. **Click** on **Format**. The Format menu will appear.

3. **Click** on **Chart Type**. The Chart Type dialog box will open with the Basic Types tab in front.

4. **Click** on a **Chart Type**. A sample will be displayed.

NOTE

Traditionally, bar charts compare item to item, pie charts compare parts of a whole item, and line charts show a trend over a period of time.

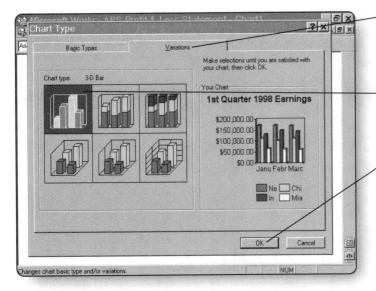

5. Click on the **Variations tab**. Options for each chart type will be displayed.

6. Click on any desired **variation**. A sample will be displayed.

7. Click on **OK**. The chart will change to the selected style.

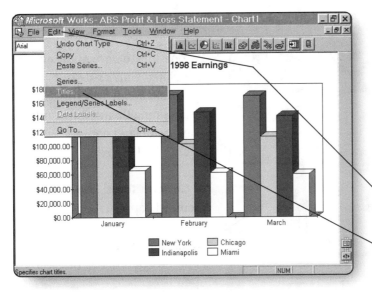

Adding Chart Titles

When you first created the chart, you had an option to give the chart a title. You can edit or delete that title, or assign other types of titles.

1. Click on **Edit**. The Edit menu will appear.

2. Click on **Titles**. The Edit Titles dialog box will open.

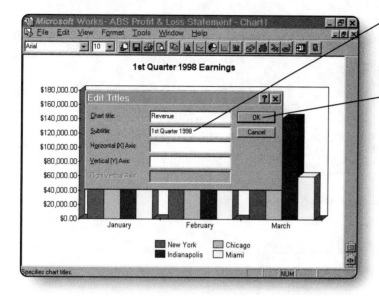

3. **Type** the **text** for any title. The title will display in the text box.

4. **Click** on **OK**. The chart titles will be changed.

NAMING A CHART

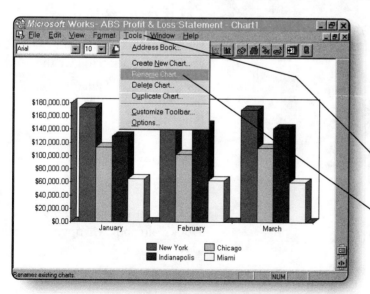

It's possible to have many charts associated with a single spreadsheet. Identify the charts by assigning them a name other than the default name; Chart1, Chart2, and so forth.

1. **Click** on **Tools**. The Tools menu will appear.

2. **Click** on **Rename Chart**. The Rename Chart dialog box will open.

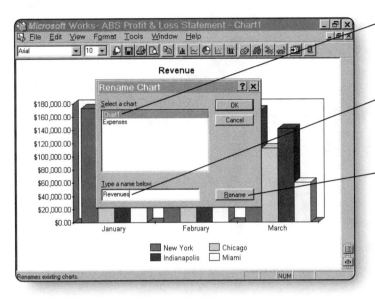

3. **Click** on the **chart** to be renamed. The chart name will be highlighted.

4. **Type** a new **name** in the Type a name below: text box. The new name will be displayed.

5. **Click** on **Rename**. The chart will be renamed.

6. **Click** on **OK**. The Rename Chart dialog box will close.

CHANGING THE CHART SERIES

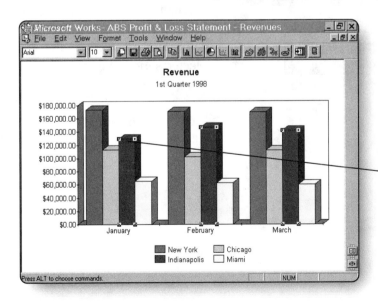

If you do not like the default colors assigned to a chart, you can change them for any series.

1. **Display** the **chart** to be modified. The chart will be displayed.

2. **Click** on any colored **bar, line,** or **series** item. Four white handles will appear around all items in the selected series.

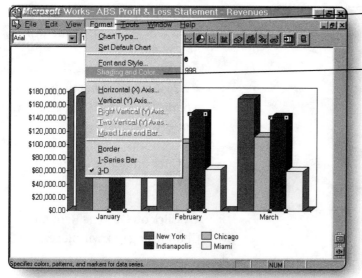

3. **Click** on **Format**. The Format menu will appear.

4. **Click** on **Shading and Color**. The Format Shading and Color dialog box will open.

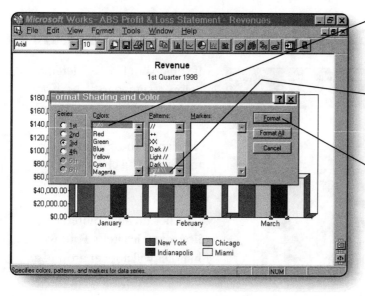

5. **Click** on a **color** for the selected series. The color will be highlighted.

6. **Click** on a **pattern** for the selected series. The pattern will be highlighted.

7. **Click** on **Format**. The chart will be updated with the new options.

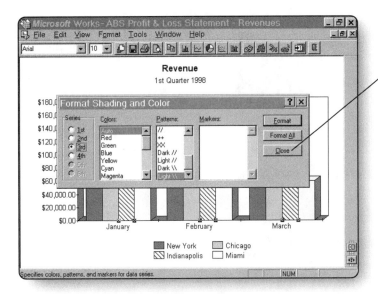

8. **Repeat steps** 3 through **5** for each series to be changed.

9. **Click** on **Close**. The Format Shading and Color dialog box will close.

PRINTING A CHART

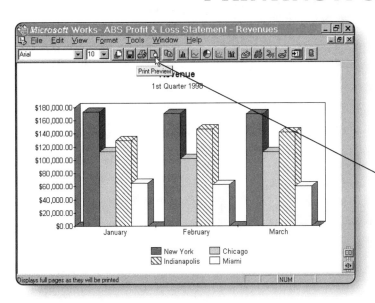

Like printing any type of document, you should preview the work before you print it.

1. **Display** the **chart** to be printed. The chart will display onscreen.

2. **Click** on the **Print Preview button**. A sample of the printed chart will display.

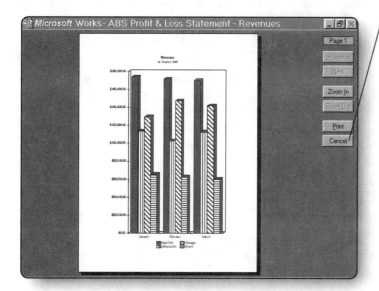

3. **Click** on **Cancel**. The screen will return to the chart display.

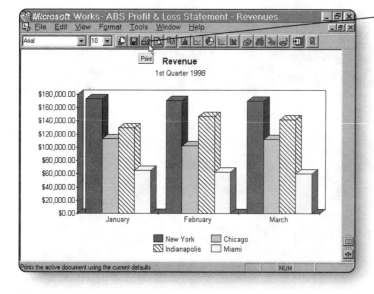

4. **Click** on the **Print button**. The chart will print with standard options.

NOTE

Set up the page size and orientation through the File menu and the Page Setup dialog box.

DELETING A CHART

If you no longer want the chart created from your spreadsheet, you can delete it.

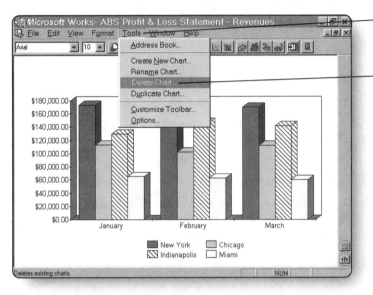

1. **Click** on **Tools**. The Tools menu will appear.

2. **Click** on **Delete Chart**. The Delete Chart dialog box will open.

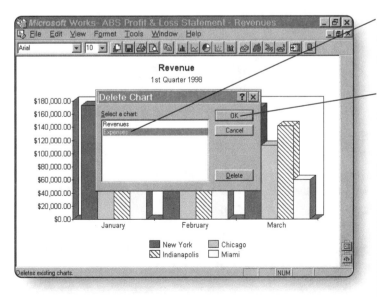

3. **Click** on the **chart** that you want to delete. The chart name will be highlighted.

4. **Click** on **OK**. A confirmation message will appear.

5. **Click** on **OK**. The chart will be deleted.

NOTE

All charts are saved with their corresponding spreadsheet.

PART III REVIEW QUESTIONS

1. Spreadsheet data is made up of what three components?
   See "Entering Data" in Chapter 10

2. What character should you type first to enter a value as a label?
   See "Entering Values into Cells" in Chapter 10

3. What function key can be pressed to edit the contents of a cell?
   See "Editing the Contents of a Cell" in Chapter 10

4. When deleting a spreadsheet column, where do the remaining columns move? *See "Deleting Rows and Columns" in Chapter 11*

5. What does the Fill feature do when you type the word January in a cell and drag across to other cells? *See "Using the Fill Feature" in Chapter 11*

6. With what character must all spreadsheet formulas begin?
   See "Creating Formulas" in Chapter 12

7. What character is used in a formula to designate an absolute reference? *See "Creating an Absolute Reference in a Formula" in Chapter 12*

8. How can you center heading text across a group of columns?
   See "Centering Headings" in Chapter 13

9. How do you tell Works that you want to print a specific area of the spreadsheet? *See "Printing a Range" in Chapter 14*

10. What styles of charts can Works create? *See "Changing a Chart Style" in Chapter 15*

PART IV

Using a Database

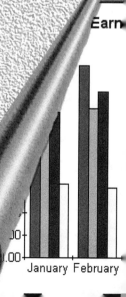

16 Creating a Database

Whether or not you realize it, you use databases every day. Your phone book is a database; your television show listing is a database; even a cookbook is a database. A database in its most simple form is an organized list of information. Works provides a simple database application that allows you to create and manage your own databases. In this chapter, you'll learn how to:

✦ Understand fields and records

✦ Create a new database

✦ Look at different database views

✦ Move a field

✦ Add or delete fields

UNDERSTANDING FIELDS AND RECORDS

Information in a database is grouped into records and fields.

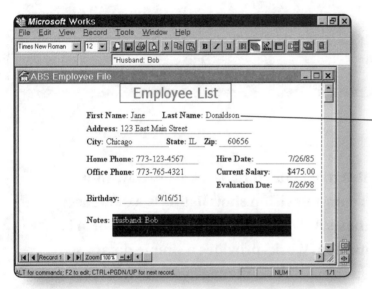

✦ A *record* is all the information about one person, product, event, and so on. Every record in a database contains the same fields.

✦ A *field* is one item in a record, such as a name or address. You can enter text, numbers, dates, or formulas in a field.

CREATING A NEW DATABASE

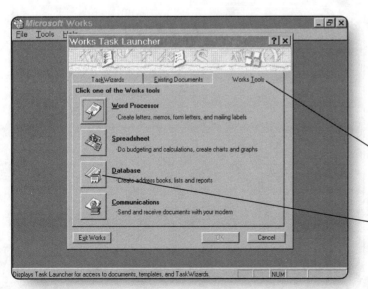

Create a new database by using the Works Task Launcher.

1. Start Microsoft Works. The Task Launcher will appear onscreen.

2. Click on the **Works Tools tab**. The Works Tools tab will come to the front.

3. Click on **Database**. A Create Database dialog box will appear.

Adding Fields

The first thing you must do when creating a new database is name your fields. If you are creating an address database, you might include fields such as name, address, or phone number. If you were creating a database to track your CD collection, you might include fields such as title, artist, or date purchased.

1. **Type** a **name** for the first field. The text will appear in the Field name: text box. Field names can be a maximum of 15 characters.

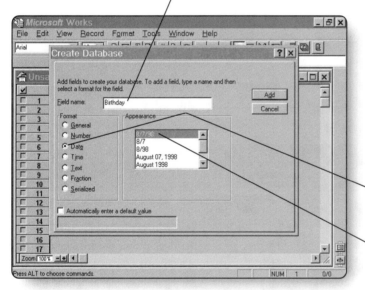

Fields can employ a variety of formats such as General, Number, or Date. Items like name, address, or telephone number have a General (text) format, data such as age have a Number format, and a hire date has a Date format.

2. **Click** on a **format type** for the field. The option will be selected.

3. **Select** any **Appearance options**. The option will be selected.

Works can automatically enter field data. For example, if you are creating an address book where most records reside in Indiana, Works can automatically enter IN or Indiana. It is then easy to change it for the few records that do not reside in Indiana.

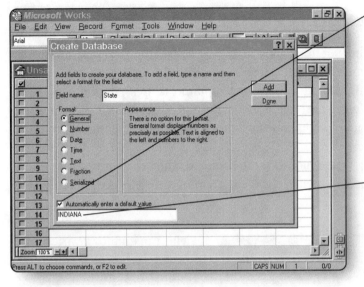

4. Optionally, **click** on **Automatically enter a default value**. The option will be checked.

5. Click on the **default value text box**. A blinking insertion point will appear.

6. Enter the **default value**. The text will display in the default value text box.

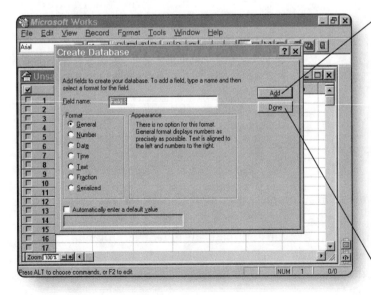

7. Click on **Add**. The field is added and you are prompted for the name of the second field.

8. Repeat steps 1 through **6** until all fields have been added.

TIP

You can edit fields, add additional fields, or delete unwanted fields later.

9. Click on **Done**. The Create Database dialog box will close.

LOOKING AT THE DIFFERENT VIEWS

When the database is first displayed, it is shown in List view.

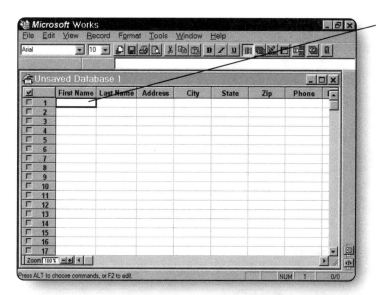

List view is similar to looking at a spreadsheet. The field names are entered as column headings. As you enter each record, the information displays in the rows. In List view, you can see multiple records at the same time.

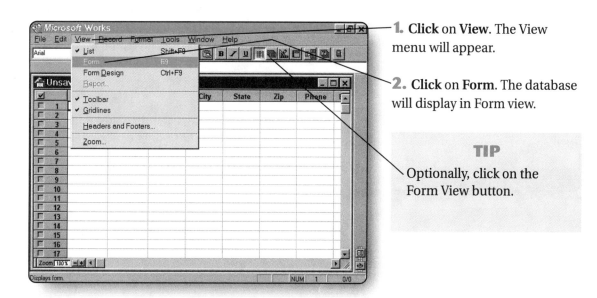

1. **Click** on **View**. The View menu will appear.

2. **Click** on **Form**. The database will display in Form view.

TIP
Optionally, click on the Form View button.

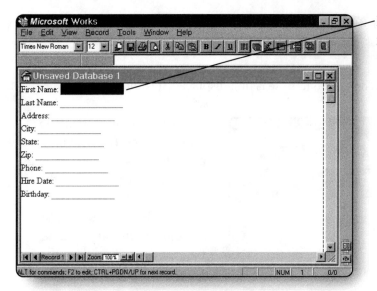

In Form view, you can see one record displayed at a time.

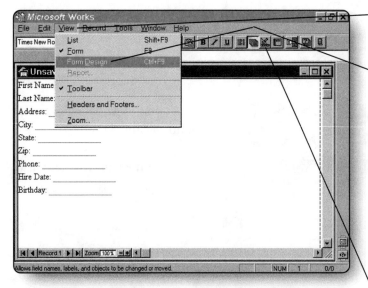

3. Click on **View**. The View menu will appear.

4. Click on **Form Design**. The database will display in Form Design view. The database design can be edited in this view.

TIP

You can edit fields, add additional fields, or delete unwanted fields later.

TIP

Optionally, click on the Form Design button.

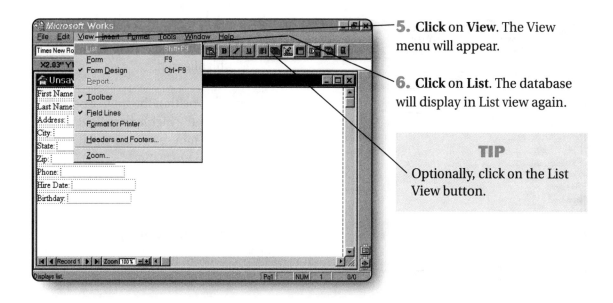

5. **Click** on **View**. The View menu will appear.

6. **Click** on **List**. The database will display in List view again.

TIP

Optionally, click on the List View button.

MOVING A FIELD

If you placed a field in the wrong position, you can move it.

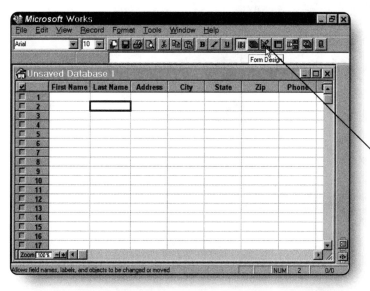

Moving a Field in the Form Design

Enhance the display of the fields by placing them in easy-to-read positions onscreen.

1. **Click** on the **Form Design button.** The database will display in Form Design view.

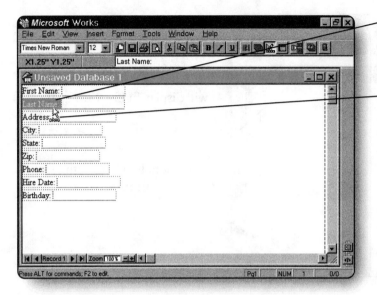

2. Click on the **field name** to be moved. The field name will be highlighted.

3. Position the **mouse pointer** over the highlighted field name. The mouse pointer will display the word "DRAG."

4. Drag the **field name** to the desired position. A box will indicate the new position.

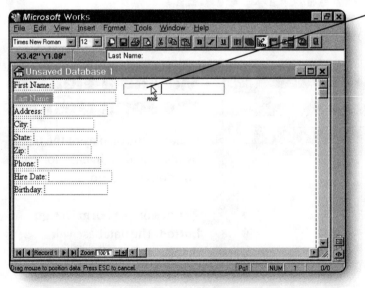

5. Release the **mouse button**. The field name and field contents will be moved.

Moving a Field in the List View

If you move a field in the Form view, it does not change the order of the fields in List view. You can use the Windows Copy and Paste commands to change the order in List view.

1. **Click** on the **List View button**. The database will display in List view.

2. **Click** on the **field name** to be moved. The column will be highlighted.

3. **Click** on **Edit**. The Edit menu will appear.

4. **Click** on **Cut**. A confirmation dialog box will appear.

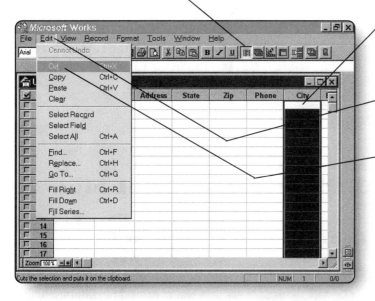

NOTE

This message box says "Permanently delete this information?" Don't be alarmed. You are not going to *permanently* delete the information. You are going to temporarily place the information on the Windows clipboard.

5. **Click** on **OK**. The column/field will be deleted.

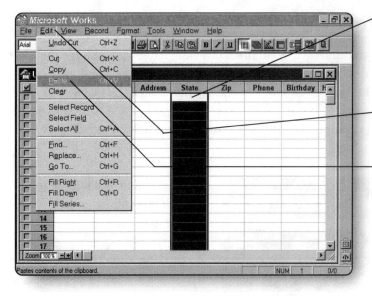

6. **Click** on the **field heading** where you want the data to be positioned. The current field will be highlighted.

7. **Click** on **Edit**. The Edit menu will appear.

8. **Click** on **Paste**. The existing field (and data) will be moved to the right and the field that you put in the Clipboard will be inserted.

ADDING ADDITIONAL FIELDS

Add as many additional fields as you need. The easiest method to add additional fields is using the List view.

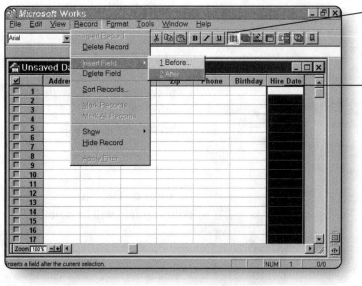

1. If necessary, **click** on the **List View button**. The database will display in List view.

2. **Click** on the **field heading** located at the position where you want the new field. The field column will be highlighted.

3. **Click** on **Record**. The Record menu will appear.

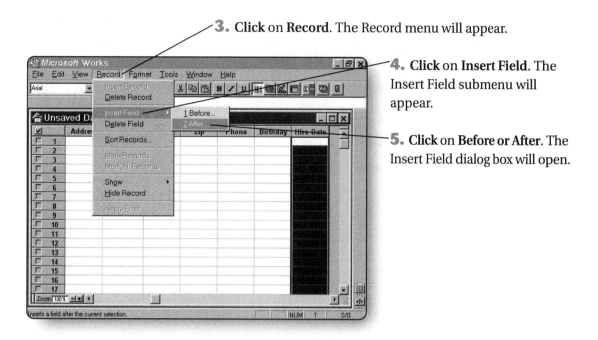

4. **Click** on **Insert Field**. The Insert Field submenu will appear.

5. **Click** on **Before or After**. The Insert Field dialog box will open.

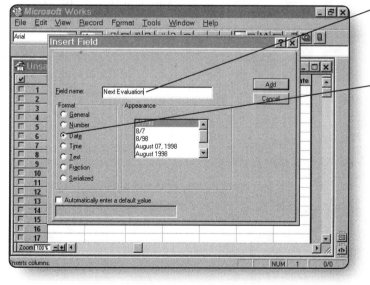

6. **Type** a **name** in the Field name: text box. The text will appear in the text box.

7. **Click** on a **Format** type. The option will be selected.

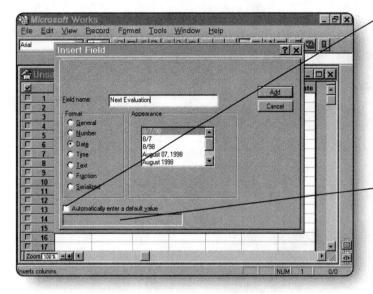

8. Optionally, **click** on **Automatically enter a default value**. The option will be checked.

9. Click in the **default value text box**. A blinking insertion point will appear.

10. Enter the **default value**. The text will display in the default value text box.

11. Click on **Add**. The field will be added.

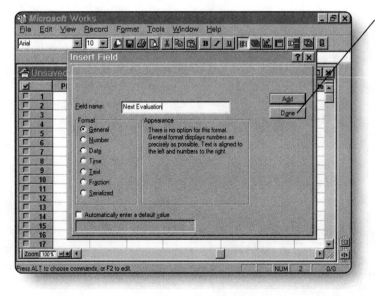

12. Click on **Done**. The Insert Field dialog box will close.

DELETING A FIELD

If a field is no longer needed, you can delete it. When you delete a field, any data for that field is also deleted.

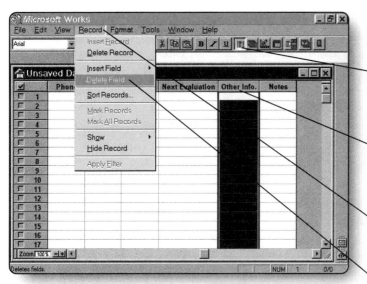

The easiest method to delete a field is using the List view.

1. If necessary, **click** on the **List View** button. The database will display in List view.

2. **Click** on the **field heading** to be deleted. The column will be highlighted.

3. **Click** on **Record**. The Record menu will appear.

4. **Click** on **Delete Field**. A confirmation message will appear.

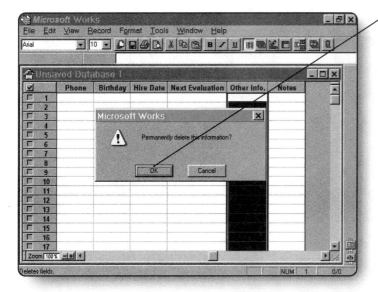

5. **Click** on **OK**. The field will be deleted.

CHANGING FIELD ORDER

When moving around in a database, you'll use the Tab key to move from field to field. By default, Works will move from field to field in the order that they were created. You can modify the tab order of the fields.

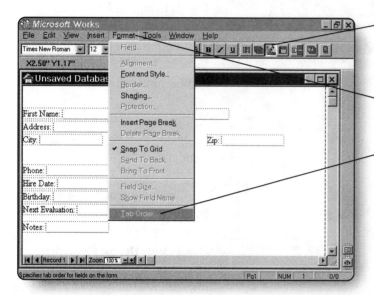

1. **Click** on the **Form Design button**. The database will display in Form Design view.

2. **Click** on **Format**. The Format menu will appear.

3. **Click** on **Tab Order**. The Format Tab Order dialog box will open.

The Set Tab Order list will display the current order of the fields.

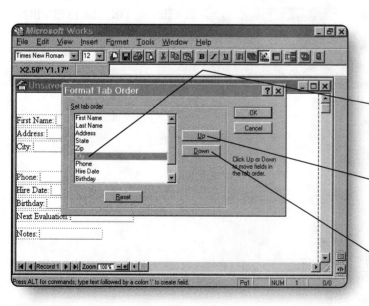

4. **Click** on the **field name** to be moved. The field name will be highlighted.

5a. **Click** on **Up**. The field will be moved up in the tab order.

OR

5b. **Click** on **Down**. The field will be moved down in the tab order.

6. **Click** on **OK**. The Format Tab Order dialog box will close.

17 Working with Data

After you create the database and form, you are ready to add and work with the data for your database. In this chapter, you'll learn how to:

✦ Enter data

✦ Move around the database

✦ Edit records

✦ Find records

✦ Sort records

✦ Delete records

WORKING WITH DATA

Record data can be entered in either List view or Form view. The number of records that can be entered is limited only by the size of your hard drive.

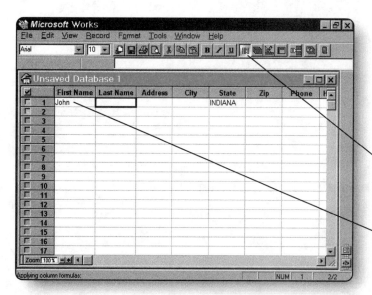

Entering Data in List View

If you are working in List view, you'll see all the records together as you enter them.

1. **Click** on the **List View button**. The database will display in List view.

2. **Type** the **data** for the first field. The data will be entered.

NOTE

When you enter a new record, any fields that you designed with a default value will be automatically entered for you. If you need a different value, highlight the default value and enter the new one.

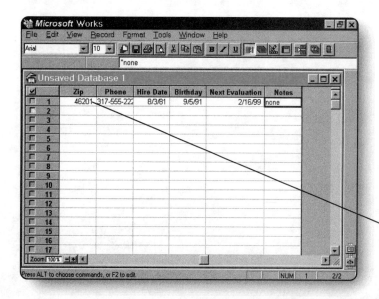

3. **Press** the **Tab key**. The next field will be selected.

4. **Type** the **data** for the next field. That data will be entered.

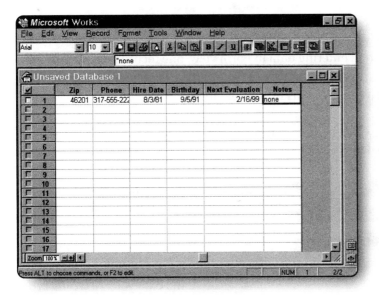

5. **Repeat steps** 3 and 4 until you have entered data for the current record.

When you are ready to add another record:

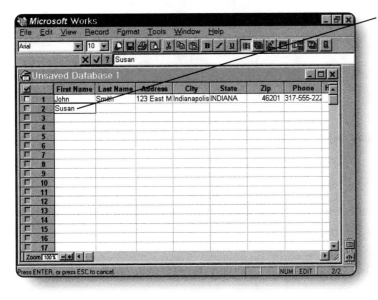

6. While in the last field, **press** the **Tab key**. Works will automatically move to the first field of the next record.

Entering Data in Form View

When entering data in Form view, one record at a time will be displayed. Form view is usually the easiest view to use if you have many fields in your database.

1. **Click** on the **Form View button**. The database will display in Form view.

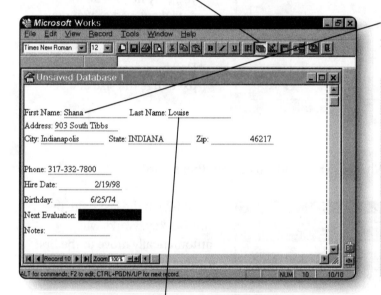

2. **Type** the **data** for the first field. The data will be entered.

> **NOTE**
>
> If the data you are typing is larger than the field size, you may not see all the data displayed or you may see a series of #### displayed. In Chapter 18, "Formatting a Database," you'll learn how to change the size of a field.

3. **Press** the **Tab key**. The next field will be selected.

4. **Type** the **data** for the next field. That data will be entered.

5. **Repeat steps 3** and **4** until you have entered data for the current record.

When you are ready to add another record:

6. **Press** the **Tab key**. Works will automatically display a blank record, ready for entering data.

NOTE

As you access any fields that you designed with a default value, the value will be automatically entered for you. If you need a different value, highlight the default value and enter the new one.

MOVING AROUND IN THE DATABASE

After several records are in the database, you may need to return to a specific record to review it.

Moving around in List View

Moving around the database in List view is similar to moving around in a Works spreadsheet. You can use your mouse or keyboard to quickly move around your database in List view.

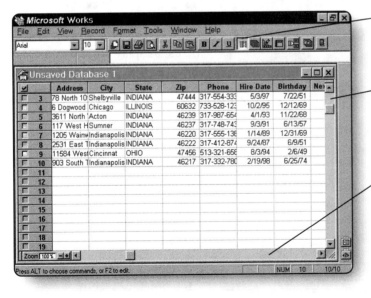

1. Click on the **List View button**. The database will display in List view.

2a. Click on the **vertical scroll bar** until the record you are looking for is visible.

OR

2b. Click on the **horizontal scroll bar** until the field you are looking for is visible.

3. Click anywhere on the **desired record**. The field within that record will be selected.

The following table describes keyboard methods for moving around in your database in List view:

KEYSTROKE	RESULT
Up/Down arrow keys	Moves one record at a time up or down
Left/Right arrow keys	Moves one field at a time left or right
Page Down	Moves one screen of records down
Page Up	Moves one screen of records up
Home	Moves to the first field of the current record
Ctrl+Home	Moves to the first field of the first record
F5	Displays the Go To dialog box

Moving around in Form View

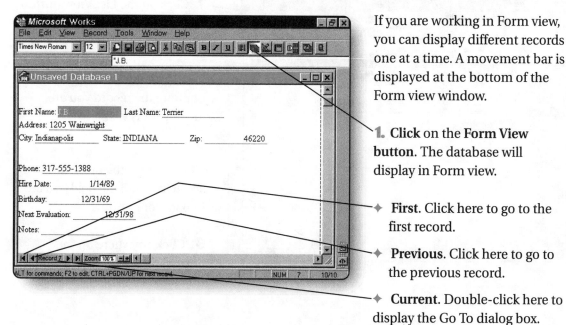

If you are working in Form view, you can display different records one at a time. A movement bar is displayed at the bottom of the Form view window.

1. Click on the **Form View button.** The database will display in Form view.

◆ **First.** Click here to go to the first record.

◆ **Previous.** Click here to go to the previous record.

◆ **Current.** Double-click here to display the Go To dialog box.

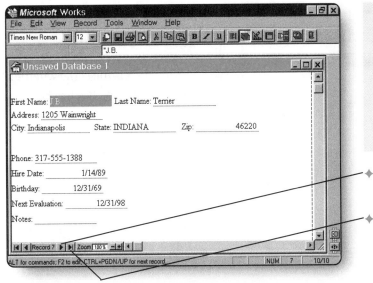

TIP

Other methods to display the Go To dialog box include pressing Ctrl+G, pressing the F5 key, or clicking on the Edit menu and selecting Go To.

◆ **Next**. Click here to go to the next record.

◆ **Last Record**. Click here to go to the last record.

Using the Go To Dialog Box

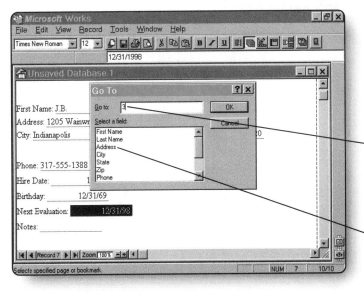

Use the Go To dialog box to quickly jump to a specific record or field.

1. Display the **Go To dialog box**. The Go To dialog box will open.

2a. Enter a **record number**. The number will be displayed in the Go To: text box.

OR

2b. Click on a **field name**. The field name will be displayed in the Go To: text box.

3. Click on **OK**. The Go To dialog box will close and the specified record or field will be displayed.

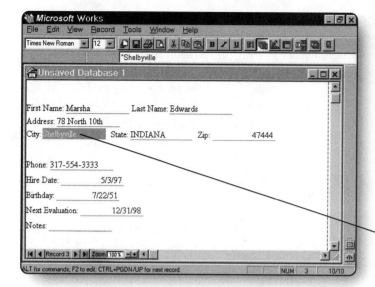

EDITING RECORDS

Editing data is the same whether you are in Form view or List view.

1. **Locate** the **record** to be edited. The current record will be displayed.

2. **Click** on the **data** to be edited. The data will be highlighted.

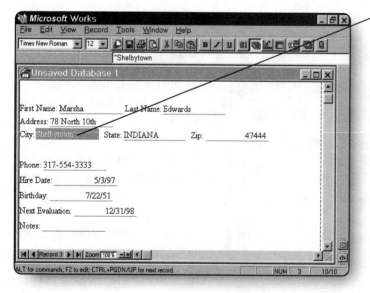

3. **Type** the **corrected information**. The new data will be displayed in the field.

4. **Press Enter**. The existing data will be replaced with the new data.

FINDING RECORDS

Need to locate a specific record? Let Works do the searching for you. An example might be to search for anyone who lives in Chicago. Finding records is slightly different from filtering records, which you will learn to do in Chapter 19, "Using Reports." The List view is an easy view to work with when finding specific records.

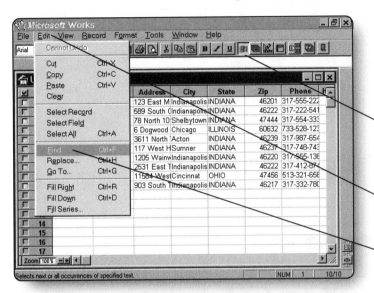

1. **Click** on the **List View button**. The database will display in List view.

2. **Click** on **Edit**. The Edit menu will appear.

3. **Click** on **Find**. The Find dialog box will open.

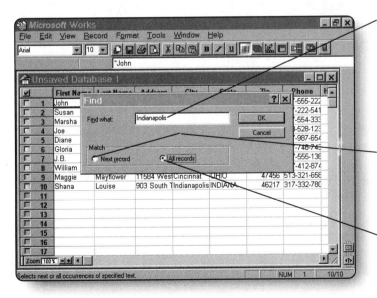

4. **Type** the **characters** you want to locate. The text will appear in the Find what: text box.

5. **Click** on one of the following Match **options**:

✦ **Next Record**. To find the next occurrence of the specified characters, but not search any further, choose Next Record.

✦ **All Records**. To find all records in the database that contain the specified characters and display those records only, choose All Records.

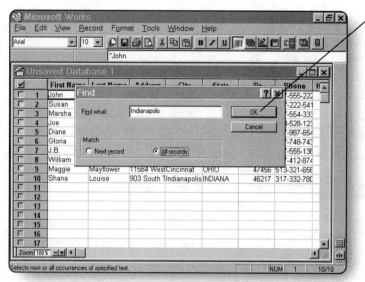

6. Click on **OK**. If you selected Next Record, the next field that contains the specified text will be highlighted. If you chose All Records, only the records matching the criteria will display.

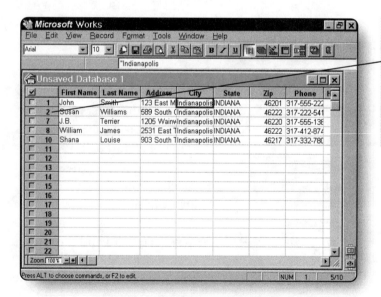

NOTE

Notice in this example, out of the 10 records originally entered, only records 1, 2, 7, 8 and 10 match the criteria.

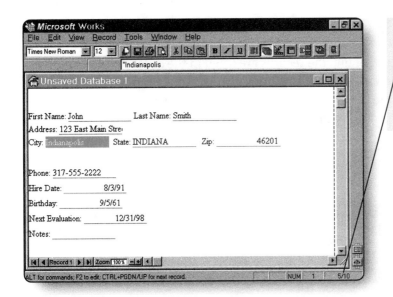

Redisplaying Records

If you selected to find All Records, only the records that matched your selection are displayed. You can easily redisplay all records.

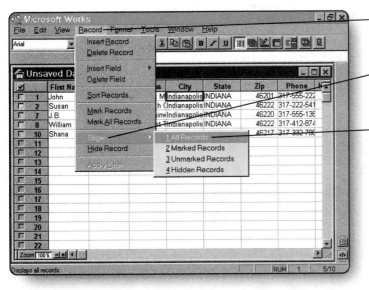

1. **Click** on **Record**. The Record menu will appear.

2. **Click** on **Show**. The Show submenu will appear.

3. **Click** on **All Records**. All records in the database will redisplay.

SORTING RECORDS

By default, the records are listed in the order that you entered them. You can sort them by any field. If multiple records have the same data in the specified field, you also can specify a second or third sorting method.

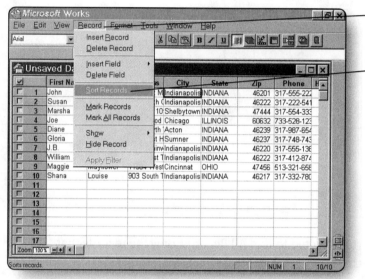

1. **Click** on **Record**. The Record menu will appear.

2. **Click** on **Sort Records**. The Sort Records dialog box will open.

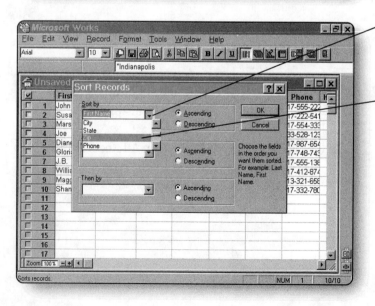

3. **Click** on the **down arrow** in the Sort By: list box. A list of fields will be displayed.

4. **Click** on the first **field** to sort by. The field name will be displayed in the Sort By: list box.

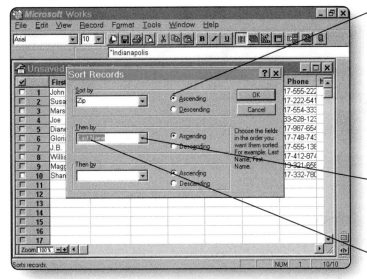

5. **Click** on **Ascending or Descending**. The option will be selected.

If multiple records have the same data in the specified field, you can also specify a second or third sorting method.

6. **Click** on the **down arrow** in the first Then by: list box. A list of fields will be displayed.

7. **Click** on the second **field** to sort by. The field name will be displayed in the first Then by: list box.

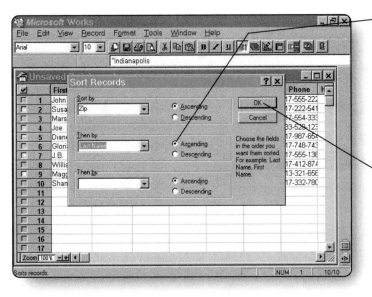

8. **Click** on **Ascending or Descending**. The option will be selected.

9. Optionally, **repeat steps 6 through 8** for the second Then by: list box.

10. **Click** on **OK**. The Sort dialog box will close.

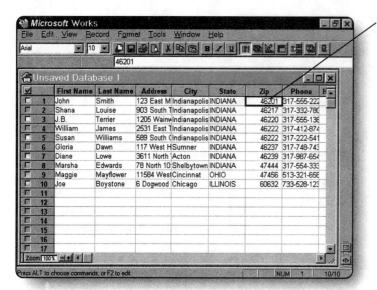

The records will be sorted and displayed in the order specified.

DELETING RECORDS

It is a simple process to delete a record. Deleting a record erases all data from all fields of the selected record only. The procedure for deleting a record is the same in List view or Form view.

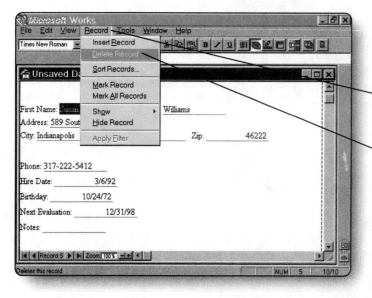

1. **Click** anywhere **on the record** to be deleted. The selected record will be displayed.

2. **Click** on **Record**. The Record menu will be displayed.

3. **Click** on **Delete Record**. The selected record will be deleted.

NOTE

If you delete a record in error, immediately go to the Edit menu and click on Undo.

18 Formatting a Database

You've learned how to create database fields and enter the records. You can make your database more noticeable with Works in several ways. You can modify and enhance its appearance by changing the look or size of fields or even adding a company logo. In this chapter, you'll learn how to:

✦ Change the field type

✦ Change the alignment or size of a field

✦ Rename a field

✦ Add non-field text

✦ Add artwork to a database

FORMATTING FIELDS

When you format fields, you change the appearance of your field data. Options for formatting include the type of contents in a field as well as the alignment, font, border, or shading options of field data.

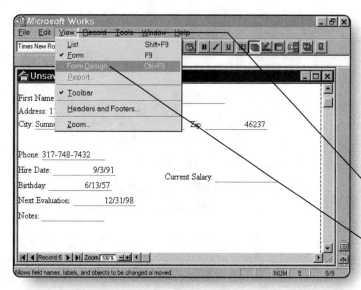

Changing the Field Type

When you first created your database, you were given several options to set the format type of the field. The format of a field can be changed at any time.

1. **Click** on **View**. The View menu will appear.

2. **Click** on **Form Design**. The database will display in Form Design view.

3. **Click** on the **field** to be modified. The field will be highlighted.

4. **Click** on **Format**. The Format menu will appear.

5. **Click** on **Field**. The Format dialog box will open with the Field tab displayed.

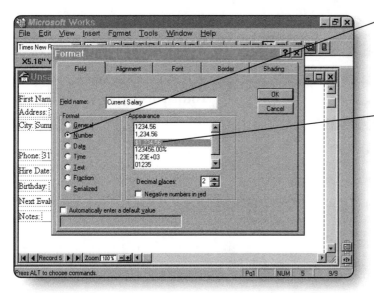

6. **Click** on a **format**. The option will be selected and any appearance options will be displayed.

7. **Click** on an **appearance option**. The option will be selected.

8. **Click** on **OK**. The Format dialog box will close.

Changing the Alignment of a Field

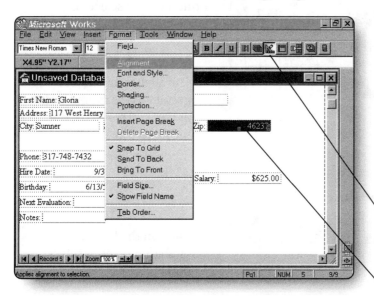

The default alignment of field contents is General. Text items will be aligned to the left whereas dates and numerically formatted fields will be aligned to the right. You can override the default alignment and set any field to line up on the right, left, or center of the field.

1. If necessary, **click** on the **Form Design button**. The database will be in Form Design view.

2. **Click** on the **field** to be modified. The field will be highlighted.

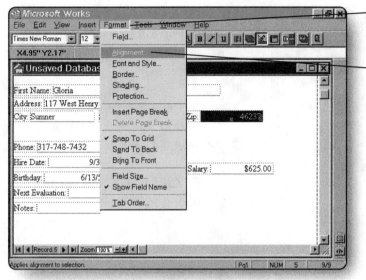

3. **Click** on **Format**. The Format menu will appear.

4. **Click** on **Alignment**. The Format dialog box will open with the Alignment tab displayed.

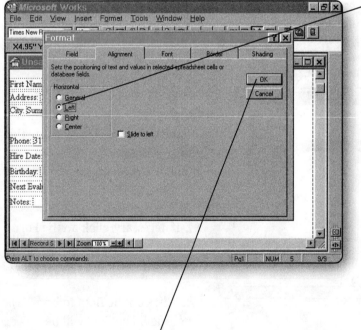

5. **Click** on an **Alignment**. The option will be selected.

NOTE

The alignment choices pertain to the overall width of the field contents, not the page. The next section discusses field width.

TIP

Click on the Font, Border, or Shading tabs to select these options.

6. **Click** on **OK**. The Format dialog box will close. The field alignment will be modified to your specifications.

CHANGING THE SIZE OF A FIELD

When the fields were first created, Works made each field the same size—twenty characters for each field. Perhaps that is too much—or not enough.

Using the Menu

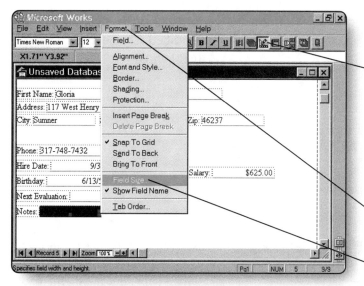

Fields can be up to 325 characters wide and 325 lines long.

1. If necessary, **click** on the **Form Design button**. The database will be in Form Design view.

2. Click on the **field** to be modified. The field will be highlighted.

3. Click on **Format**. The Format menu will appear.

4. Click on **Field Size**. The Format Field Size dialog box will open.

5. Type a **size** in the Width: text box. The new value will be displayed.

6. Press the **Tab** key. The Height: text box will be highlighted.

7. Type a **size** for the field height. The new value will be displayed.

8. Click on **OK**. The dialog box will close and the field will change to the specified width and height.

Changing Field Size by Dragging

Visually resize the field using the mouse.

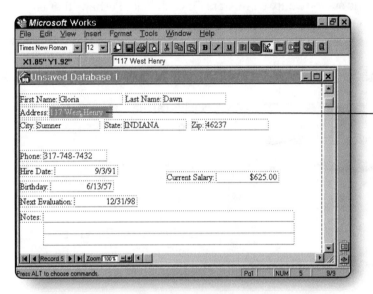

1. If necessary, **click** on the **Form Design button**. The database will be in Form Design view.

2. **Click** on the **field** to be modified. The field will be highlighted.

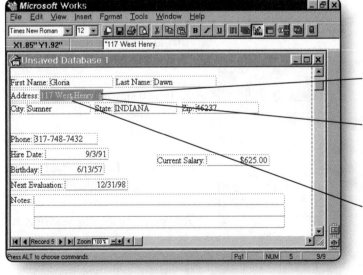

Notice the three size boxes that appear around the perimeter of a field when it is highlighted:

✦ The top box on the right is used to change the field width

✦ The bottom box on the right is used to change both the height and width at the same time.

✦ The box at the bottom is used to change the field height.

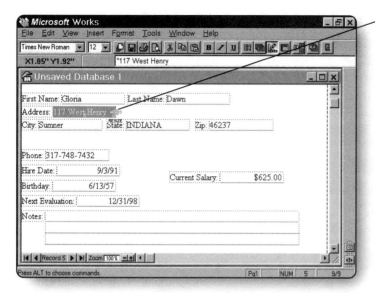

3. Position the **mouse pointer** on one of the size boxes. The mouse pointer will change to an arrow with the word "RESIZE" displayed.

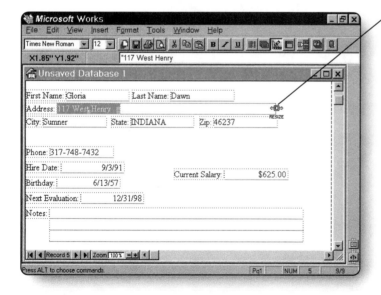

4. Drag the **size box** to the desired size. A dotted box will indicate the new size.

5. Release the **mouse button**. The field will be resized.

NOTE

Field text that was previously unable to display because the field size was too small may now appear.

RENAMING A FIELD

The name originally assigned to a field can be changed. Field names can be up to 15 characters including spaces and punctuation.

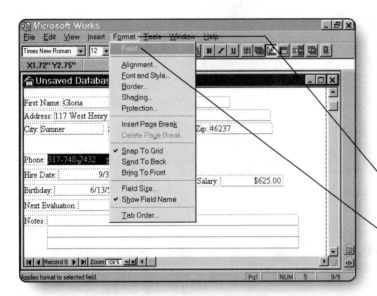

1. If necessary, **click** on the **Form Design button**. The database will be in Form Design view.

2. Click on the **field** to be modified. The field will be highlighted.

3. Click on **Format**. The Format menu will appear.

4. Click on **Field**. The Format dialog box will open with the Field tab displayed.

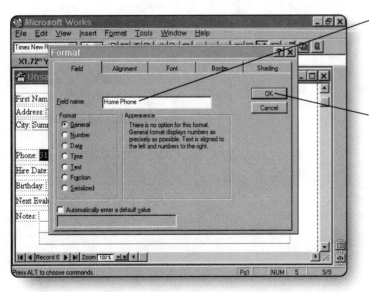

5. Type a new **name** in the Field name: text box. The text will be displayed in the Field name: text box.

6. Click on **OK**. The field name will be changed.

NOTE

No data is changed when renaming a field.

ADDING NON-FIELD TEXT

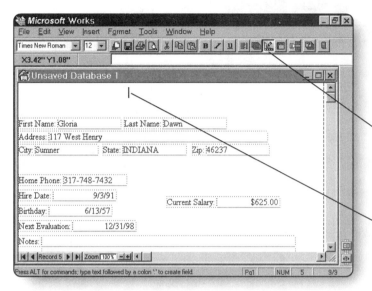

Text that is not related to a field can be added. Add items like your company name or a description of the information you're storing in the database.

1. If necessary, **click** on the **Form Design button**. The database will be in Form Design view.

2. Click the **mouse** where you want the text to be located. A blinking insertion point will appear.

3. Type text. The text will be displayed and highlighted.

NOTE

Do not type any colons (:) in the text. Works will treat items with a colon as a new field.

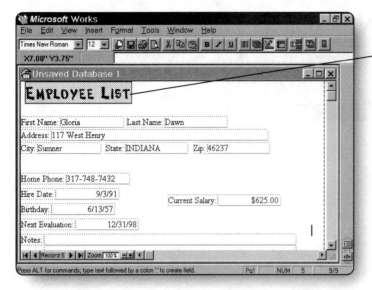

TIP

Non-field text can be formatted or moved in the same manner as field text.

ADDING ARTWORK TO A DATABASE

Enhance the appearance of your database by adding artwork to the design. Any artwork added will appear on each record in the database.

Adding a Logo

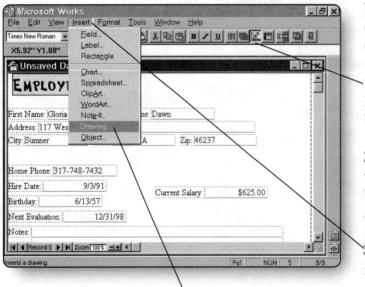

You can add your company logo or other graphic to be displayed on each record of the database.

1. If necessary, **click** on the **Form Design button**. The database will be in Form Design view.

2. **Click** the **mouse** where you want the logo to be located. A blinking insertion point will appear.

3. **Click** on **Insert**. The Insert menu will appear.

4. **Click** on **Drawing**. A Microsoft Drawing window will be displayed.

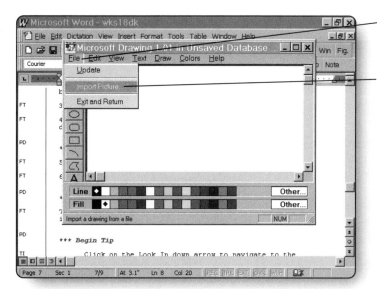

5. Click on **File**. The File menu will appear.

6. Click on **Import Picture**. The Open dialog box will open.

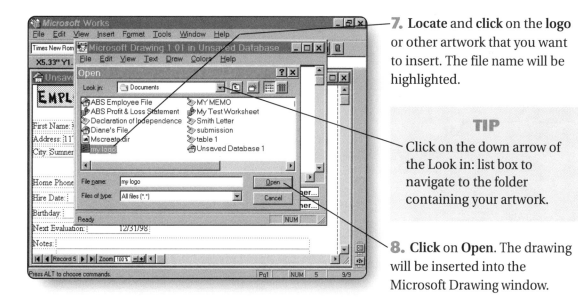

7. Locate and **click** on the **logo** or other artwork that you want to insert. The file name will be highlighted.

TIP

Click on the down arrow of the Look in: list box to navigate to the folder containing your artwork.

8. Click on **Open**. The drawing will be inserted into the Microsoft Drawing window.

The next step is to insert the drawing into the database window.

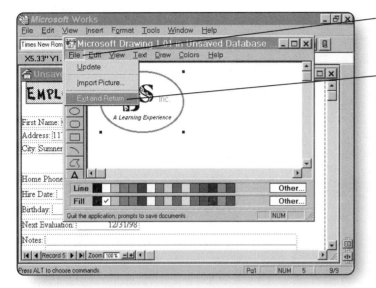

9. Click on **File**. The File menu will appear.

10. Click on **Exit and Return**. A message box will open.

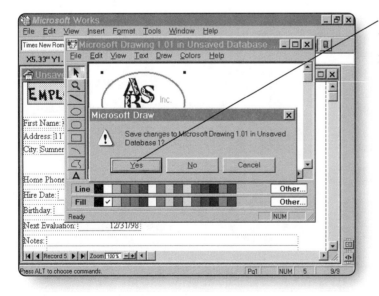

11. Click on **Yes**. The image will be inserted into the database form.

TIP

Resize artwork by clicking and dragging on one of the eight handles surrounding the image.

Adding Clip Art

Don't want to insert a logo? You can still enhance your database by adding one of the many pieces of clip art or photographs supplied with Microsoft Works.

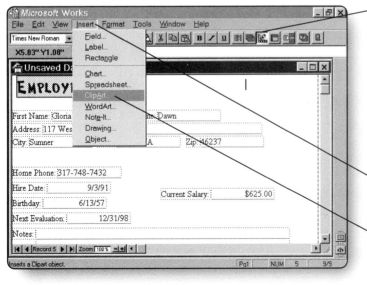

1. If necessary, **click** on the **Form Design button**. The database will be in Form Design view.

2. **Click** the **mouse** where you want the artwork to be located. A blinking insertion point will appear.

3. **Click** on **Insert**. The Insert menu will appear.

4. **Click** on **ClipArt**. The Microsoft Clip Gallery dialog box will open.

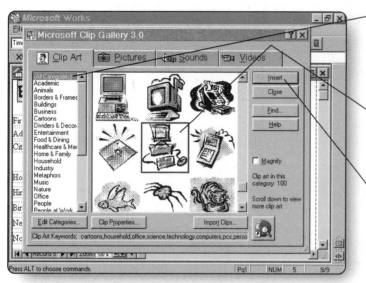

5. **Click** on the type of **image** that you want to use. The selection of available artwork will display.

6. **Click** on the **image** you want to insert. The selection will be surrounded by a black box.

7. **Click** on **Insert**. The clip art image or picture will be inserted into your database.

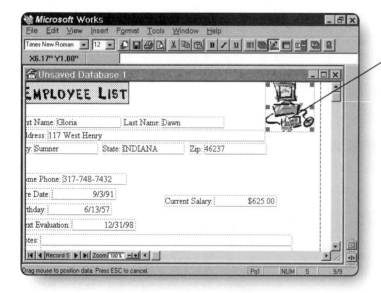

TIP

Move the artwork by placing the mouse pointer in the middle of the artwork and dragging it to the desired location.

19 Using Reports

Works allows you to decide how your printed data should look by letting you create reports. Using reports, you can control the format of the report, which fields and records are included in the report, and whether you want totals. In this chapter, you'll learn how to:

✦ Filter records

✦ Create a report

✦ Print a report

✦ Save a database

FILTERING RECORDS

Filtering records is the process of letting Works know which records to select from the database. For example, you could create a filter named "Chicago Smiths" that includes only the people named Smith who live in Chicago. You could create another filter named "Youth" that includes only the people under 21 years of age.

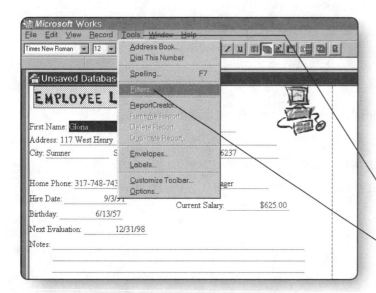

Creating a Filter the First Time

The first time you create a filter in the database, a Filter Name box will appear. This box does not appear on subsequent filters.

1. **Click** on **Tools**. The Tools menu will appear.

2. **Click** on **Filters**. The Filter Name dialog box will open.

3. **Enter** a **name** for the filter. The default name is Filter1.

4. **Click** on **OK**. The Filter dialog box will open.

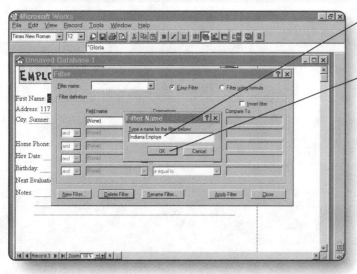

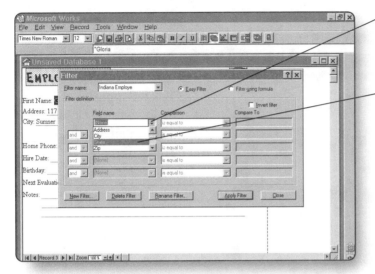

5. **Click** on the **Field name down arrow**. A list of field names will display.

6. **Click** on the first **Field name** that you want to filter. The name will display in the Field name: text box.

7. **Press** the **Tab key**. The highlight will jump to the Comparison box.

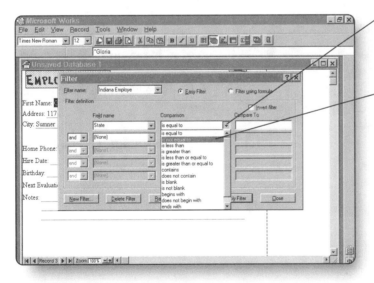

8. **Click** on the **Comparison down arrow**. A list of comparison types will display.

9. **Click** on the desired **option**. The option will display in the comparison box.

10. **Press** the **Tab key**. The highlight will jump to the Compare To box.

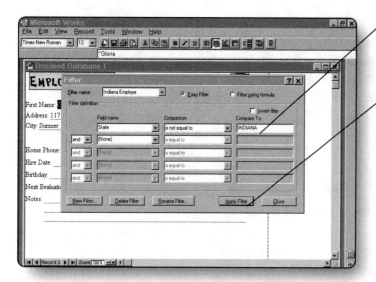

11. **Type** the **value or criterion** to be compared. You can type text or numbers.

12. **Click** on **Apply Filter**. The Filter dialog box will close and only records that match the filter will be displayed.

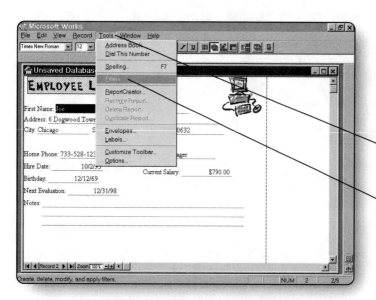

Creating Additional Filters

A database can have up to eight filters.

1. **Click** on **Tools**. The Tools menu will appear.

2. **Click** on **Filters**. The Filter dialog box will open with the last filter you created.

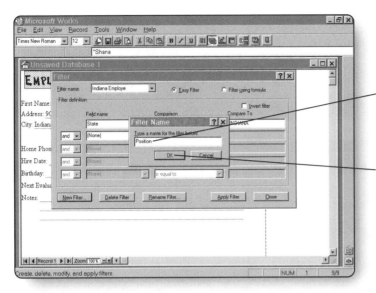

3. **Click** on **New Filter**. The Filter Name dialog box will open.

4. **Enter** a **name** for the new filter. The name will display in the dialog box.

5. **Click** on **OK**. The Filter Name dialog box will close.

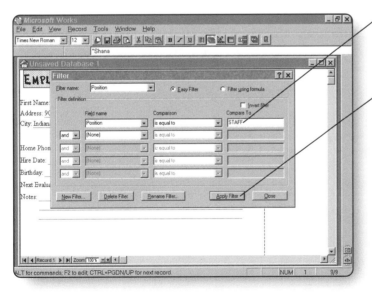

6. **Apply** the **filter information** as you learned in the previous section.

7. **Click** on **Apply Filter**. The Filter dialog box will close and only records that match the filter will be displayed.

Selecting Multiple Criteria

You can define up to five criteria for Works to match. Each additional criterion will use the logical operators AND or OR. For Example, you could choose the last name Smith AND he must live in the City of Chicago. This would exclude a person named Smith who lives in Indianapolis. If you use OR in the above example, the criteria would include anyone named Smith (regardless of where they live) and it would include anyone who lives in Chicago, regardless of whether their last name is Smith, Jones, Koers or whatever.

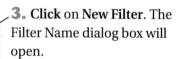

1. **Click** on **Tools**. The Tools menu will appear.

2. **Click** on **Filters**. The Filter dialog box will open with the last filter you created.

3. **Click** on **New Filter**. The Filter Name dialog box will open.

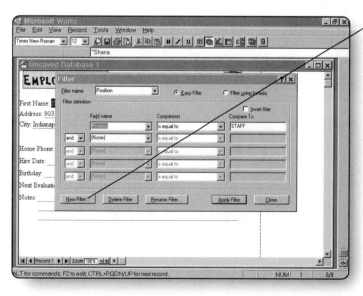

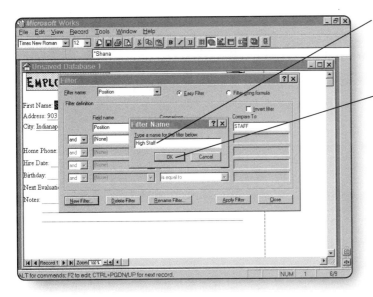

4. **Enter** a **name** for the new filter. The name will display in the dialog box.

5. **Click** on **OK**. The Filter Name dialog box will close.

6. **Choose** a **Field name** for the first criteria. The Field name will display.

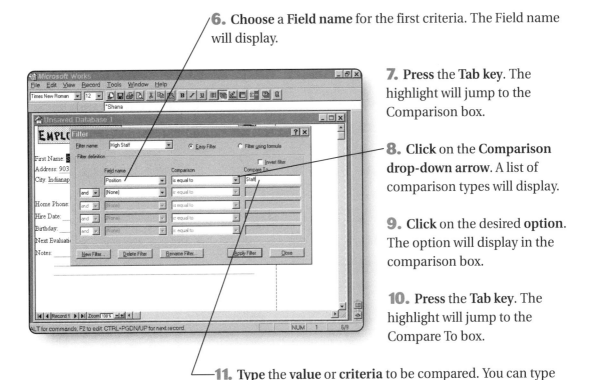

7. **Press** the **Tab key**. The highlight will jump to the Comparison box.

8. **Click** on the **Comparison drop-down arrow**. A list of comparison types will display.

9. **Click** on the desired **option**. The option will display in the comparison box.

10. **Press** the **Tab key**. The highlight will jump to the Compare To box.

11. **Type** the **value** or **criteria** to be compared. You can type text or numbers.

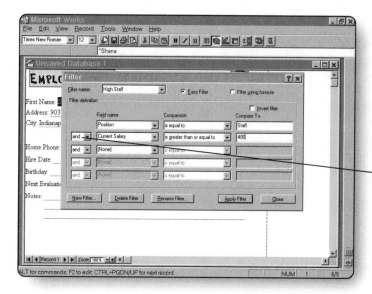

12. Press the **Tab key**. The highlight will move to the second criterion line.

13. Click on the **Comparison drop-down arrow**. A selection of choices will display.

14. Click on **AND** or **OR**. The option will be displayed.

15. Press the **Tab key**. The highlight will move to the second Field name box.

16. Repeat steps 6 through 13 for each criterion that you want to specify.

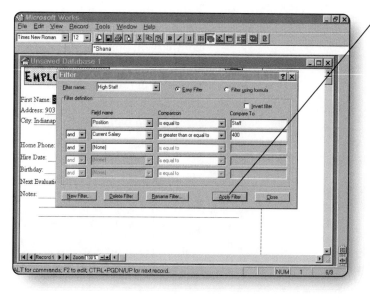

17. Click on **Apply Filter**. The Filter dialog box will close and only records that match the filter will be displayed.

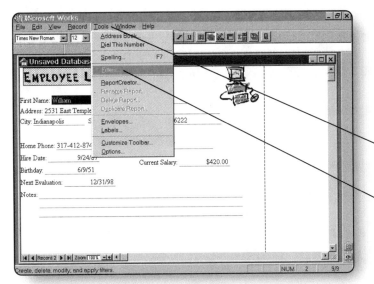

Applying a Filter

If you wish to select records from a filter that you previously created, Works will allow you to select the filter from a list.

1. **Click** on **Tools**. The Tools menu will appear.

2. **Click** on **Filters**. The Filter dialog box will open.

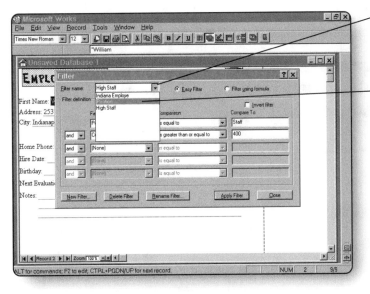

3. **Click** on the **Filter name drop-down arrow**. A list of current filters will display.

4. **Click** on the **Filter name** to be used. The filter information will display.

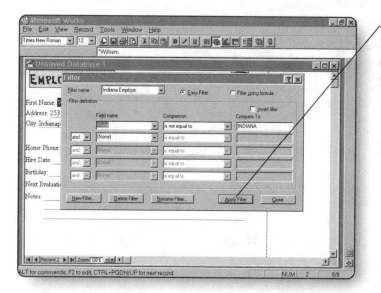

5. **Click** on **Apply Filter**. The Filter dialog box will close and only the records that match the filtered criteria will display.

RENAMING A FILTER

If the name you originally selected for your filter doesn't quite seem appropriate, rename it. Filters can be renamed at any time.

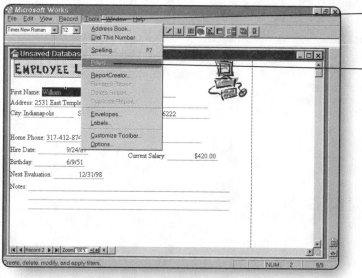

1. **Click** on **Tools**. The Tools menu will appear.

2. **Click** on **Filters**. The Filter dialog box will open.

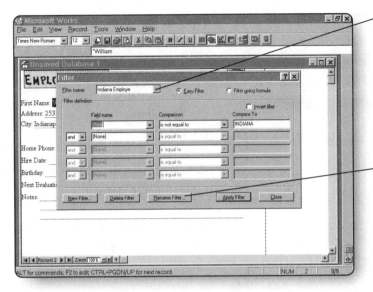

3. **Click** on the **Filter Name drop-down arrow**. A list of current filters will display.

4. **Click** on the **Filter name** to be renamed. The filter information will be displayed.

5. **Click** on **Rename Filter**. The Filter Name dialog box will open.

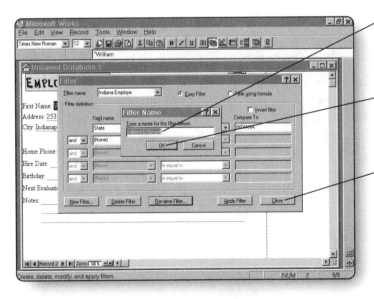

6. **Type** a **new name** for the filter. The text will appear in the text box.

7. **Click** on **OK**. The Filter Name dialog box will close and the filter will be renamed.

8. **Click** on **Close**. The Filter dialog box will close.

DELETING A FILTER

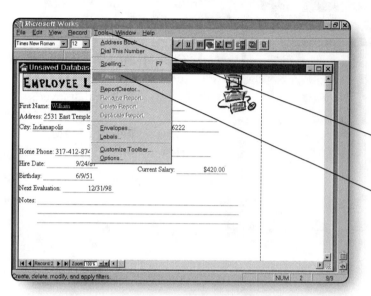

You can easily delete filters. When you delete a filter, you are not deleting any records or fields, only the instructions to filter it.

1. Click on **Tools**. The Tools menu will appear.

2. Click on **Filters**. The Filter dialog box will open.

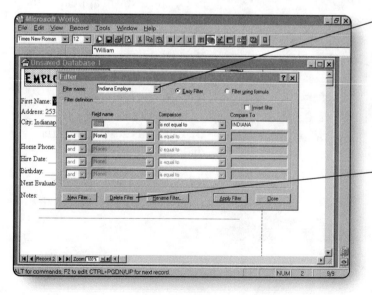

3. Click on the **Filter name: drop-down arrow**. A list of current filters will display.

4. Click on the **Filter name** to be deleted. The filter information will be displayed.

5. Click on **Delete Filter**. A confirmation box will open.

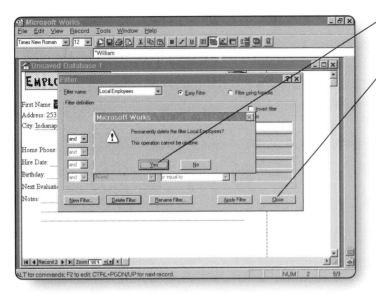

6. **Click** on **Yes**. The filter will be removed from the filter list.

7. **Click** on **Close**. The Filter dialog box will close.

CREATING A REPORT

Reports organize and summarize the database information. When you create a report, you can specify which fields to print and where on the page to print them. You can also sort and group information as well as include calculations such as totals or averages.

Each database can include up to eight reports.

Using the ReportCreator

Use the ReportCreator to create a database report that is sorted and formatted.

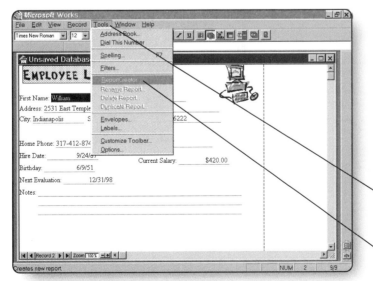

1. **Click** on **Tools**. The Tools menu will appear.

2. **Click** on **ReportCreator**. The Report Name dialog box will open.

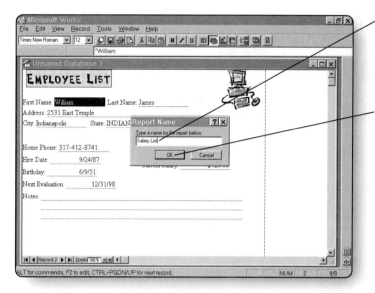

3. **Enter** a **name** for the report. Report names can be up to 15 characters in length including spaces.

4. **Click** on **OK**. The ReportCreator wizard will open.

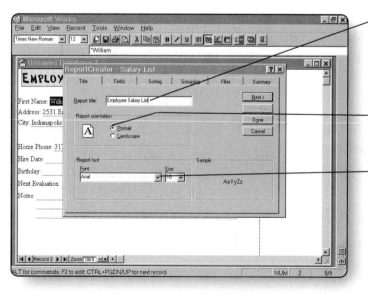

5. **Type** a **title** for your report. The title will print on the report and can be up to 255 characters including spaces.

6. **Click** on an **orientation**. The option will be selected.

7. **Click** on the **Font drop-down arrow**. A list of available fonts will appear.

8. **Click** on a **Font**. The font name will be displayed.

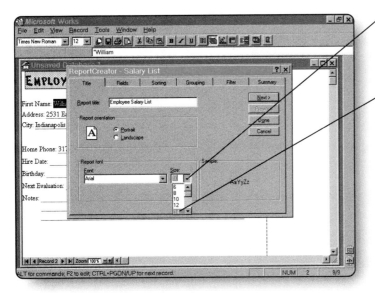

9. Click on the **Size drop-down arrow.** A list of available font sizes will appear.

10. Click on the **Size** that you want for your font. The size will be displayed.

11. Click on **Next.** The Fields tab will come to the front.

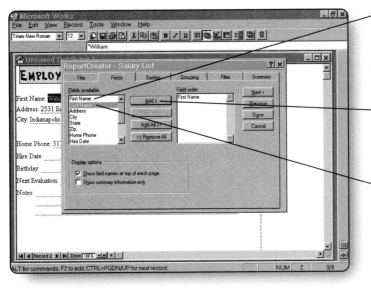

12. Click on the **first field name** that you want to display in the report. The field name will be highlighted.

13. Click on **Add.** The field name will be added to the Field order list.

14. Click on the **next field name** to be in the report. The field name will be highlighted.

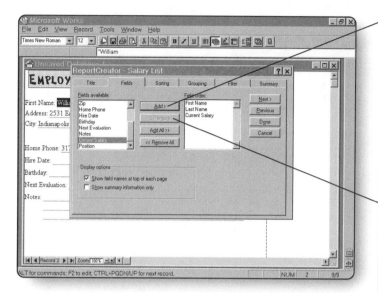

15. Click on **Add**. The field name will be added to the Field order list.

16. Repeat steps 14 and **15** for each field to be included in the report.

TIP

To remove a field from the report, click on the field name in the Field order list, then click on Remove. The field will only be removed from the report, not from the database.

17. Click on **Next**. The Sorting tab will come to the front.

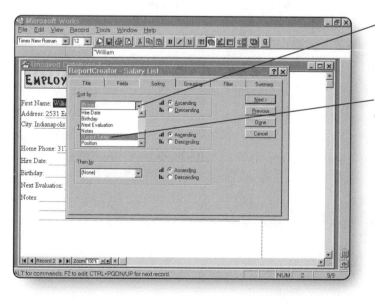

18. Click on **Sort by down-arrow**. A list of field names will appear.

19. Click on the **field** to sort by. The field name will display.

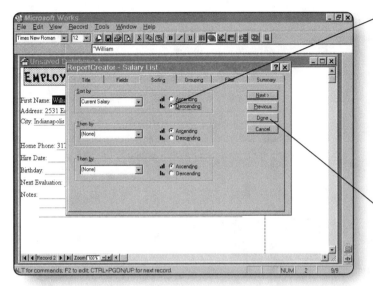

20. **Click** on **Ascending** or **Descending**. The option will be selected.

21. **Click** on **Done**. A message box will display.

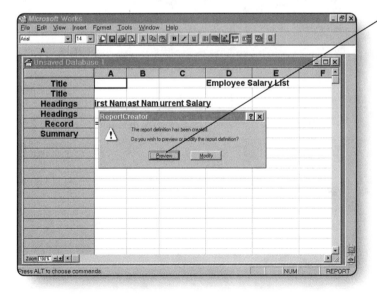

22. **Click** on **Preview**. The report will display with the data as specified.

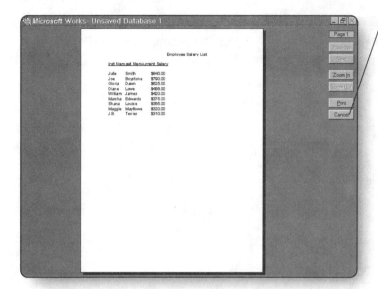

23. Click on Cancel. The database report layout will display.

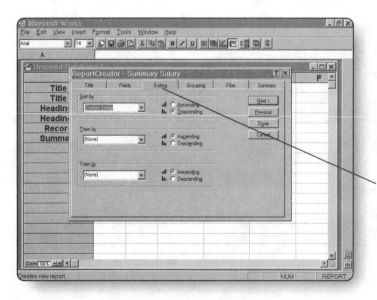

Creating Summary Reports

Let a Works report summarize your data with totals or averages.

1. Create a report following steps 1 through 20.

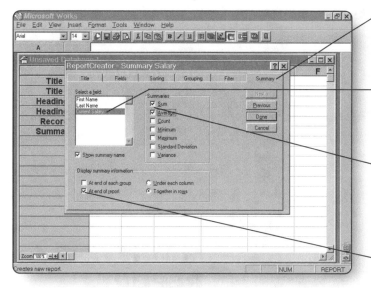

2. Click on the **Summary tab**. The Summary tab will come to the front.

3. Click on the **field name** to summarize by. The field name will be highlighted.

4. Click on the **summary types** that you would like in your report. Selected options will display a check mark.

5. Click on a **location** for the summary information. The options will be selected.

6. Click on **Done**. A message box will display.

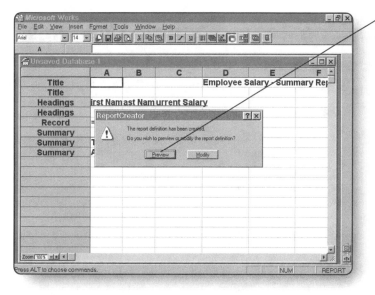

7. Click on **Preview**. The report will display with the specified data.

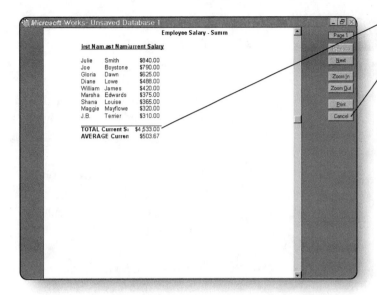

The summarized fields are displayed.

8. Click on **Cancel**. The database report layout will display.

MODIFYING A REPORT

You may want to modify the appearance of the report data. Working in the report editor is very similar to working with a Works spreadsheet except that instead of row numbers, the rows are named with the type of data to be displayed.

Editing Report Column Headings

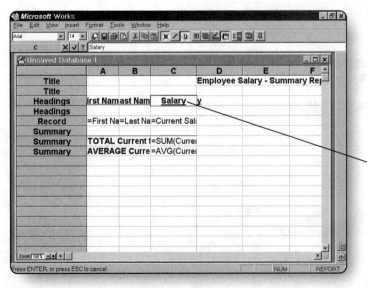

By default, each column in a report is displayed with the field name, which you can easily edit.

1. Click on the **heading** that you want to modify. The cell will be selected.

2. Type a **new heading**. The new text will display.

3. Press the **Enter key**. The new heading will replace the old heading.

Changing Column Width

Use your mouse to widen a column width. A line located at the right edge of each column heading divides the columns. You will use this line to change the column width.

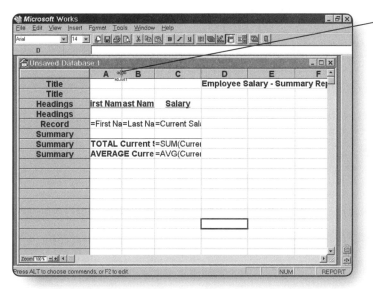

1. **Position** the **mouse pointer** on the right column line for the field that you want to change. The mouse pointer will become a double-headed white arrow with the word "ADJUST" displayed under it.

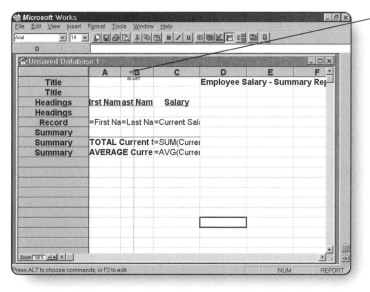

2. **Press** and **hold** the **mouse button** and **drag** the column line. If you drag it to the right, the column width will increase; if you drag it to the left, the column width will decrease.

3. **Release** the **mouse button**. The column width will be changed.

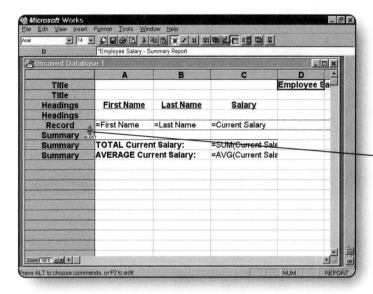

Increasing Row Height

Add additional room between each record in your report by increasing row height.

1. **Position** the **mouse pointer** on the lower row line for the row that you want to change. The mouse pointer will become a double-headed white arrow with the word "ADJUST" displayed under it.

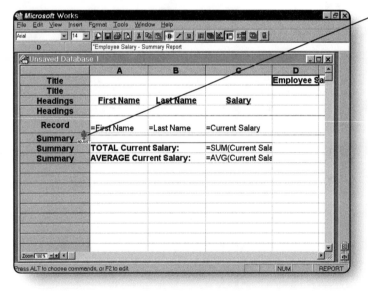

2. **Press** and **hold** the **mouse button** and **drag** the column line. If you drag it down, the row height will increase; if you drag it up, the row height will decrease.

3. **Release** the **mouse button**. The column width will be changed.

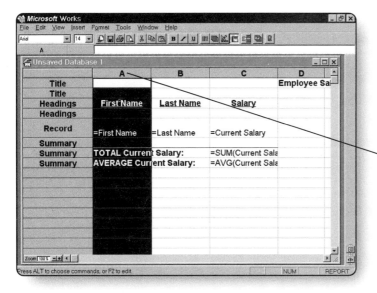

Modifying Alignment

Change the alignment of any field column, row, or individual field data.

1. **Click** on a **field column, row,** or **cell** to modify. The column, row, or cell will be highlighted.

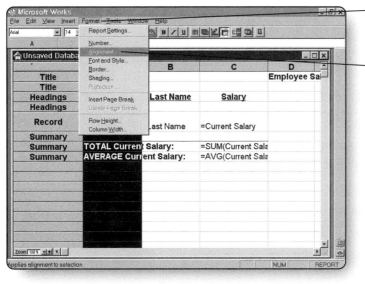

2. **Click** on **Format**. The Format menu will appear.

3. **Click** on **Alignment**. The Format dialog box will open with the Alignment tab in front.

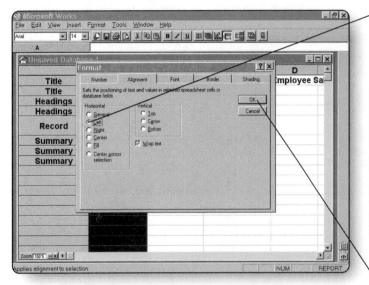

4. **Click** on an **Alignment** option. The option will be selected.

5. **Click** on **OK**. The Format dialog box will close and the selected options will be applied.

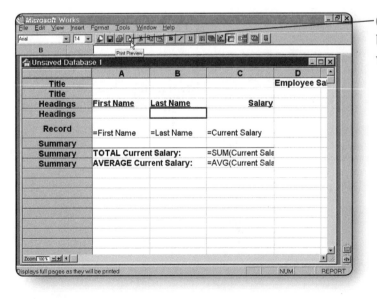

6. **Click** on the **Print Preview button**. The complete report will be displayed.

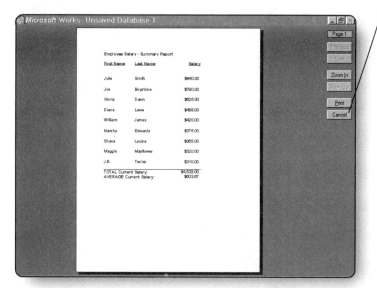

7. **Click** on **Cancel**. The database report layout will display.

DELETING A REPORT

Because you are limited to eight reports per database, you may need to delete unwanted or old reports.

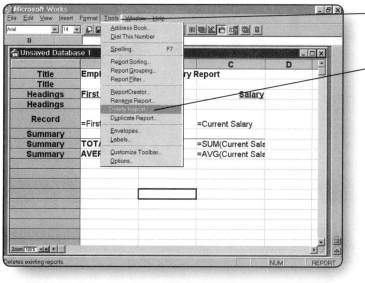

1. **Click** on **Tools**. The Tools menu will appear.

2. **Click** on **Delete Report**. The Delete Report dialog box will open.

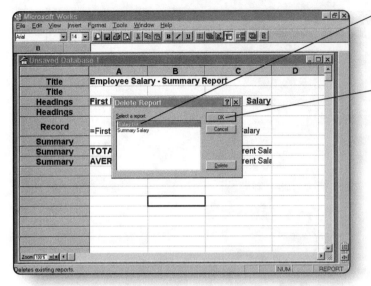

3. **Click** on the **Report name** to be deleted. The report name will be highlighted.

4. **Click** on **OK**. A confirmation message will appear.

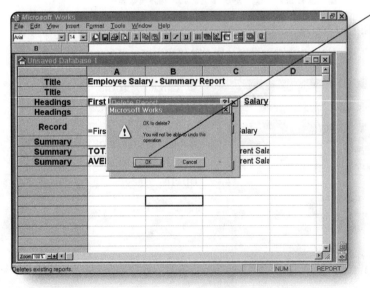

5. **Click** on **OK**. The report will be deleted.

PRINTING A REPORT

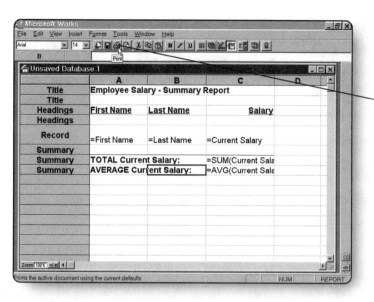

Print a hard copy of your report for your files and/or distribute to others.

1a. **Click** on the **Print button**. The report will print with standard options.

OR

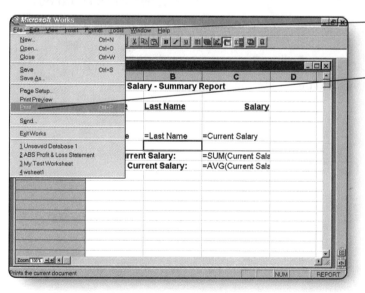

1b. **Click** on **File**. The File menu will appear.

2. **Click** on **Print**. The Print dialog box will open.

Many options are available from the Print dialog box.

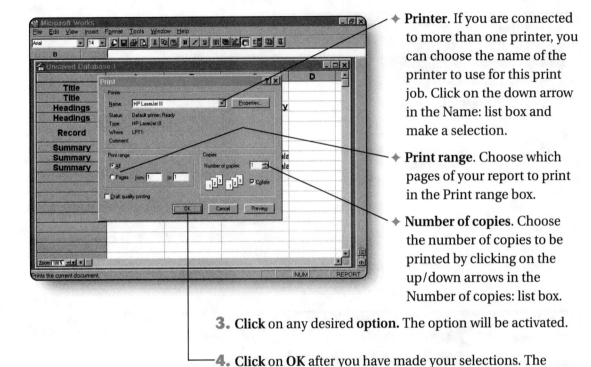

♦ **Printer.** If you are connected to more than one printer, you can choose the name of the printer to use for this print job. Click on the down arrow in the Name: list box and make a selection.

♦ **Print range.** Choose which pages of your report to print in the Print range box.

♦ **Number of copies.** Choose the number of copies to be printed by clicking on the up/down arrows in the Number of copies: list box.

3. **Click** on any desired **option.** The option will be activated.

4. **Click** on **OK** after you have made your selections. The report will be sent to the printer.

20 Completing a Database

Now that you've learned how to create and work in a database, you'll need to do a few other tasks. In this chapter, you'll learn how to:

✦ Save a database

✦ Close a database

✦ Open a database

SAVING A DATABASE

Just like the other components of Microsoft Works, when you create a file, you should save it for future use.

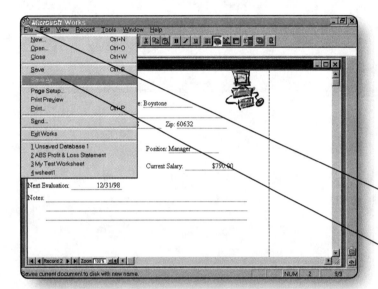

Saving a Database the First Time

When you first create a document, it has no name. If you want to use that document later, it must have a name so Works can find it.

1. **Click** on **File**. The File menu will appear.

2. **Click** on **Save As.** The Save As dialog box will open.

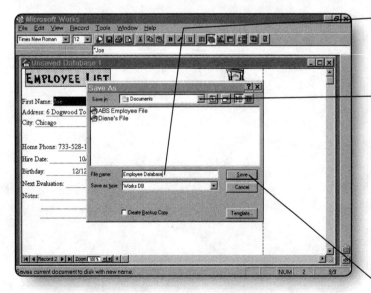

3. **Type** a **name** for your file in the File name: text box. The file name will be displayed.

The Save in: drop-down list box lists the folder where the file will be saved. The default folder that appears is Documents. If you don't want to save to this folder or if you want to save your database to another disk, you can select another one. Click on the down arrow to browse.

4. **Click** on **Save**. Your database will be saved and the name you specified will appear in the title bar.

Resaving a Database

As you continue to work on your database, you should resave your database every ten minutes or so. This will ensure that you do not lose any changes.

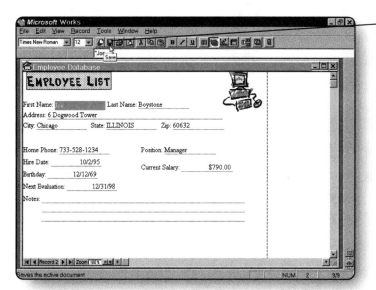

1. **Click** on the **Save button**. The database will be resaved with any changes. No dialog box will appear because the database is resaved with the same name and in the same folder as previously specified.

NOTE

If you want to save the database with a different name or in a different folder, click on File, then choose Save As. The Save As dialog box will prompt you for the new name or folder. The original document will remain, as will the new one.

CLOSING A DATABASE

When you finish working on a database, you should close it. Closing is the equivalent of putting it away for later use. When you close a database, you put the database away—not the program. Works is still active and ready to work for you.

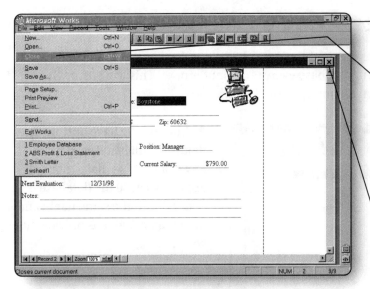

1. **Click** on **File**. The File menu will open.

2. **Click** on **Close**. The database will close; however, the Works program still will be active.

If no other documents are currently open, the Task Launcher will appear.

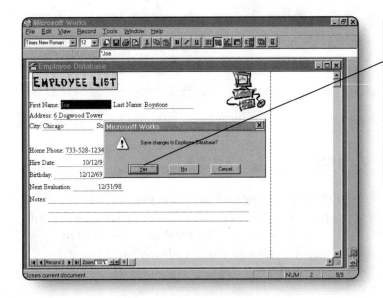

OPENING A SAVED DATABASE

To edit a database you have already closed, you must open that database again. If you want to open a database when you begin the Works program, the screen will look different from the screen that appears if you are already in a database and want to open another one.

Opening a Database from Another Document

Even if you already have a Works document open onscreen, you can open another. In fact, you can have up to eight documents open at a time. These documents could be any combination of spreadsheets, word processing documents, or database files.

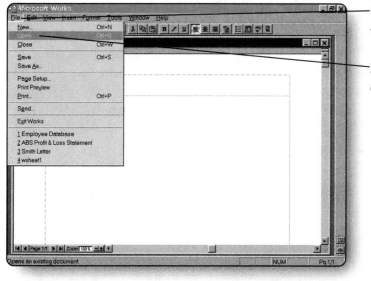

1. Click on **File**. The File menu will appear.

2. Click on **Open**. The Open dialog box will open.

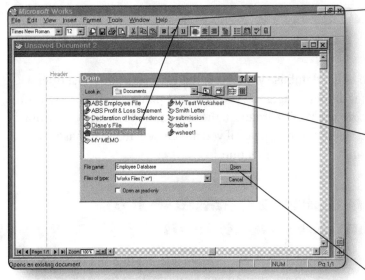

3. **Click** on the **file name** that you wish to open. The file name will be highlighted and will appear in the File name: text box.

NOTE

If your file is located in a different folder than the one displayed in the Look in: list box, click on the down arrow to navigate to the proper folder.

4. **Click** on **Open**. The file will be placed on your screen, ready for you to edit.

Opening a Database from the Task Launcher

You can open a document from the Works Task Launcher which appears when you first start the Works program.

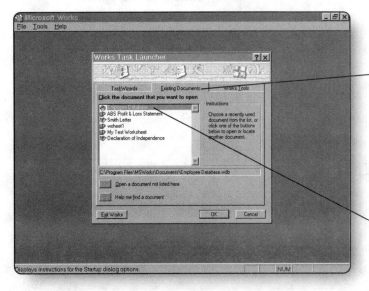

1. **Start Microsoft Works**. The Task Launcher will appear.

2. **Click** on the **Existing Documents tab**. The Existing Documents tab will come to the front.

If the database you want to open is listed:

3a. **Click** on the **file name** that you want to open. The file name will be highlighted.

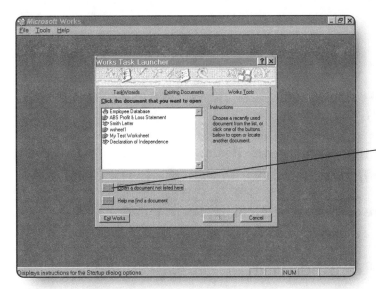

4a. **Click** on **OK**. The file will be placed onscreen, ready for you to edit.

If the database you want to open is not listed:

3b. **Click** on **Open a document not listed here**. The Open dialog box will open.

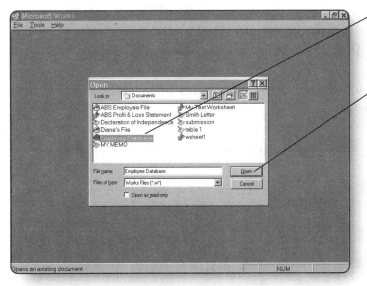

4b. **Click** on the **file name** you wish to open. The file name will be highlighted.

5b. **Click** on **Open**. The database will be placed onscreen, ready for you to edit.

PART IV REVIEW QUESTIONS

1. In a database, what is a record? *See "Understanding Fields and Records" in Chapter 16*

2. What view must be active to change the design of a form? *See "Looking at the Different Views" in Chapter 16*

3. How many records are displayed when using Form View? *See "Entering Data in Form View" in Chapter 17*

4. How many ways can records be sorted? *See "Sorting Records" in Chapter 17*

5. What is the maximum size of a field? *See "Changing Field Size by Using the Menu" in Chapter 18*

6. When adding graphics to a database, on what records will the graphic display? *See "Adding Artwork to a Database" in Chapter 18*

7. How many filters can a database have? *See "Creating Additional Filters" in Chapter 19*

8. What do reports do to database information? *See "Creating a Report" in Chapter 19*

9. What feature does Works provide to assist you in creating a report? *See "Using the ReportCreator" in Chapter 19*

10. How can a report summarize your data? *See "Creating Summary Reports" in Chapter 19*

PART V
Putting It All Together

21 Working with Graphics

Included in Works are several ways to add graphics to your document. One method is to use the Microsoft Draw program to create your own simple graphics. Another interesting tool is the WordArt program. In this chapter, you'll learn how to:

✦ Create a WordArt object

✦ Enhance a WordArt object

✦ Draw objects with Microsoft Draw

✦ Edit drawn objects

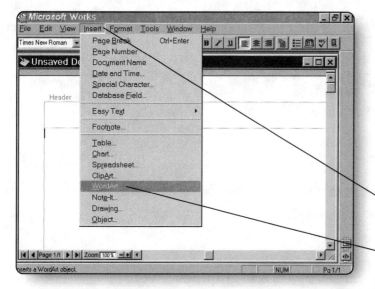

USING WORDART

Works includes a tool to reshape, rotate, and add special effects to text. Make your text come alive with the shapes that you create with WordArt!

1. **Click** on **Insert**. The Insert menu will appear.

2. **Click** on **WordArt**. A WordArt window will display.

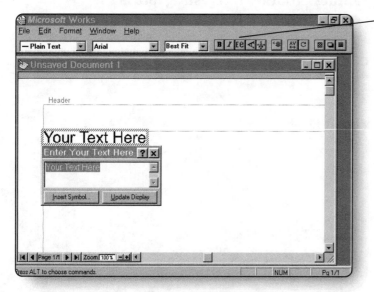

Notice that both the menu bar and toolbar have changed.

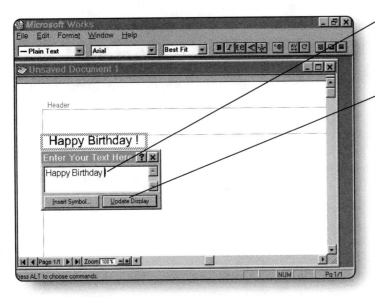

3. **Type** the **text** to be used. The text will appear in the WordArt window.

4. **Click** on **Update Display**. The text will appear in the document.

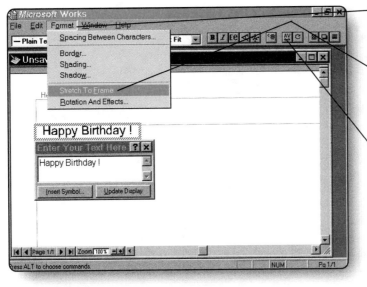

5. **Click** on **Format**. The Format menu will appear.

6. **Click** on **Stretch To Frame**. The text you typed will expand.

TIP

Optionally, click on the Stretch To Frame button.

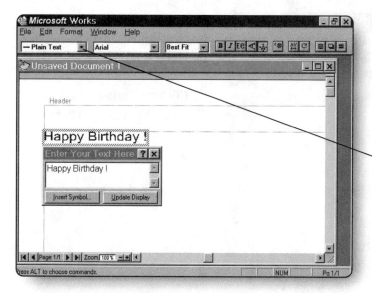

Shaping WordArt Text

Change the shape of the typed text to circular, triangular, or any other shape.

1. **Click** on the **Style drop-down arrow**. A collection of shapes will appear.

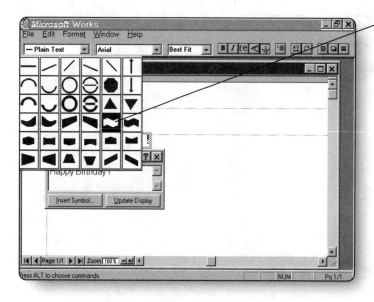

2. **Click** on the **shape** you want your text to take. The text will be reshaped.

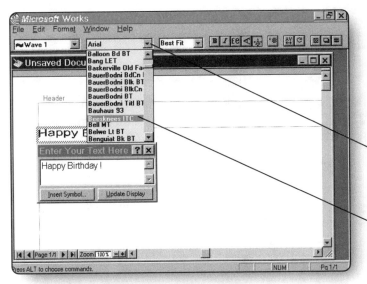

Changing the Font of WordArt

WordArt text can be displayed in any font that you have available on your computer.

1. **Click** on the **Font drop-down arrow**. A list of available fonts will display.

2. **Click** on the desired **font**. The text will be modified to the selected font.

> **NOTE**
> Your list of fonts may vary from the ones shown.

Adding a Fill to WordArt Text

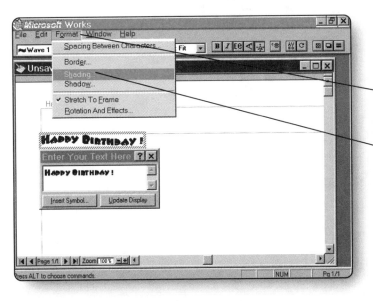

Adding a shading (fill) pattern to your WordArt can give the WordArt texture.

1. **Click** on **Format**. The Format menu will appear.

2. **Click** on **Shading**. The Shading dialog box will open.

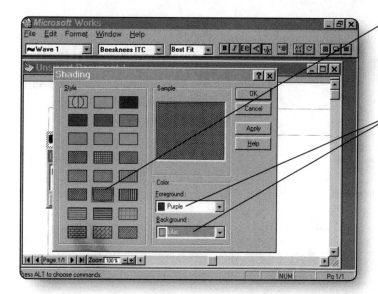

3. **Click** on a shading **Style**. The option will be selected.

TIP

Optionally, choose a background or foreground color for the text pattern.

4. **Click** on **OK**. The Shading dialog box will close.

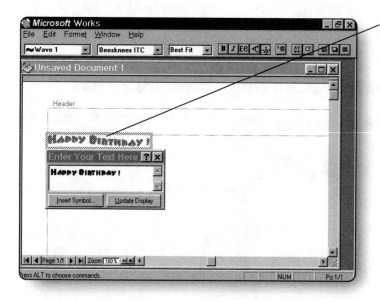

The selected shading effect will be applied to the WordArt object.

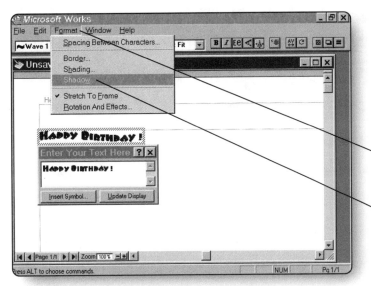

Adding a Text Shadow

Give depth and a 3-D effect to your WordArt by adding a shadow.

1. Click on **Format**. The Format menu will appear.

2. Click on **Shadow**. The Shadow dialog box will open.

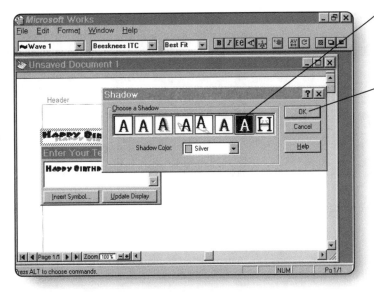

3. Click on a **shadow effect**. The selected effect will be highlighted.

4. Click on **OK**. The Shadow dialog box will close and the shadow will be applied to your WordArt.

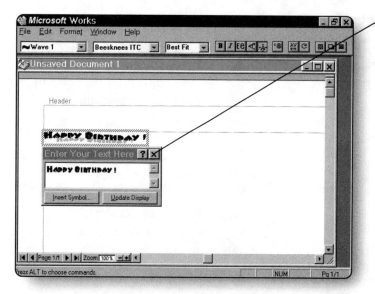

5. **Click** on the WordArt **Close button**. The WordArt box will close.

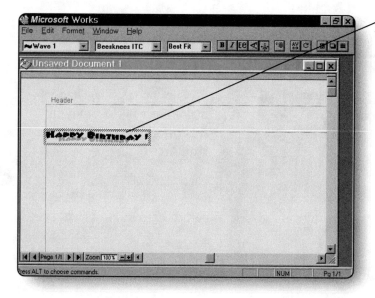

The WordArt object will appear in your document. The object will still be selected, ready for you to modify.

Resizing a WordArt Object

A WordArt object has eight handles for resizing the object. The handles on the top or bottom will resize the height of the object, whereas the handles on the left or right side will change the width of the object. The four corner handles will resize both the width and height at the same time.

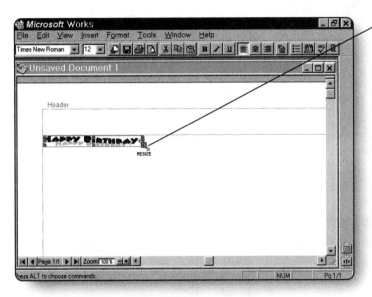

1. Position the **mouse** over one of the handles. The mouse will change to a double-headed arrow displaying the word "RESIZE." Depending on the object size, font, and other attributes, these handles may be difficult to see.

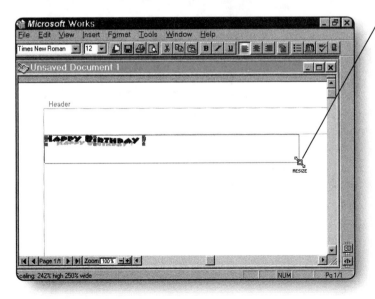

2. Click and **drag** the **handle** until the object is the desired size. A dotted line will indicate the new object size.

3. Release the **mouse button**. The object will be resized.

4. **Click anywhere** outside of the WordArt object. The object will be deselected.

TIP

Double-click on the object to edit the text, shape, shadow, color, or fill of the object.

Deleting a WordArt Object

It is easy to delete a WordArt object.

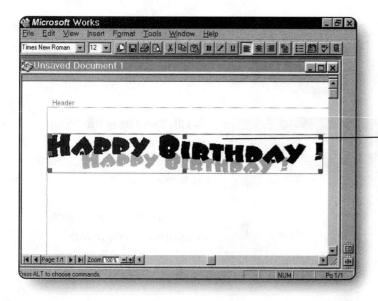

1. **Click** on a WordArt **object**. The object will be selected.

2. **Press** the **Delete key**. The object will be deleted.

USING MICROSOFT DRAW

Even if you think that you can't draw a straight line, you can with Microsoft Draw. Use Microsoft Draw to create maps and other drawings to be included in a Works document.

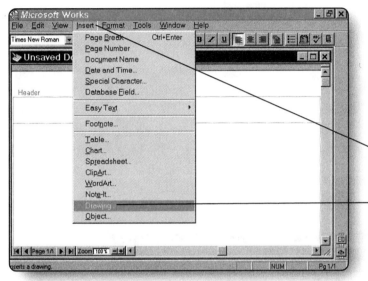

Starting Microsoft Draw

Microsoft Draw creates an embedded drawing right into your Microsoft Works document.

1. Click on **Insert**. The Insert menu will appear.

2. Click on **Drawing**. The Microsoft Drawing window will display.

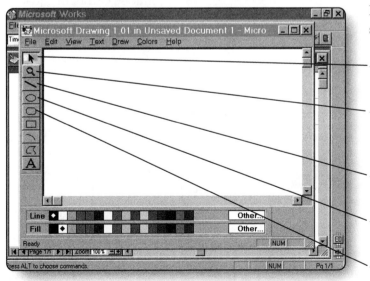

Drawing Tools appear on the left side of the screen:

✦ **Pointer**. Use this tool to select a drawn object to modify.

✦ **Zoom**. Use this tool to change the magnification of the drawing.

✦ **Line**. Use this tool to draw straight lines.

✦ **Oval**. Use this tool to draw ovals or circles.

✦ **Rounded Rectangle**. Use this tool to draw rectangles and squares with rounded corners.

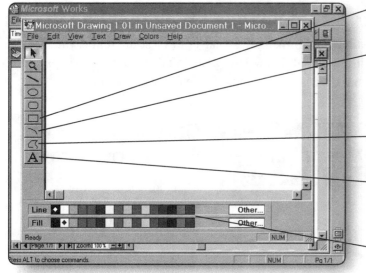

✦ **Rectangle**. Use this tool to draw rectangles and squares.

✦ **Arc**. Use this tool to draw arcs that are 90° segments (quadrants) of ellipses. A filled arc has a wedge shape.

✦ **Freeform**. Use the Freeform tool to draw freehand objects.

✦ **Text**. Use this tool to add a single line text object to your drawings.

The color pallettes are used to select the inside fill color or the outside line color of a drawn object.

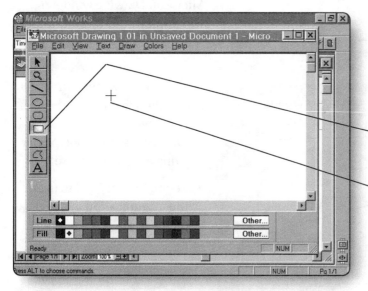

Drawing Rectangles

Draw rounded corner or square corner rectangles.

1. **Click** on the **Rectangle tool**. The tool will be selected.

2. **Position** the **pointer** at one corner of the rectangle that you want to draw. The mouse pointer will change to a black cross.

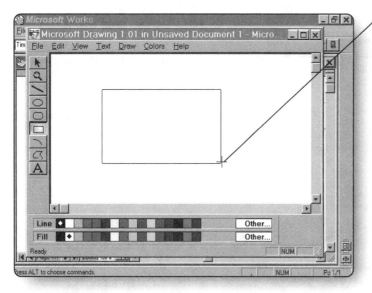

3. **Click** and **drag** the mouse. An outline of a rectangle will appear.

4. **Release** the **mouse button**. The rectangle will display.

TIP

To draw a rectangle from its center rather than from a corner, press the CTRL key and hold it down as you drag.

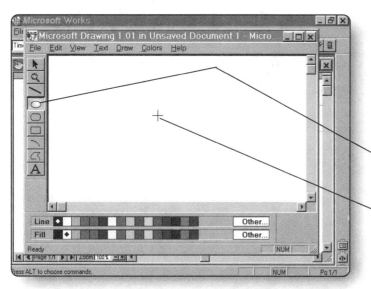

Drawing Perfect Circles

Using the Oval tool and your keyboard, you can draw perfectly shaped circles!

1. **Click** on the **Oval tool**. The tool will be selected.

2. **Position** the **mouse pointer** where you want to begin drawing the circle. The mouse pointer will change to a black cross.

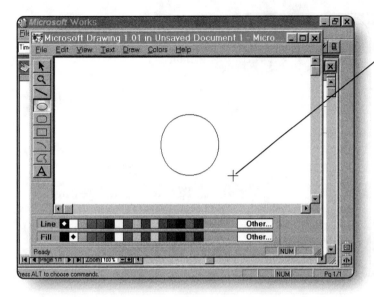

3. **Press** and **hold** the **Shift key**.

4. **Click** and **drag** the mouse. An outline of a circle will appear.

5. **Release** the **mouse button.**

6. **Release** the **Shift key**. The circle will display.

TIP

Hold the Shift key while drawing with the Rectangle tool to draw a perfect square.

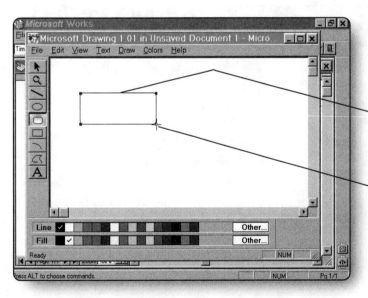

Resizing Objects

Four handles surround a drawn object and allow you to resize it.

1. **Click** on the **object** to be resized. The object will be selected.

2. **Position** the tip of the **mouse pointer** over one of the handles. The mouse pointer will change to a black cross.

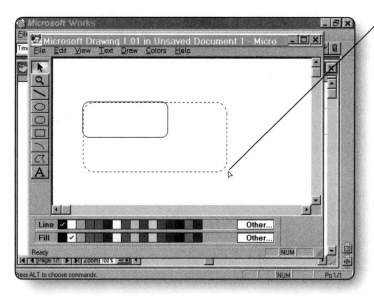

3. **Press** the **mouse button** and **drag** the **handle**. A dotted line will indicate the new object size.

4. **Release** the **mouse button**. The object will be resized.

Moving Objects

You can move a drawn object to a different position on the page.

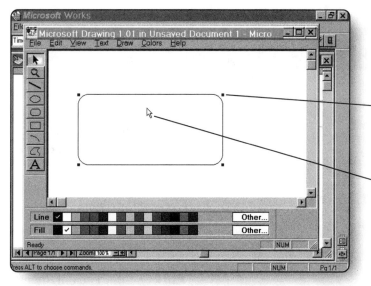

1. **Click** on the **object** to be moved. The object will be selected.

2. **Position** the **mouse pointer** over the object to be moved. Do *not* position it over one of the sizing handles.

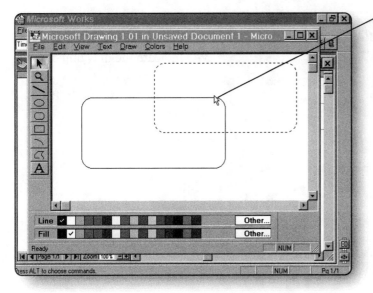

3. **Press** the **mouse button** and **drag** the **object** to the new location. A dotted line will indicate the new object position.

4. **Release** the **mouse button**. The object will be moved.

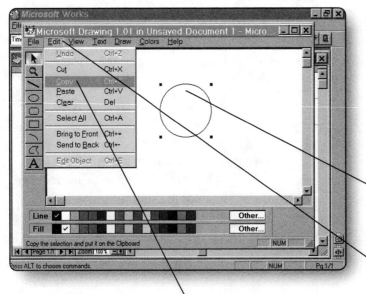

Duplicating Shapes

If you've drawn an object and would like to duplicate it without starting from scratch, use the Windows Copy and Paste commands.

1. **Click** on the **object** to be duplicated. The object will be selected.

2. **Click** on **Edit**. The Edit menu will appear.

3. **Click** on **Copy**. The object will be copied to the Windows Clipboard.

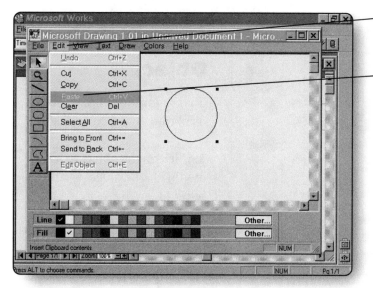

4. **Click** on **Edit**. The Edit menu will appear.

5. **Click** on **Paste**. The second object will be placed on top of the first.

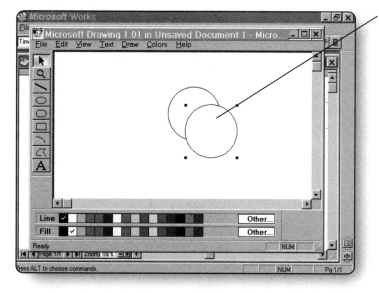

You can now move the second object to the desired position.

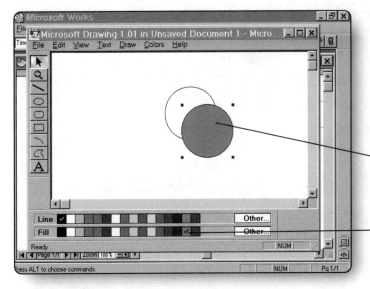

Changing the Fill Color of an Object

Change any object to any color displayed on the color palette.

1. **Click** on the **object** to be modified. The object will be selected.

2. **Click** on the **desired color** from the fill color palette. The fill color of the object will be changed.

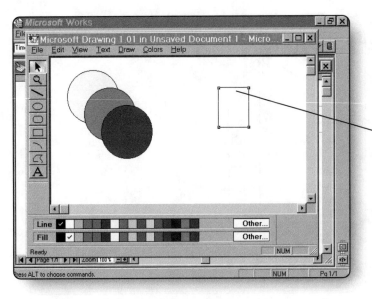

Deleting Objects

If an object is no longer needed in a drawing, you can delete it with just the push of a key.

1. **Click** on the **object** to be deleted. The object will be selected.

2. **Press** the **Delete key**. The object will be deleted.

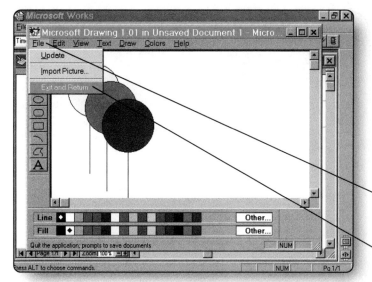

Adding the Drawing to a Document

When your drawing is complete, you can return to your Microsoft Works document with the drawing included.

1. Click on **File**. The File menu will appear.

2. Click on **Exit and Return**. A message dialog box will display.

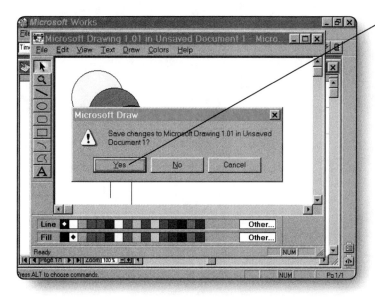

3. Click on **Yes**. The Microsoft Draw program will close and your Works document will be displayed.

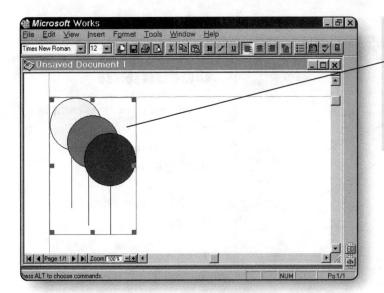

TIP

Double-click on the drawing object to return to the Microsoft Draw program for further editing of the selected object.

22 Creating Form Letters Using Mail Merge

Form letters are multiple printed copies of the same document, with different information such as names and addresses printed on each copy automatically.

We've all received such letters—like the ones telling us, "You may already be a winner." If this seems like an intimidating task, you can relax. In Part II, "Using the Word Processor," you learned how to create a document using the word processing feature of Works, and in Part IV, "Using a Database," you learned how to create and work with a database. By combining a document and a database, you can create form letters for mass mailings. In this chapter, you'll learn how to:

✦ Use the Form Letter Wizard

✦ Print form letters

PREPARING TO MERGE

When preparing a document for merging, leave the space blank where the variable information, such as name and address, will appear.

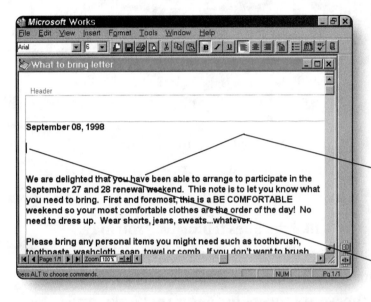

USING THE FORM LETTER WIZARD

The Form Letter Wizard will assist you in preparing a form letter.

1. Open or **create** the **letter** with the common information. The document will be active in the Works window.

2. Click the **mouse** where the first field is to appear. The blinking insertion point will appear.

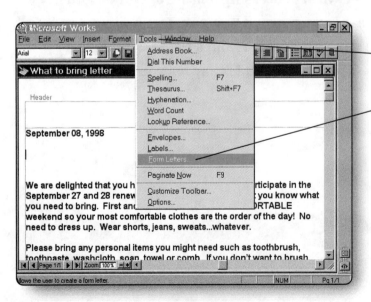

3. Click on **Tools**. The Tools menu will appear.

4. Click on **Form Letters**. The Form Letter Wizard will open.

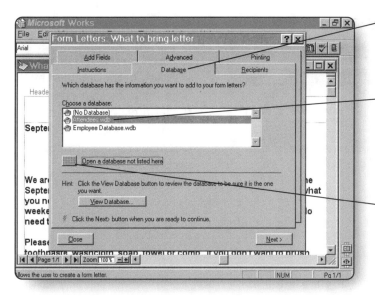

5. Click on the **Database tab**. The Database tab will come to the front.

6. Click on the **Database** to merge. The database will be selected.

TIP

If the database you want to use does not appear in the Choose a database list, click on Open a database not listed here to locate and select your database. Click on OK when the database is selected.

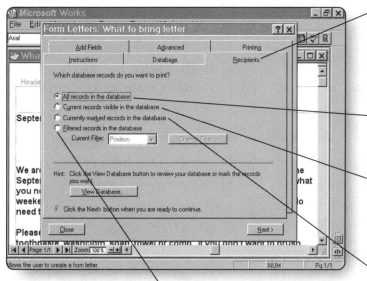

7. Click on the **Recipients tab**. The Recipients tab will come to the front.

8. **Choose one** of the following:

✦ **All records in the database**. This option will create a letter for each record in the database.

✦ **Current records visible in the database**. This option will create a letter for each record as specified by a search.

✦ **Currently marked records in the database**. This option will create a letter for each record marked in the database.

✦ **Filtered records in the database**. This option will create a letter for each record as specified by a filter. You'll need to specify which filter to use.

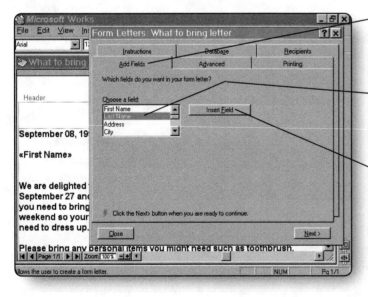

9. Click on the **Add Fields tab**. The Add Fields tab will come to the front.

10. Click on the **first field** to be added in the form letter. The field will be highlighted.

11. Click on **Insert Field**. A field name placeholder will be added to the Works document.

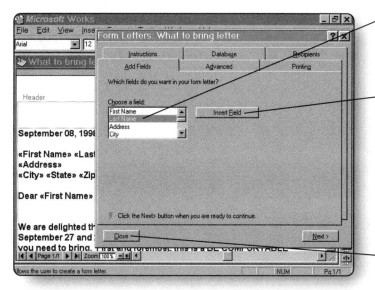

12. **Click** on the **next field** to be added to the form letter. The field name will be highlighted.

13. **Click** on **Insert Field**. The field name will be inserted into the Works document.

14. **Repeat steps 12** and **13** until all fields have been added.

NOTE

If you need to reposition the insertion point, click on Close; reposition the insertion point and then return to Tools, Form Letters.

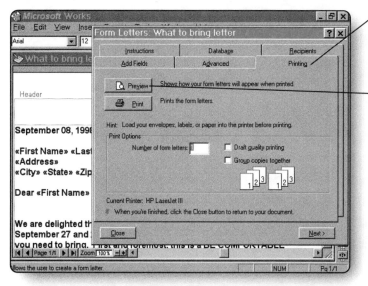

15. **Click** on the **Printing tab**. The Printing tab will come to the front.

16. **Click** on **Preview**. An information box will open.

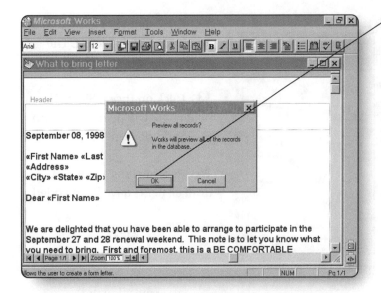

17. **Click** on **OK**. The first merged record will appear in Print Preview.

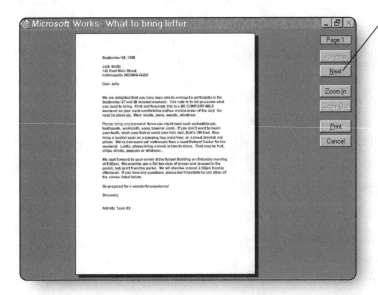

18. **Click** on **Next**. The next merged record will appear in Print Preview.

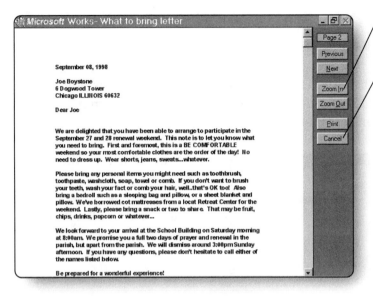

19. **Click** on **Zoom In**. You'll be able to read the text of the letter.

20. **Click** on **Cancel**. The Form Letter Wizard will reappear.

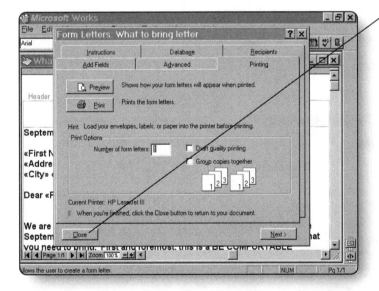

21. **Click** on **Close**. The Form Letter Wizard will close.

PRINTING MERGED RECORDS

When you are ready to print your merged records, Works will automatically insert the requested information from the database into the document.

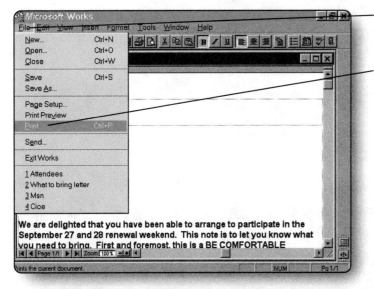

1. **Click** on **File**. The File menu will appear.

2. **Click** on **Print**. The Print dialog box will open.

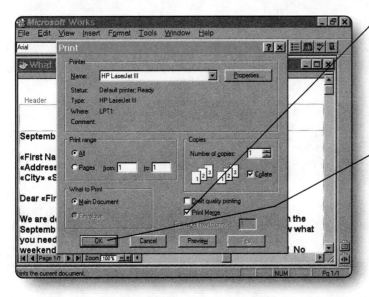

3. **Click** on the **Print Merge box**. A check mark will appear in the Print Merge box.

4. **Change** any other desired printing **options**.

5. **Click** on **OK**. The form letters will print.

23 Inserting a Chart into a Report

Inserting a graphic into a report can visually intensify the document. Because almost everyone likes charts (and charts are a type of graphic), you can create a chart using your spreadsheet or your word processor and include the same chart in your report. In this chapter, you'll learn how to:

✦ Include a chart created from a Works worksheet

✦ Create a new chart from a word processing document

✦ Edit an embedded chart

✦ Update an embedded chart

INSERTING A CHART FROM A SPREADSHEET

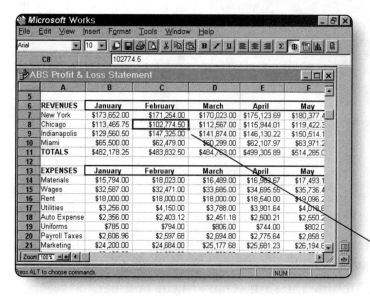

In Chapter 15, "Creating Charts," you learned how to create a chart from a Works spreadsheet. You can now insert that chart into a word processing document. The chart will be *linked* to the spreadsheet, which means that if the data in the spreadsheet changes, the chart in the word processing document also changes.

1. **Open** the **spreadsheet** which contains the chart. The spreadsheet will appear in the Works window.

NOTE

The Spreadsheet must be saved before you can insert the chart.

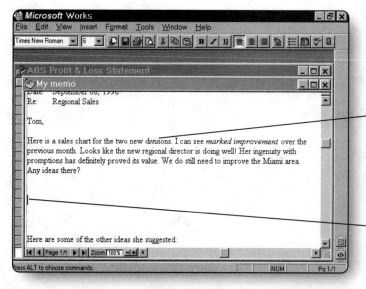

2. **Open** the word processing **document** that is to contain the chart. The word processing document will appear in the Works window.

3. **Click** the **mouse** where you want to insert the chart. The blinking insertion point will appear.

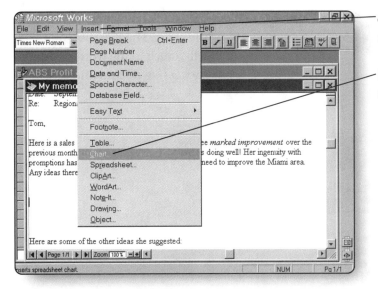

4. **Click** on **Insert**. The Insert menu will appear.

5. **Click** on **Chart**. The Insert Chart dialog box will open.

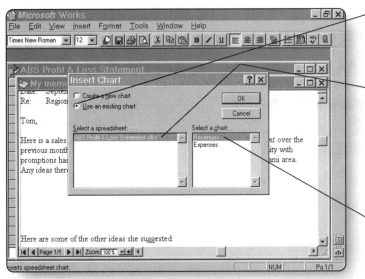

6. **Click** on **Use an existing chart**. The option will be selected.

7. **Click** on the **spreadsheet** that contains the chart that you want to include. The file name will be highlighted and a list of charts in the selected spreadsheet will appear.

8. **Click** on the **chart name** that you want to include. The chart name will be highlighted.

9. **Click** on **OK**. The chart will be included in the word processing document.

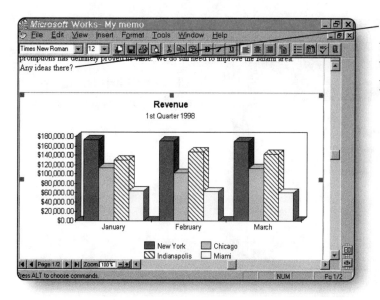

10. Click **anywhere** outside of the chart. The insertion point will return to the word processing document.

CREATING AND EMBEDDING A NEW CHART

If you want to create a chart but don't have a created worksheet, you can produce a new one.

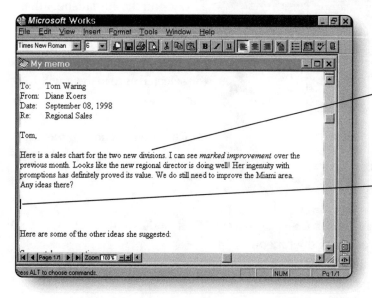

1. Open or create a word processing document. The document will appear in the Works window.

2. Click the mouse where you want to insert the chart. The blinking insertion point will appear.

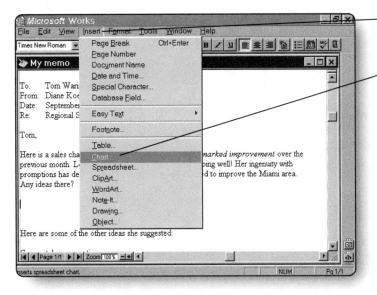

3. **Click** on **Insert**. The Insert menu will appear.

4. **Click** on **Chart**. The Insert Chart dialog box will open.

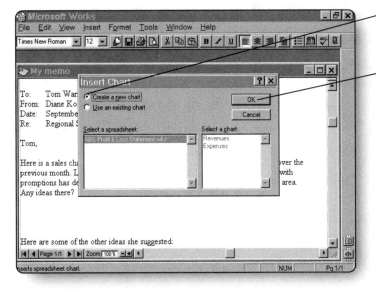

5. **Click** on **Create a new chart**. The option will be selected.

6. **Click** on **OK**. A message box will open.

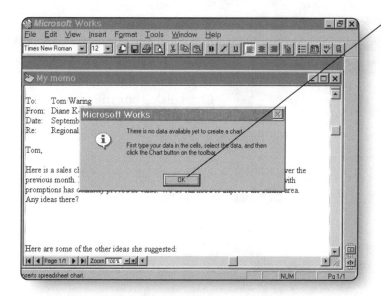

7. **Click** on **OK**. The message box will close and a small spreadsheet will appear.

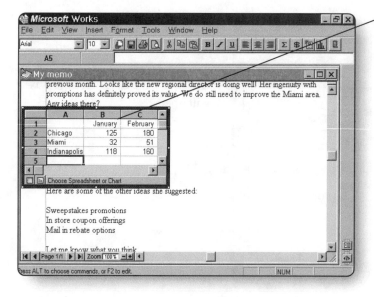

8. In the spreadsheet, **type** the **data** for the chart. The data will appear in the spreadsheet.

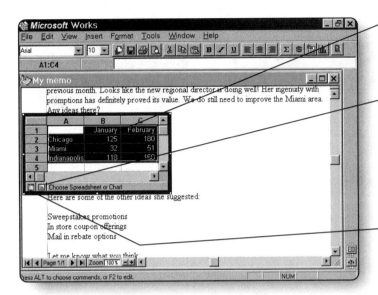

9. **Select** the spreadsheet **cells** that you want to chart. The cells will be highlighted.

10. **Click** on the **chart icon** at the bottom of the spreadsheet box. The New Chart dialog box will open.

TIP

Click on the Spreadsheet icon if you want to insert just the data and not a chart.

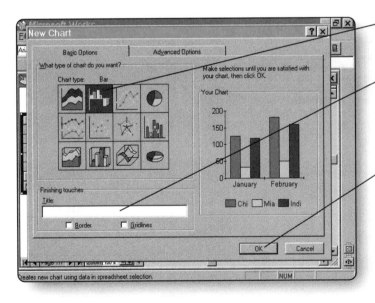

11. **Click** on a **chart style**. A sample will display.

12. Optionally, **add** a **title**, **border,** or **gridlines**. A sample will display in the Your Chart area.

13. **Click** on **OK**. The chart will be created.

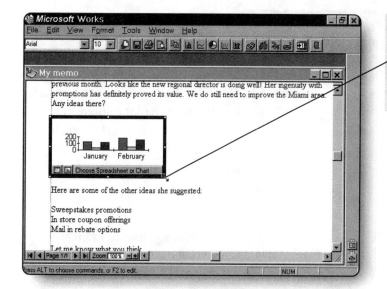

Resize the chart by
dragging any one of the
eight selection handles.

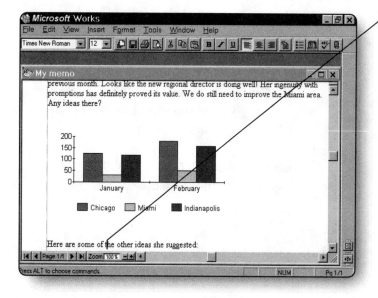

14. **Double-click anywhere**
outside of the chart. The
insertion point will return to the
word processing document.

EDITING AN EMBEDDED CHART

When a chart is embedded into a document, you can easily edit the chart data.

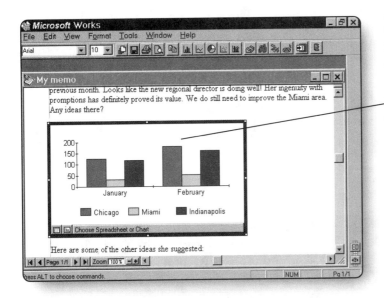

Editing a Chart Created in a Document

1. **Double-click** on the **chart**. The chart will be selected.

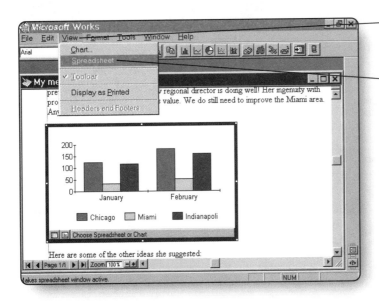

2. **Click** on **View**. The View menu will appear.

3. **Click** on **Spreadsheet**. The spreadsheet cells will be displayed.

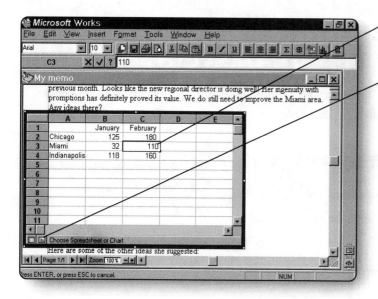

4. **Change** the desired **cells**. The data will be modified.

5. **Click** on the **chart icon** at the bottom of the spreadsheet box. The spreadsheet turns back into a chart.

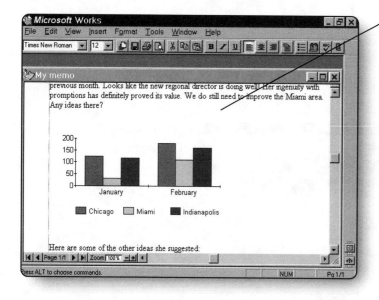

6. **Double-click anywhere** outside of the chart. The insertion point will return to the word processing document.

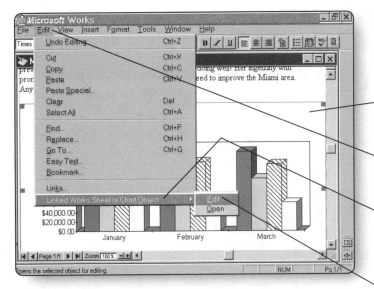

Editing a Chart Created from a Spreadsheet

1. **Click** on the **chart** to be edited. The chart will be selected.

2. **Click** on **Edit**. The Edit menu will appear.

3. **Click** on **Linked Works Sheet or Chart Object**. A submenu will appear.

4. **Click** on **Edit**. The original spreadsheet will be opened and the chart will appear on top.

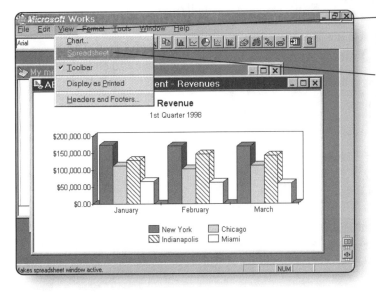

5. **Click** on **View**. The View menu will appear.

6. **Click** on **Spreadsheet**. The spreadsheet cells will be displayed.

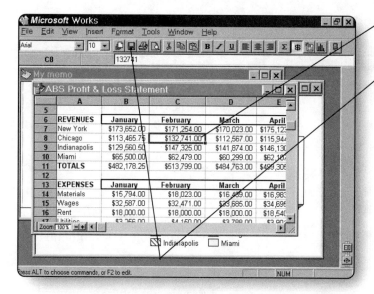

7. Change the desired **cells**. The data will be modified.

8. Click on the **Save button**. The File will be saved.

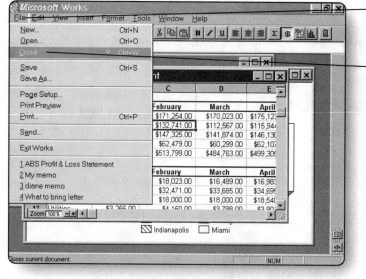

9. Click on **File**. The File menu will open.

10. Click on **Close**. The spreadsheet and chart will close.

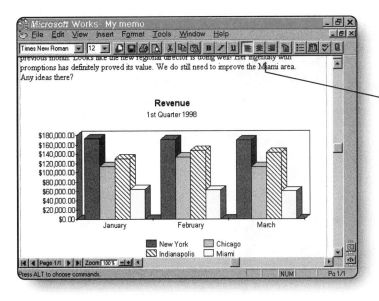

The word processing document will reappear with the chart reflecting the changes.

11. Click anywhere outside of the chart. The insertion point will return to the word processing document.

UPDATING AN EMBEDDED CHART

If you make changes to a spreadsheet that is linked to a word processing document, Works will advise you to update the links when the word processing document is reopened.

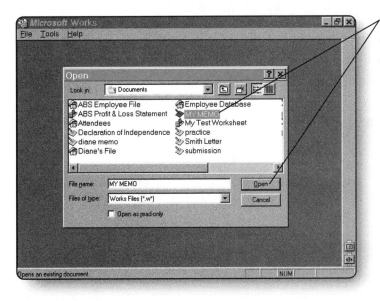

1. Open the word processing **document**. A message box will appear.

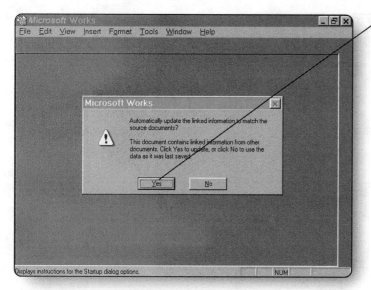

2. **Click** on **Yes**. The message box will close.

The spreadsheet and chart will be examined for changes and the word processing document will be opened and updated.

DELETING AN EMBEDDED CHART

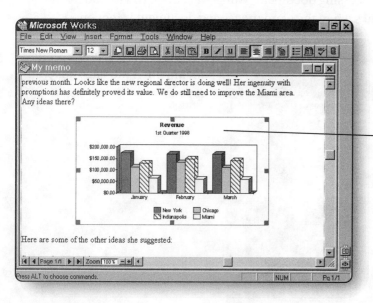

Deleting an unwanted chart is only a keyboard stroke away. Removing a chart created from a spreadsheet does not delete the original chart.

1. **Click** on the **chart** to be deleted. The chart will be selected.

2. **Press** the **Delete key**. The chart will be removed.

24 Using the Works Calendar

Do you need to track when and where your child has practice? Do you lose track of time or forget appointments? An appointment is anything that requires your time during a specific period. Items like meetings, calls to clients, or interviews are considered appointments. Works has a brand new calendar program. In this chapter, you'll learn how to:

✦ **View the Calendar**

✦ **Add and delete appointments**

✦ **Assign reminders to appointments**

✦ **Work with appointment categories**

✦ **Find appointments**

✦ **Print a calendar**

STARTING THE WORKS CALENDAR

The Works Calendar is included with the Microsoft Works program but it runs separately. There are two ways to launch the Works Calendar program.

Starting from the Desktop

When Works Calendar was installed, an option appeared to place a shortcut to the calendar on the Windows desktop. See Appendix A for information on Installing Microsoft Works.

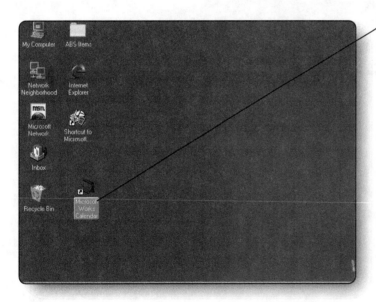

1. Double-click on the **Works Calendar icon.** The calendar will open in Month view.

> **NOTE**
>
> The first time the Calendar is opened, a message will display, asing if you would like to make Works your default calendar. Click on Yes. The message box will disappear.

Beginning from the Start Menu

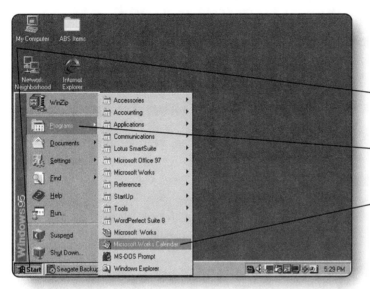

The Works Calendar will appear in two locations on the Start menu.

1. **Click** on **Start**. The Start menu will appear.

2. **Click** on **Programs**. The Programs menu will appear.

3a. **Click** on **Microsoft Works Calendar**. The calendar will open in Month view.

OR

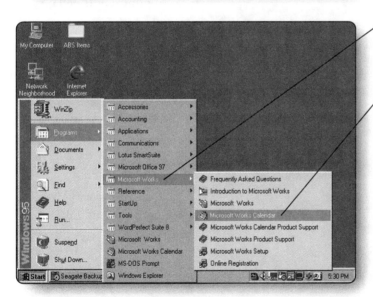

3b. **Click** on **Microsoft Works**. The Microsoft Works menu will appear.

4. **Click** on **Microsoft Works Calendar**. The calendar will open in Month view.

VIEWING THE CALENDAR

Although the calendar opens in Month view—allowing you to see the appointments for an entire month—you can also view it in Day or Week view.

Viewing by Week

To see your appointments for seven consecutive days, switch to Week view.

1. Click on View. The View menu will open.

2. Click on Week. A list of your weekly appointments will be displayed.

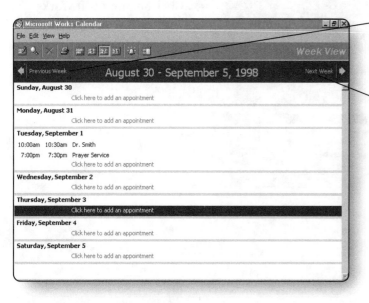

3. Click on Previous Week. The prior week's appointments will be displayed.

4. Click on Next Week. The next week's appointments will be displayed.

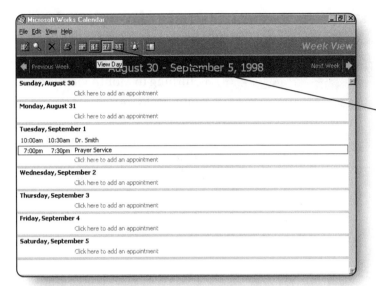

Viewing by Day

View your appointments hour by hour with the daily view.

1. **Click** on the **View Day button**. Appointments will be displayed for the day.

2. **Click** on **Previous Day**. The previous day's appointments will be displayed.

3. **Click** on **Next Day**. The next day's appointments will be displayed.

4. **Click** on **Go To Today**. Today's date will be highlighted on the calendar.

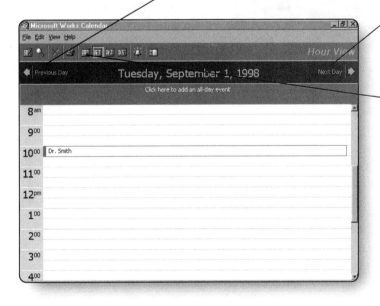

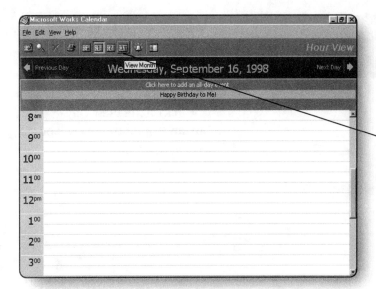

Viewing by Month

Returning to Month View is only a mouse click away.

1. **Click** on the **View Month button**. Appointments will be displayed for a month.

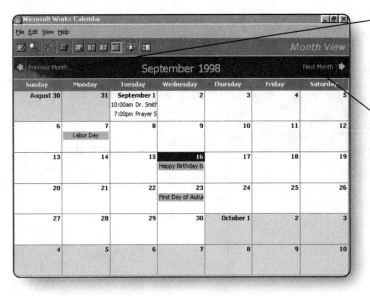

2. **Click** on **Previous Month**. The appointments for the previous month will be displayed.

3. **Click** on **Next Month**. The appointments for the next month will be displayed.

CREATING A NEW APPOINTMENT

Appointments can be created with a specified starting and/or ending time, as an all day event, or as a recurring event such as a birthday or weekly meeting.

Adding an All Day Event

Do you want to take an extra day off to enjoy the sunshine? You can add that as an all day event in your calendar. Appointments can be added from any view: daily, weekly, or monthly.

1. **Click** on the **New Appointment button**. The New Appointment dialog box will open.

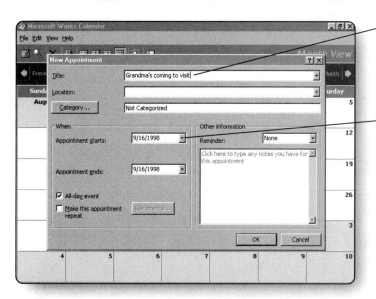

2. **Type** a **description** of the appointment in the Title: text box. The description will display in the Title: text box.

3. **Click** on the **Appointment starts: down arrow**. A monthly calendar will appear.

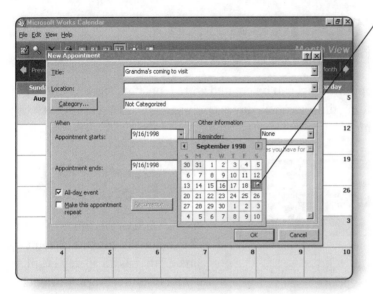

4. **Click** on the **starting date** for the appointment. The date will display in the Appointment starts: text box.

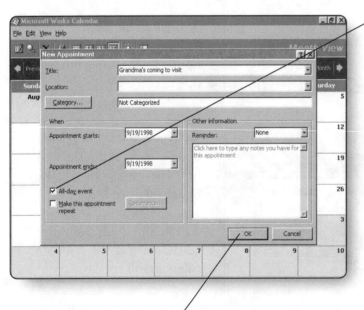

5. If necessary, **click** in the **All-day event check box**. A check mark will appear in the box.

TIP

To create an appointment that spans multiple days (such as a vacation), click on the Appointment ends: down arrow and choose an ending date.

6. **Click** on **OK**. The appointment will be added.

Adding a Timed Appointment

When creating an appointment, you can specify a beginning and/or ending time for the appointment.

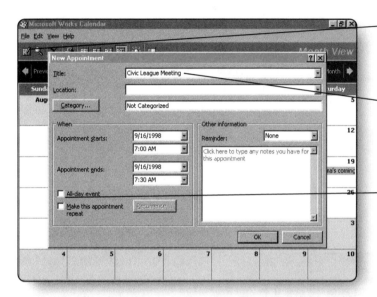

1. **Click** on the **New Appointment button**. The New Appointment dialog box will open.

2. **Type** a **description** of the appointment in the Title: text box. The description will display in the Title: text box.

3. If necessary, **click** to remove the check mark in the **All-day event box**. No check mark will appear in the box.

NOTE

If the All-day event box is checked, no starting and ending times will be displayed.

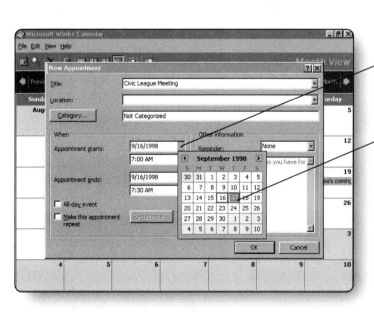

4. **Click** on the **Appointment starts: down arrow**. A monthly calendar will appear.

5. **Click** on the **date** for the appointment. The date will display in the Appointment starts: text box.

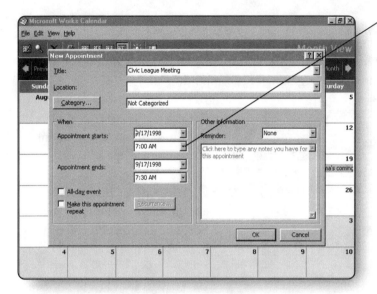

6. Click on the **starting time down arrow** in the box below the Appointment starts: text box. A list of times will display.

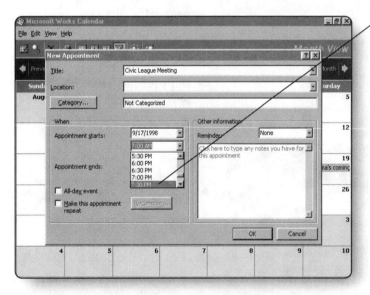

7. Click on the **starting time** for the appointment. The time will display in the starting time text box.

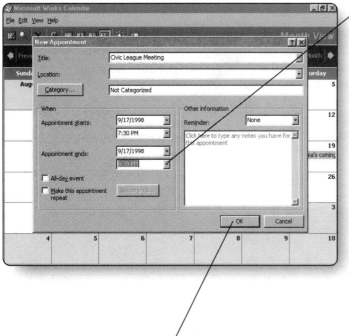

8. **Click** on the **ending time down arrow**. A list of times will display.

9. **Click** on the **ending time** for the appointment. The time will display in the ending time text box.

TIP

To create a timed appointment that spans multiple days, click on the Appointment ends: down arrow and choose an ending date.

10. **Click** on **OK**. The appointment will be added.

Adding a Recurring Appointment

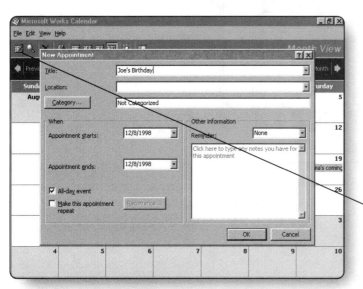

A recurring appointment is one that you schedule at the same time every day, week, month, and so on. This saves you the effort of having to enter the appointment repeatedly. An example of a recurring appointment might be a birthday or weekly sales meeting.

1. **Click** on the **New Appointment button**. The New Appointment dialog box will open.

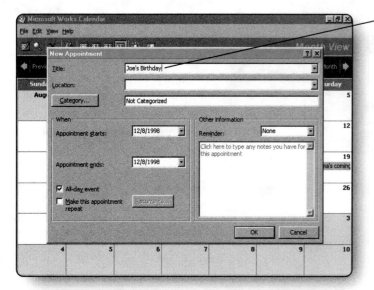

2. Type a **description** of the appointment in the Title: text box. The description will display in the Title: text box.

TIP

Decide on the starting and ending dates and times and mark the event as an all day event, if necessary, before proceeding to step 3.

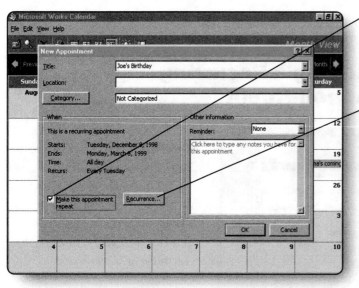

3. Click on **Make this appointment repeat.** A check mark will appear in the check box.

4. Click on **Recurrence.** The Recurrence Options dialog box will open.

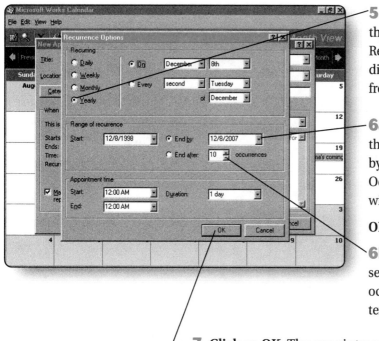

5. **Click** on a **frequency** using the drop-down arrows under the Recurring options. The options displayed will vary with the frequency selected.

6a. **Type** an **ending date** using the drop-down arrow in the End by: text box under the Range of Occurrence options. The date will be displayed.

OR

6b. **Click** on the **down arrow** to select the maximum number of occurrences in the End after: text box.

7. **Click** on **OK**. The appointment will be repeated at the specified intervals.

REMINDING YOURSELF

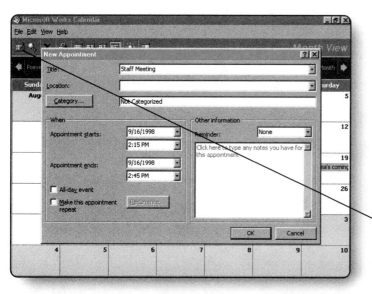

If you want Works to remind you of an appointment, you can set an alarm. At the assigned time before the appointment, an alarm will sound and a dialog box will appear.

Setting Reminders

1. **Click** on the **New Appointment button**. The New Appointment dialog box will open.

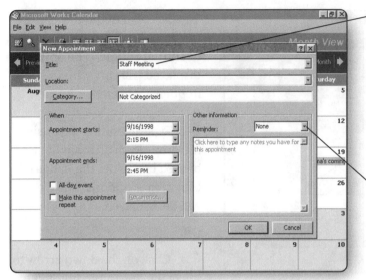

2. **Enter** the necessary appointment **information** in the Title: text box. The information will display in the Title: text box.

Next you'll need to select how early you want to be reminded of your appointment.

3. **Click** on the **Reminder down arrow** under the Other information option area. A list of time intervals will display.

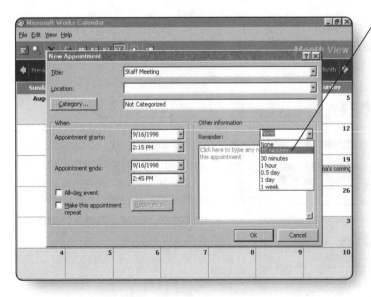

4. **Click** on a **time interval**. The time will display.

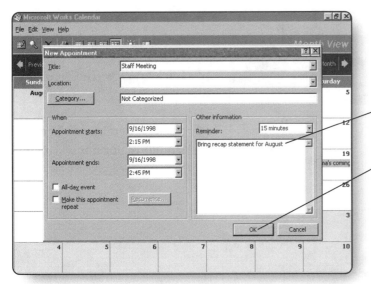

5. **Click** in the **notes text box** under the Reminder: text area. The blinking insertion point will display.

6. **Type** any reminder note **text**. The text will display.

7. **Click** on **OK**. The New Appointment dialog box will close.

Viewing Reminders

Any applicable reminders will be displayed whether you are in the Calendar program or any other Windows program. Reminders will also display when the calendar program is started, or you can display them at any time during the usage of the application.

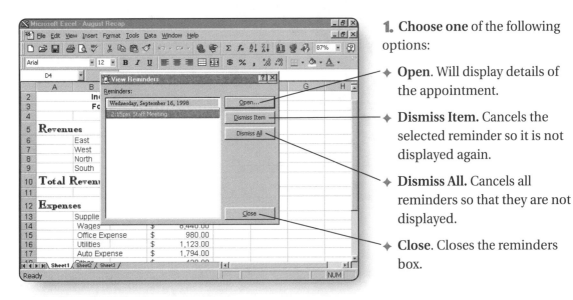

1. **Choose one** of the following options:

◆ **Open**. Will display details of the appointment.

◆ **Dismiss Item.** Cancels the selected reminder so it is not displayed again.

◆ **Dismiss All.** Cancels all reminders so that they are not displayed.

◆ **Close**. Closes the reminders box.

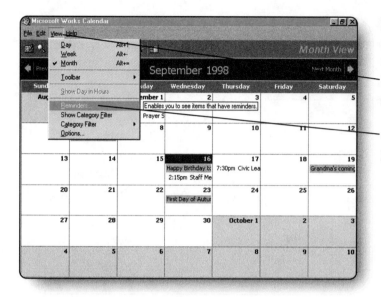

2. Start Works Calendar. The Calendar program will open.

3. Click on **View**. The View menu will open.

4. Click on **Reminders**. The Reminders dialog box will open.

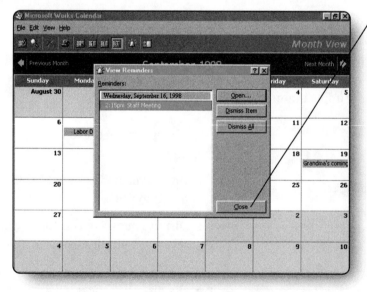

5. Click on **Close**. The Reminders dialog box will close.

WORKING WITH CATEGORIES

Organize your appointments by using Categories. Calendar comes with nine pre-defined categories but you can also add others.

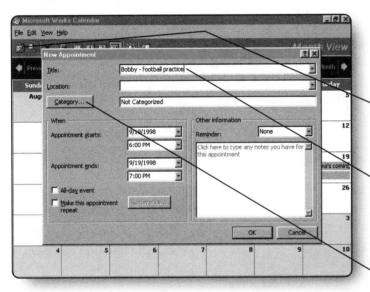

Adding a Category to an Appointment

1. **Click** on the **New Appointment button**. The New Appointment dialog box will open.

2. **Enter** the necessary appointment **information** in the Title: text box. The information will display in the Title: text box.

3. **Click** on **Category**. The Choose Categories dialog box will open.

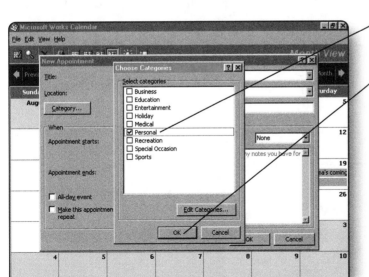

4. **Click** on a **Category**. The option will display a check mark.

5. **Click** on **OK**. The appointment will have a category assigned to it.

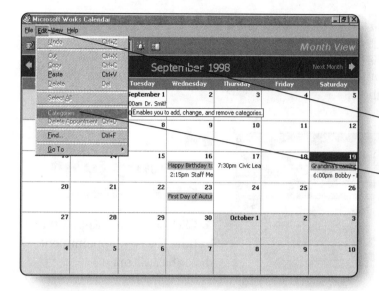

Adding New Categories

Add a new category of your own.

1. **Click** on **Edit**. The Edit menu will open.

2. **Click** on **Categories**. The Edit Categories dialog box will open.

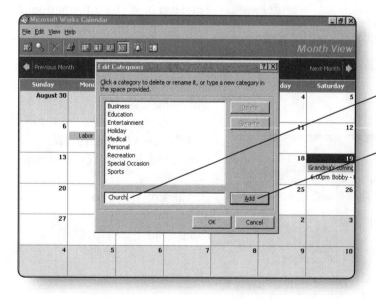

3. **Click** the **mouse** in the blank text box. The blinking insertion point will appear.

4. **Type** a new **category name**. The text will display in the box.

5. **Click** on **Add**. The new category will be displayed.

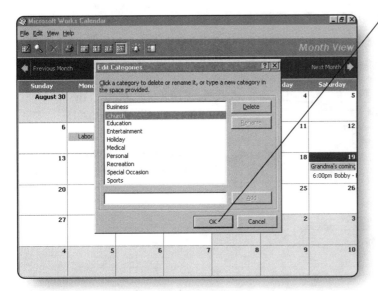

6. **Click** on **OK**. The Edit Categories dialog box will close.

Deleting Categories

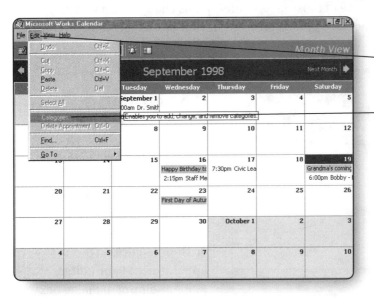

Delete any unwanted categories.

1. **Click** on **Edit**. The Edit menu will open.

2. **Click** on **Categories**. The Edit Categories dialog box will open.

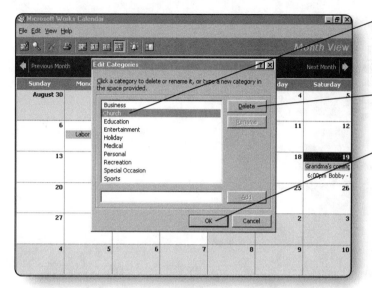

3. **Click** on the **category** to be deleted. The category name will be highlighted.

4. **Click** on **Delete**. The category will be deleted.

5. **Click** on **OK**. The Edit Categories dialog box will close.

EDITING APPOINTMENTS

It's one of those facts of life—plans change. It's a very simple process to update an event in your Works calendar.

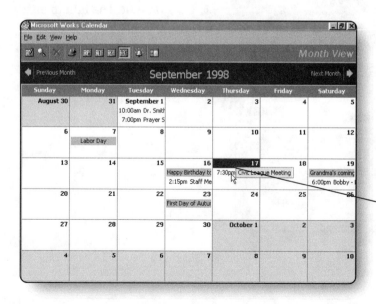

Editing Appointment Information

If you need to change the text or reminder information of an appointment, you'll use the Edit Appointment dialog box.

1. **Double-click** on the **appointment** to be edited. The Edit Appointment dialog box will open.

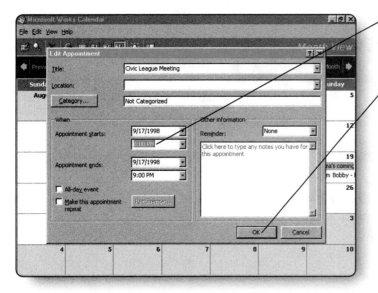

2. Make any **changes** to the appointment. The changes will appear in the dialog box.

3. Click on **OK**. The Edit Appointment dialog box will close.

Rescheduling Events to Another Day

If your company picnic has been postponed to the next weekend, move it by using the Month View.

1. If necessary, **click** on **Month View**. The calendar will be displayed by the month.

2. Press and **hold** the **mouse** over the **event** to be moved. The event will be highlighted.

3. **Drag** the **event** to the new date. Both the new and old dates will be highlighted.

4. **Release** the **mouse button**. The event will be rescheduled.

Rescheduling Appointments for the Same Day

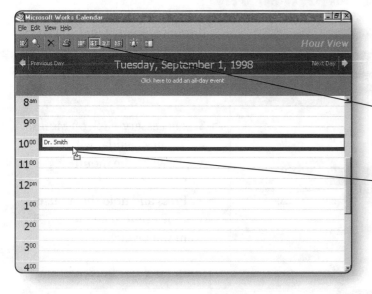

If you're moving your appointment to a different time the same day, move it in the day view.

1. **Click** on **Day View**. The calendar will be displayed by the day.

2. **Press** and **hold** the **appointment** to be rescheduled. The appointment will be surrounded by a heavy border.

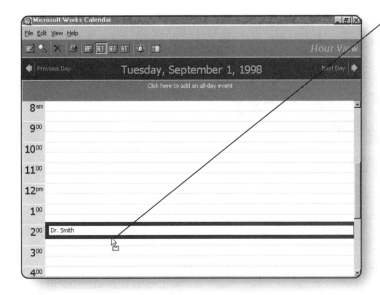

3. Drag the **appointment** to the new scheduled time. The appointment appears at the new time.

4. Release the **mouse button**. The appointment will be moved.

DELETING APPOINTMENTS

If an appointment has been canceled, delete it from your calendar. It doesn't matter which view you are using.

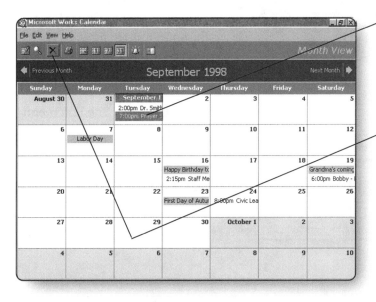

1. Click on the **appointment** to be deleted. The appointment will be highlighted or a blinking insertion point will be displayed on the appointment.

2. Click on the **Delete button**. A confirmation box will appear.

3. **Click** on **Yes**. The appointment will be permanently deleted.

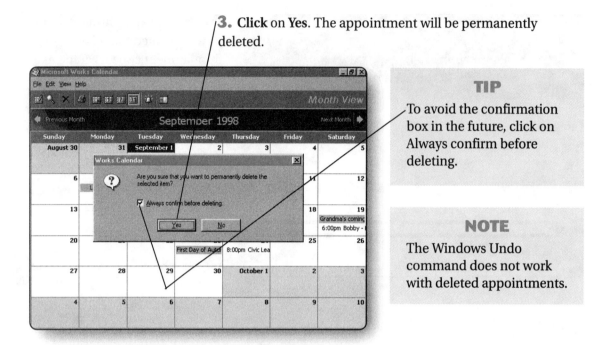

TIP

To avoid the confirmation box in the future, click on Always confirm before deleting.

NOTE

The Windows Undo command does not work with deleted appointments.

FINDING APPOINTMENTS

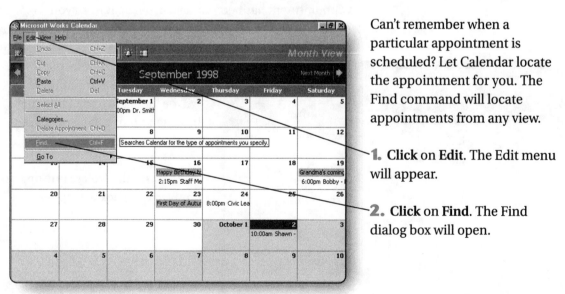

Can't remember when a particular appointment is scheduled? Let Calendar locate the appointment for you. The Find command will locate appointments from any view.

1. **Click** on **Edit**. The Edit menu will appear.

2. **Click** on **Find**. The Find dialog box will open.

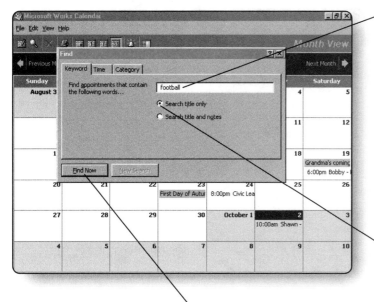

3. **Type** the **search text** under the Keyword tab. The text will appear in the Find appointments that contain the following words: text box.

4. **Click** on a search location **option**. The option will be selected.

5. **Click** on **Find Now**. A list of all appointments that match the criteria will be displayed.

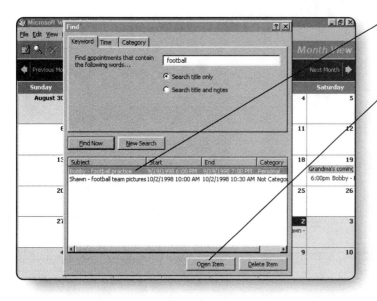

6. **Click** on the **item to be viewed**. The appointment will be highlighted.

7. **Click** on **Open Item**. The appointment information will be displayed.

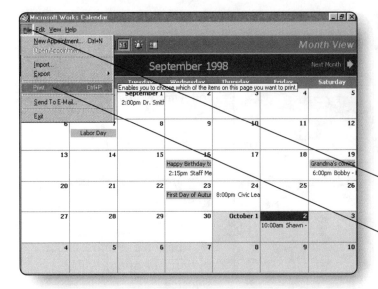

PRINTING A CALENDAR

If you need a paper copy of your calendar, you can print it by the day, week, month, or even hour of the appointments.

1. Click on **File**. The File menu will appear.

2. Click on **Print**. The Print dialog box will open.

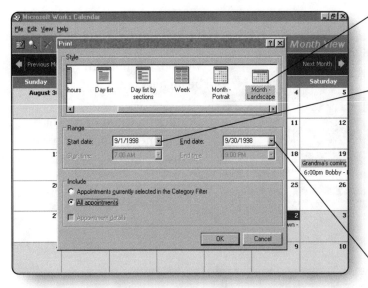

3. Click on the calendar **Style** to be printed. The style will be highlighted.

4. Click on the **Start date down arrow**. A monthly calendar will appear.

5. Click on the **starting date** that you want to print. The date will display in the Start date: text box.

6. Click on the **End date down arrow**. A monthly calendar will appear.

7. Click on the **ending date** that you want to print. The date will display in the End date: text box.

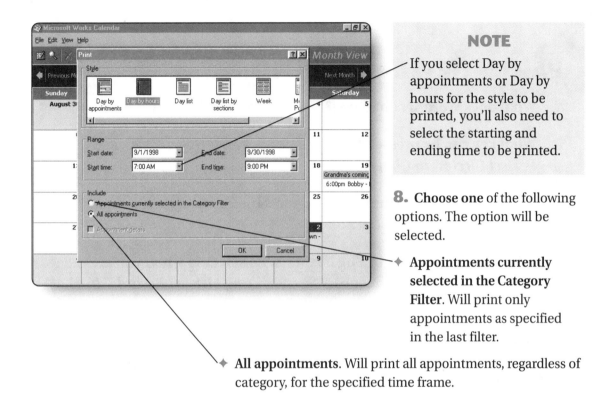

If you select Day by appointments or Day by hours for the style to be printed, you'll also need to select the starting and ending time to be printed.

8. Choose one of the following options. The option will be selected.

✦ **Appointments currently selected in the Category Filter**. Will print only appointments as specified in the last filter.

✦ **All appointments**. Will print all appointments, regardless of category, for the specified time frame.

9. Click on **OK**. The calendar will print with the options that you specified.

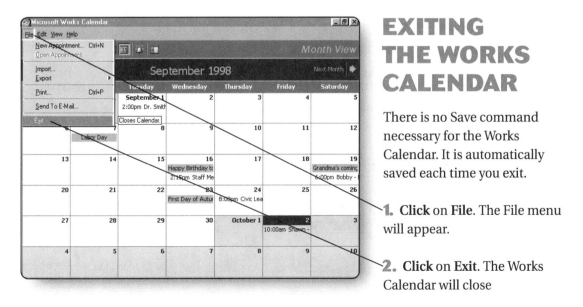

EXITING THE WORKS CALENDAR

There is no Save command necessary for the Works Calendar. It is automatically saved each time you exit.

1. Click on **File**. The File menu will appear.

2. Click on **Exit**. The Works Calendar will close

PART V REVIEW QUESTIONS

1. **What does WordArt do to text?** *See "Using WordArt" in Chapter 21*

2. **What key can be pressed to draw a perfect circle?** *See "Drawing Perfect Circles" in Chapter 21*

3. **What two types of documents are combined to do a mail merge?** *See "Creating Form Letters Using Mail Merge" in Chapter 22*

4. **What box in the Print Dialog box must be selected when you are ready to print merged records?** *See "Printing Merged Records" in Chapter 22*

5. **When the data in the spreadsheet changes, what happens to a linked chart that is a word processing document?** *See "Inserting a Chart from a Spreadsheet" in Chapter 23*

6. **Other than the Month view, what other views are provided by Calendar?** *See "Viewing the Calendar" in Chapter 24*

7. **What is a recurring appointment?** *See "Adding a Recurring Appointment" in Chapter 24*

8. **How does Calendar remind you when an appointment is coming up?** *See "Reminding Yourself" in Chapter 24*

9. **What feature does Calendar provide to help you locate a scheduled appointment?** *See "Finding Appointments" in Chapter 24*

10. **Does the Save command need to be used with Calendar?** *See "Exiting the Works Calendar" in Chapter 24*

Installing Works

Installing Microsoft Works is a painless process. In this chapter, you'll learn how to:

✦ **Install Microsoft Works 4.5**

✦ **Uninstall Microsoft Works 4.5**

SYSTEM REQUIREMENTS

Works 4.5 has specific requirements to run properly. The following table lists these specifications:

COMPONENT	REQUIREMENT
Processor	Multimedia PC P90 or higher
Operating System	Win 95, 98, or NT
Memory	16MB RAM
Disk Space	105MB disk
CD	2X or higher CD-ROM Drive
Monitor	Super VGA 256 color
Mouse	Microsoft Mouse or compatible pointing device

INSTALLING WORKS 4.5

Microsoft Works 4.5 comes on a single CD. The Works installation disk includes the Works program, the Works Calendar program, and Internet Explorer version 4.

NOTE

See Prima Tech's *Internet Explorer 4.0 Fast & Easy* for assistance with Internet Explorer.

TIP

Before installing Microsoft Works 4.5, be sure to temporarily disable any anti-virus programs running on your system.

1. **Place** the **Installation CD** into your CD-ROM drive. If you have autoplay enabled, the setup program will automatically begin.

If setup appears, skip to step 6. If the setup program does not begin, you'll have to start it manually.

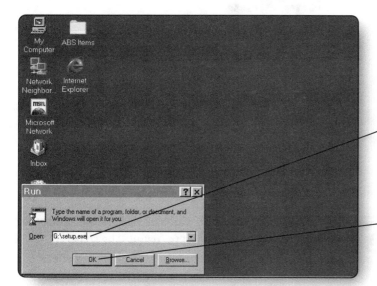

2. **Click** on **Start**. The Start menu will appear.

3. **Click** on **Run**. The Run dialog box will open.

4. **Type G:\setup.exe** in the Open: text box, substituting G: for the drive letter for your CD-ROM drive.

5. **Click** on **OK**. The Microsoft Works 4.5 Setup wizard will begin.

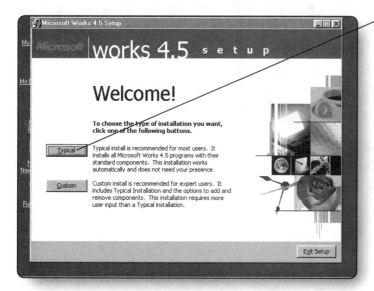

6. **Click** on **Typical**. The next screen will prompt you for your CD Code.

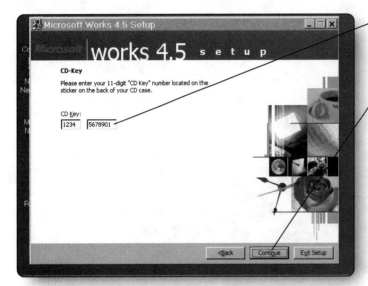

7. **Enter** the **CD Code**. The CD Code is the 11 digit number located on the CD case.

8. **Click** on **Continue**. The next setup screen will appear.

NOTE

If other applications are active, Works will advise you to close them before continuing. Close the applications and click on Continue.

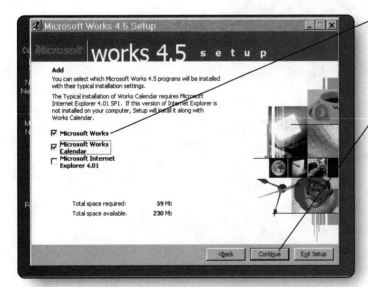

9. **Click** on the **components** you want to install. The selected components will have a check mark next to them.

10. **Click** on **Continue**. The files will be copied and installed.

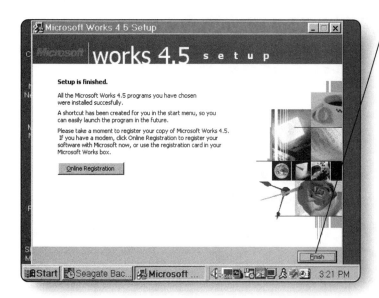

11. **Click** on **Finish**. The setup program will close and you will return to the Windows desktop.

UNINSTALLING WORKS 4.5

If you no longer want Microsoft Works on your system, you can easily uninstall it.

1. **Place** the **Installation CD** into your CD-ROM drive. If you have autoplay, the setup program will automatically begin. If setup appears, skip to step 6. If the setup program does not begin, you'll have to start it manually.

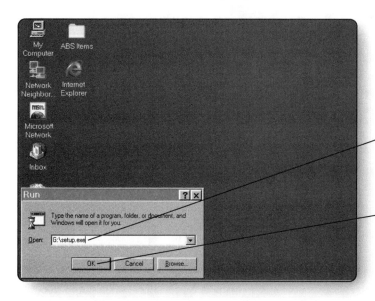

2. **Click** on **Start**. The Start menu will appear.

3. **Click** on **Run**. The Run dialog box will open.

4. **Type G:\setup.exe**. Substitute G: for the drive letter to your CD-ROM drive.

5. **Click** on **OK**. The Microsoft Setup Wizard will begin in Maintenance Mode.

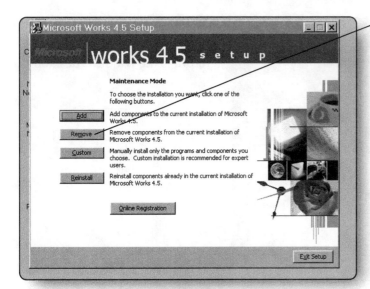

6. Click on **Remove**. A list of installed components will display.

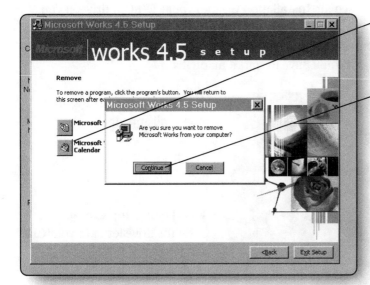

7. Click on a **component** you want to uninstall. A confirmation message will appear.

8. Click on **Continue**. The program will be removed and a message box will appear.

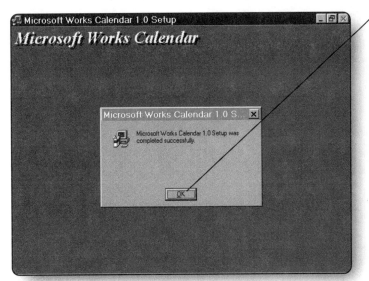

9. Click on OK. You will return to the Setup Wizard.

10. Repeat steps 7 through 9 until all components to be removed have been selected. The setup box will appear advising you that the components have been removed.

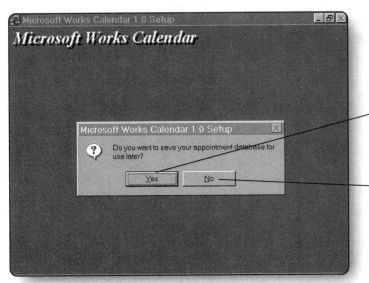

If you elected to remove the Works calendar, you will be prompted to save your appointment database.

11a. Click on Yes. Your calendar information will be saved.

OR

11b. Click on No. Your calendar information will be discarded.

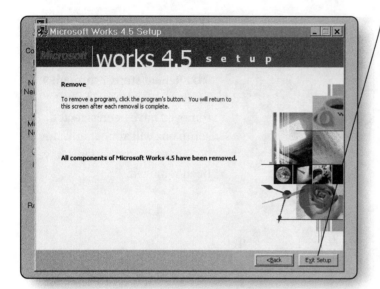

12. **Click** on **Exit Setup**. A confirmation box will open.

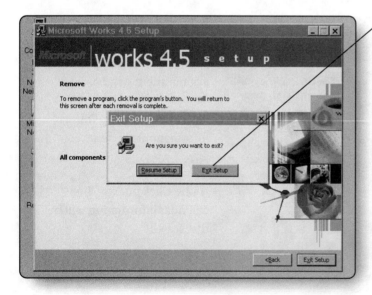

13. **Click** on **Exit Setup**. The Setup program will close and you will return to your Windows desktop.

B Using Task Wizards and Templates

Over 35 task Wizards and over 100 templates are included with the Microsoft Works program that can be used for home, business, employment, educational, volunteer, and civic activities. In this chapter, you'll learn how to:

✦ Use a Task Wizard to create a loan analysis spreadsheet.

✦ Use the Garage Sale Flyer template.

USING A TASK WIZARD

A Task Wizard is a shortcut for creating a document. You'll be able to make a few choices and the Task Wizard will set up a document for you. You can then edit the document as usual.

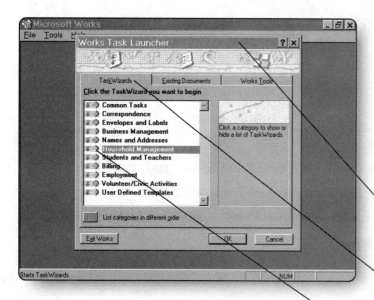

Creating a Loan Analysis Spreadsheet

Discover how much the payments would be on that new house or car you've been thinking about!

1. **Open Works** or **click** on the **Task Launcher button**. The Task Launcher will open.

2. **Click** on the **TaskWizards tab**. The TaskWizards tab will appear in front.

3. **Click** on the **diamond** next to **Household Management**. A list of wizards under the Household management category will display.

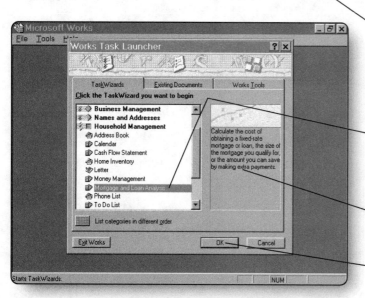

4. **Click** on a **Mortgage and Loan Analysis**. The item will be selected.

A description of each wizard will appear as you click on it.

5. **Click** on **OK**. A Works Task Launcher message box will open.

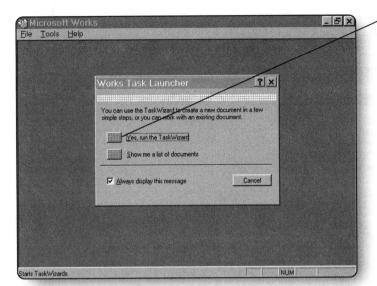

6. Click on **Yes, run the Task Wizard**. The Task Wizard will appear.

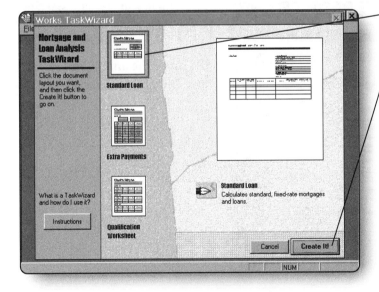

7. Click on **Standard Loan**. A green box will appear around the selection.

8. Click on **Create It!** A loan schedule using a Works spreadsheet will be created for you.

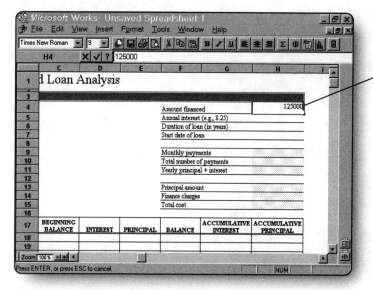

9. Click in **cell H4**. The cell will be selected.

10. Enter the **amount of loan** to be financed. The value will be displayed.

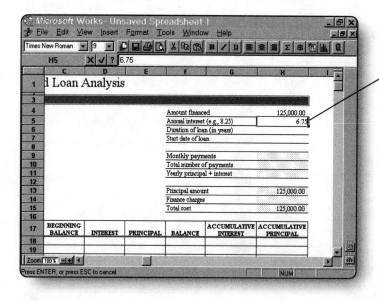

11. Click in **cell H5**. The cell will be selected.

12. Enter the annual **interest rate**. The value will be displayed.

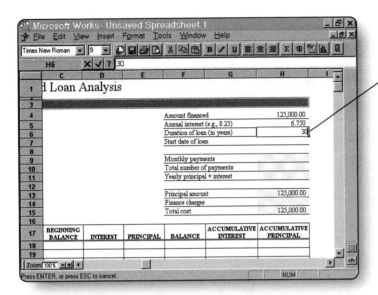

13. **Click** in **cell H6.** The cell will be selected.

14. **Enter** the **duration** of the loan in years. The value will be displayed.

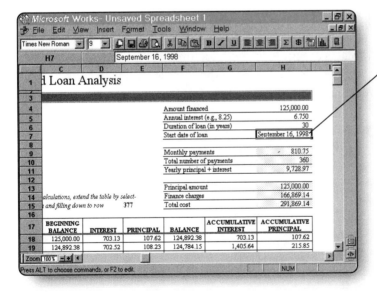

15. **Click** in **cell H7.** The cell will be selected.

16. **Enter** the **starting date** of the loan. The value will be displayed.

17. **Press** the **Enter key.** The loan amounts will be calculated.

NOTE

Do not change any other cells but H4 through H7. Doing so can alter the structure of the spreadsheet.

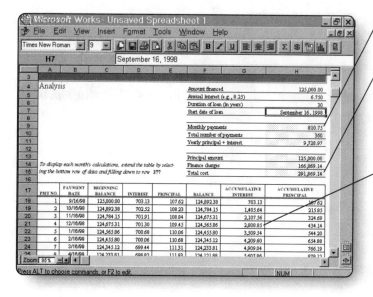

Your monthly payment amount.

Your total cost of the purchase—including interest.

Amortization of the payments.

USING A TEMPLATE

Templates are pre-designed documents that you can use. All you need to do is replace the sample data with your information.

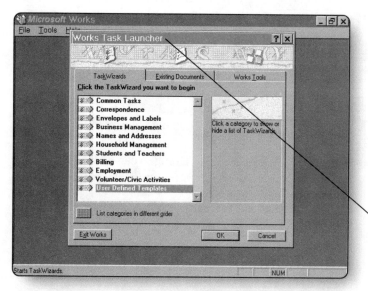

Creating a Garage Sale Flyer

Having a Garage Sale? There's a lot to do—so save yourself some time by using the Works pre-defined template to create a flyer you can distribute.

1. **Open Works** or **click** on the **Task Launcher button**. The Task Launcher will open.

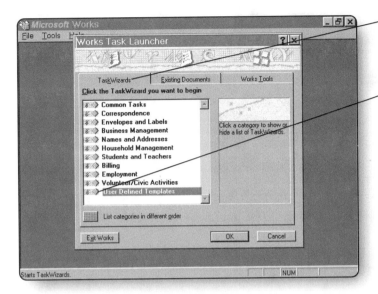

2. **Click** on the **TaskWizards tab**. The TaskWizards tab will appear in front.

3. **Click** on the **diamond** next to **User Defined Templates**. A list of Templates will display.

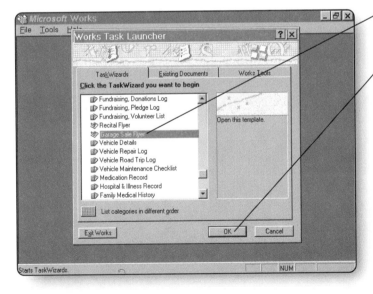

4. **Click** on **Garage Sale Flyer**. The item will be selected.

5. **Click** on **OK**. A new Works document will be created with sample information supplied.

6. **Replace** the **sample information** with your information. Your Garage Sale flyer will be complete.

Glossary

=AVG. A Works function that calculates the average of a list of values. SYNTAX: =AVG(*list*)

=COUNT. A Works function that counts the non-blank cells in a list of ranges. SYNTAX: =COUNT(*list*)

=MAX. A Works function that finds the largest value in a list. SYNTAX: =MAX(*list*)

=MIN. A Works function that finds the smallest value in a list. SYNTAX: =MIN(*list*)

=SUM. A Works function that adds a range of cells. *See also* AutoSum. SYNTAX: =SUM(*list*)

Absolute reference. In a formula, a reference to a cell that does not change when copying the formula. An absolute reference always refers to the same cell or range. It is designated in a formula by the dollar sign ($).

Active cell. The selected cell in a worksheet. It is designated with a border surrounding the cell.

Address Book. Stores names, addresses, and phone numbers in one handy location.

Alignment. The position of data in a document, cell, range, or text block; for example, centered, right-aligned, or left-aligned. Also called justification.

Attributes. Items that determine the appearance of text such as bolding, underlining, italics, or point size.

AutoSum. A function on the toolbar that adds a row or column of figures. Same as =SUM.

Axes. Lines that form a frame of reference for the chart data. Most charts have an x-axis and a y-axis.

Bar chart. A type of chart that uses bars to represent values. Normally used to compare items.

Bold. A font attribute that makes text thicker and brighter.

Bookmark. Used to mark a place in a document to locate it quickly.

Border. A line surrounding paragraphs, pages, table cells, or objects.

Browser. A software program designed for viewing Web pages on the Internet.

Bullet. A small black circle or other character that precedes each item in a list.

Cell. The area where a row and column intersect in a worksheet or table.

Chart. A graphic representation of data. Also called graph.

Choose. To use the mouse or keyboard to pick a menu item or option.

Circular reference. A cell that has a formula that contains a reference to itself.

Click on. To use the mouse or keyboard to pick a menu item or option in a dialog box.

Clip art. Drawings that can be inserted into a Works application.

Clipboard. An area of computer memory where text or graphics can be temporarily stored.

Close button. Used to shut down or exit a dialog box, window, or application.

Column. A set of cells that appear vertically on a worksheet. A single Works worksheet has 256 columns.

Columns. Vertical divisions of text on a page.

Comment. To add annotations to a document or spreadsheet cell. Comments do not print.

Compound Formula. A formula, usually in a spreadsheet, that has multiple operators. An example might be A2*C2+F4.

Copy. To take a selection from the document and duplicate it on the Clipboard.

Cut. To take a selection from the document and move it to the Clipboard.

Data. The information to be entered into a spreadsheet.

Database. A file composed of records, each containing fields together with a set of operations for searching or sorting.

Default. A setting or action predetermined by the program unless changed by the user.

Desktop. The screen background and main area of Windows where windows, icons, and dialog boxes appear.

Dialog box. A box that appears that displays warnings or messages, or requests information from the user.

Document. A letter, memo, proposal, or other file that is created in the Works program.

Drag-and-drop. To move text or an object, position the mouse pointer on the item to move, press and hold the mouse button, move the mouse, and then release the mouse button to drop the material into its new location.

Easy Formats. A process used by Works to simplify formatting of documents. It allows the application of formats from other documents, without recreating the format from the beginning.

Easy Text. Stored phrases or paragraphs of text that can be recalled into a Works word processing document with the F3 key.

Export. The ability to copy data from one program to another.

Field. A piece of information used in a database.

File format. The arrangement and organization of information in a file. File format is determined by the application that created the file.

File. Information stored on a disk under a single name.

Fill Data. A function that allows Works to automatically complete a series of numbers or words based on an established pattern.

Fill. The changing of interior colors and patterns, or the completion of data in a series of spreadsheet cells.

Font. A group of letters, numbers, and symbols with a common typeface.

Footer. Text repeated at the bottom of each page of a document or spreadsheet.

Footnote. Reference information that prints at the bottom of the page.

Form Design View. The view in a Works database that allows the structure of the database to be modified.

Form View. A view in a Works database where one record displays at a time.

Form. A type of database document with spaces reserved for fields to enter data.

Format. To change the appearance of text or objects with features such as the font, style, color, borders, and size.

Formula bar. The location where all data and formulas are entered for a selected cell.

Formula. An entry in a worksheet that performs a calculation on numbers, text, or other formulas.

Freezing. The preventing of sections of a worksheet from scrolling off the screen when the page moves down.

Function. A series of predefined formulas used in Works spreadsheets. Functions perform specialized calculations automatically.

Go To. A feature that enables the user to jump to a specific cell or worksheet location quickly.

Graph. *See* Chart.

Greater than. A mathematical operator that limits the results of a formula to be higher than a named number or cell.

Gridlines. The lines dividing rows and columns in a table or worksheet.

Handles. Small black squares which enable the resizing of an object.

Header. Text entered in an area of the document for display at the top of each page of the document.

Hide. To temporarily turn off the display of certain cells, rows, or columns.

Hypertext link. Used to provide a connection from the current document to another document or to a document on the Web.

Icon. A small graphic image that represents an application, command, or a tool. An action is performed when an icon is clicked or double-clicked.

Import. The ability to receive data from another application.

Indent. To move a complete paragraph one tab stop to the right.

Justification. *See* Alignment.

Label. Any cell entry that begins with a letter or label-prefix character.

Landscape. Orientation of a page in which the long edge of the paper runs horizontally.

Legend. A box containing symbols and text that explains what each data series represents. Each symbol is a color pattern or marker that corresponds to one data series in the chart.

Less than. A mathematical operator that limits the results of a formula to be lower than a named number or cell.

Line Spacing. The amount of space between lines of text.

List View. A view in a Works database that allows the records to be viewed in a vertical format similar to a spreadsheet.

Mail Merge. A feature that uses data from a data file and combines it with a word processing document to produce personalized letters.

Margin. The width of blank space from the edge of the page to the edge of the text. All four sides of a page have margins.

Mouse pointer. A symbol that indicates a position onscreen as the mouse moves on the Desktop.

Object. A picture, map, or other graphic element that can be placed in a Works application.

Open. To start an application, to insert a document into a new document window, or to access a dialog box.

Operator. The element of a formula that suggests an action to be performed, such as addition (+), subtraction (–), division (/), multiplication (*), greater than (>) or less than (<).

Orientation. A setting that designates whether a document will print with text running along the long or short side of a piece of paper. *See also* portrait *or* landscape.

Page Break. A command that tells the application where to begin a new page.

Page Setup. A command that tells the application the paper size, orientation, margins, and other items applicable to the entire document.

Paste. The process of retrieving the information stored on the Clipboard and inserting a copy of it into a document.

Patterns. Pre-defined shading and line arrangements used to format cells in a worksheet.

Pie chart. A round chart type in which each pie wedge represents values.

Point size. A unit of measurement used to indicate font size. One point is $1/72$ inch in height.

Point. To move the mouse until the tip of the mouse pointer rests on an item.

Portrait. The orientation of the page in which the long edge of the page runs vertically.

Print area. The designated portion of a worksheet that will print.

Print Preview. Shows how the printed document will look onscreen before it prints.

Properties. The characteristics of text, objects, or devices. Text properties might include font, size, or color.

Range name. An "English" name that identifies a range and that can be used in commands and formulas instead of the range address.

Range. A collection of cells that ranges from the first named cell to the last.

Record. The collection of field information about one particular element. For example, Joe Smith's record might include field information such as name, address, and phone number.

Redo. To reverse the last Undo action.

Reference. In a formula, a name or range that refers the formula to a cell or set of cells.

Relative. In a formula, a reference to a cell or a range that changes when the formula is copied. A relative reference refers to the location of the data in relation to the formula. A relative reference can be an address or range name.

Right align. To line up text with the right side of a cell, tab setting, or document margin, as with a row of numbers in a column.

Row. Cells running from left to right across a worksheet.

Ruler. A feature that allows page format elements to change, such as tabs and margins.

Save As. To save a previously saved document with a new name or properties.

Save. To take a document residing in the memory of the computer and create a file to be stored on a disk.

Scroll bars. The bars on the right side and bottom of a window that allow vertical and horizontal movements through a document.

Shape. An item such as a circle, rectangle, line, polygon, or polyline in the document.

Simple Formula. A formula, usually in a spreadsheet that has only one operator. An example might be B4+B5.

Sort. To arrange data in alphabetical or numeric order.

Spell Checker. A feature that checks the spelling of words in the document against a dictionary and flags possible errors for correction.

Spreadsheet. The component in Works that handles calculations and data needing to be placed in a columnar or linear format. Data is stored in small locations called cells.

Status bar. The line at the bottom of a window that shows information, such as the current page in a document.

Style. A way to format similar types of text such as headings and lists.

Symbols. Characters that are not on the keyboard, such as iconic symbols, phonetic characters, and characters in other alphabets.

Syntax. The exact structure of functions and formulas.

Table. A set of rows and columns of cells that are filled in with text, numbers, or graphics.

Tabs. Settings in the document that determine where the insertion point moves when the tab key is pressed or the indent feature used.

TaskWizards. An interactive Help feature that prompts the user for key pieces of required information to complete a project.

Template. A predesigned file with customized formatting, content, and features.

Thesaurus. A feature used to find synonyms (words that are alike) and antonyms (words that are opposite).

Titles. Descriptive pieces of text. Used in charts and spreadsheets.

Toolbar. Appears at the top of the application window and is used to access many of the commonly used features of the Works applications.

Undo. To reverse the last editing action.

Unhide. To display cells, rows, or columns previously hidden in a worksheet.

Uppercase. A capital letter.

Value. An entry that is a number, formula, or function.

Views. Ways to display documents in different perspectives.

WordArt. A feature that allows blocks of text to be manipulated into varying shapes and formats.

Word Processing. The ability to type, edit, and save a document.

Word Processor. The component in Microsoft Works that allows the user to do word processing.

Word Wrap. To let text in a paragraph automatically flow to the next line when it reaches the right margin.

World Wide Web. A series of specially designed documents—all linked together—to be viewed over the Internet.

Wrapping. A function that causes text to automatically wrap to the next line when it reaches the right edge of a cell or page margin.

X-axis. In a chart, a reference line marked in regular intervals to display the categories with descriptive labels.

Y-axis. In a chart, a reference line marked in regular intervals to display the values of a chart.

Zoom. To enlarge or reduce the way the text displays onscreen. It does not affect how the document will print.

Index